# SUCCESSFUL SERVICE-LEARNING PROGRAMS

*New Models of Excellence
in Higher Education*

# SUCCESSFUL SERVICE-LEARNING PROGRAMS

## New Models of Excellence in Higher Education

**Edward Zlotkowski**

*Editor*

ANKER PUBLISHING COMPANY, INC.
Bolton, MA

# SUCCESSFUL SERVICE-LEARNING PROGRAMS
*New Models of Excellence in Higher Education*

ISBN 1-882982-16-9


Composition by Keller & Keller *Designs in Print*
Cover design by Boynton Hue Studio


Anker Publishing Company, Inc.
176 Ballville Road
P. O. Box 249
Bolton, MA 01740-0249

*To Gavriel*
*for his commitment to others*
*and his love of learning*

# ABOUT THE EDITOR

Edward Zlotkowski received his B.A. in English and his Ph.D. in Comparative Literature from Yale University. He is Professor of English at Bentley College and in 1990 founded the Bentley Service-Learning Project, an institution-wide program that involves all of the college's undergraduate academic departments, more than a quarter of its full-time faculty, and several thousand students. Zlotkowski has lectured and written on a variety of service-learning topics. He has consulted to Campus Compact and the Massachusetts Commission on Community Service as well as to individual colleges and universities across the country. As a Senior Associate at the American Association for Higher Education, he serves as general editor of a new monograph series exploring the relationship between service-learning and individual academic disciplines.

# CONTRIBUTORS

**EDWARD ZLOTKOWSKI** is Founding Director of the Bentley Service-Learning Project, Bentley College.

**RICHARD M. BATTISTONI** is Director of the Feinstein Institute for Public Service, Providence College.

**LEE BENSON** is Professor of History, University of Pennsylvania.

**JAMES CARIGNAN** is Dean of the College, Bates College.

**AMY DRISCOLL** is Director of Community/University Partnerships, Portland State University.

**IRENE S. FISHER** is Director of the Lowell Bennion Community Service Center, University of Utah.

**IRA HARKAVY** is Director of the Center for Community Partnerships, University of Pennsylvania.

**ROGER K. HENRY** is Director, Center for Service-Learning, Brevard Community College.

**GARRY HESSER** is Director of Experiential Education, Augsburg College.

**BEVERLY W. JONES** is Director of the Community Service Program, North Carolina Central University.

**WILLIAM J. WOOD, S.J.** is Assistant Rector of the Jesuit Community at the University of San Francisco. Formerly, he was Director of the Eastside Project at Santa Clara University.

# TABLE OF CONTENTS

# APPENDICES

# FOREWORD

For most of the latter half of the 20th century, colleges and universities in this country have been portrayed as remarkable success stories—described most often as the "envy of the world." In recent years, however, the spotlight of public criticism has turned increasingly toward higher education. Particularly biting is the charge that American universities and colleges have become disconnected from the larger purposes of the society. There is the widespread perception that institutions of higher learning exist primarily for private gain, cut off from the public good. For too many, the university is seen as the place where individuals go to pursue competitive advantage in an increasingly Darwinian environment.

*Successful Service-Learning Programs: New Models of Excellence in Higher Education* presents a different perspective—a different reality that affirms higher education's fundamental connectedness to community and society. Each of the institutional stories told here—whether it's the University of Pennsylvania, Portland State, or Santa Clara—begins with the basic purposes of that particular university, the shared visions that led to its founding. In these institutions, service-learning is not merely another educational experiment added on to the margins, but is rooted in the *raison d'être* of American higher education, both public and private.

The innovative work collected in this volume is the best defense against the accusation that higher education has become disengaged from the wider community. And where there is truth to the charge that faculty have become so highly specialized that they have become largely self-referential—speaking only to themselves—and that students are being prepared to pursue narrow, self-centered interests, indifferent to the needs of others, presented here are counter examples drawn from a diverse set of colleges and universities.

More important, in this nexus of activities now identified as service-learning is the beginning of a movement that could bring coherence and direction to higher education at a time when it is most needed. Edward Zlotkowski is right when he contends in the introductory chapter that a new model of excellence is emerging. It is grounded in the historic commitment to service, whatever the roots of that commitment. Intellectually, this incipient movement grows out of an indigenously American strain of democratic pragmatism that is currently experiencing its own resurgence, a philosophical tradition running from Emerson and Dewey to, more recently, Richard Rorty, Cornel West, and Benjamin Barber. Service-learning is not only anchored in the basic missions of our colleges and universities, but also has the potential to bring to the engaged campus an intellectual rationale and depth of understanding that has been missing.

What intrigues me most about service-learning is the promise it holds for the quality of student learning. I am convinced that we are—as rash as it sounds—on the threshold of a pedagogical revolution. Instructional technology is going to transform the way faculty go about their work, and new approaches to collaborative learning will have students learning from their peers, as well as faculty, as never before. Experience-based learning—which is at the heart of the service-learning model—will complement and merge with these other powerful pedagogies to transform the faculty role and the way we organize for learning.

As an experience-based approach to education, service-learning builds on the best that we are learning about learning from cognitive and developmental psychology, as well as the most recent work in educational assessment. What can happen to students engaged in the movement from reflection to practice in the service-learning process is caught best for me, however, not by the cognitive sciences, but in these lines from the poet William Butler Yeats:

> The human soul is always moving outward into the external world and inward into itself, and this movement is double because the human soul would not be conscious were it not suspended between contraries. The greater the contrast, the more intense the consciousness.

Service-learning, carried out in the ways exemplified in the programs described in this book, immerses students in the tension between intellectual reflection and active engagement, creating a learning situation in which, to use Yeats' words, "the greater the contrast, the more intense the consciousness." If colleges and universities of the future are serious about organizing for learning, service-learning has a vital contribution to make.

A major strength of this book is that it describes innovative programs that, in their creation, challenge boundaries that have for too long been taken for granted. A prime example is the work of Penn's Center for Community Partnerships, where a genuine effort is being made to bring about in practice the intellectually, socially, and morally engaged university. In the "communal participatory action research" being conducted there, the roles of faculty, student, and community member are reconfigured. Teaching, research, and service take on different meanings and have an interrelated coherence that is seldom found, particularly in a leading research university.

Three other examples: At Portland State, service-learning has moved from the periphery of the institution—its usual home—to the very heart of the campus, integrated throughout the curriculum, providing a primary learning experience for all students. At Bentley, the project has successfully built bridges between the business disciplines and critical community service needs. And, in the moving story of the Eastside Project at Santa Clara University, we see how community service in the university's own neighborhood led to the cultivation of a global perspective, where all involved became increasingly aware of the rich diversity, the painful struggles of immigration, and the widening gap between the privileged and the poor.

Service-learning is gathering steam around the country because it is congruent with a key mission of our institutions; whets the imaginations of students, faculty, and community participants; is pedagogically effective; and meets important community needs. Service-learning is moving forward as a concerted national endeavor, however, because there are individuals who have persistently championed this educational model and invested their lives in orchestrating collaboration across campuses, disciplines, and professional associations. No one has done more to make the case for service-learning than Edward Zlotkowski. This collection of essays is an extension of that commitment and good work. He deserves our gratitude.

R. Eugene Rice
*Director, Forum on Faculty Roles and Rewards*
*American Association for Higher Education*

# PREFACE

*Successful Service-Learning Programs: New Models of Excellence in Higher Education* grows out of two originally unrelated needs assessments. After almost two decades of studying and teaching at liberal arts institutions, I found myself working in the business-oriented culture of Bentley College, and I was amazed to discover that there is more to ideas than their intrinsic merit. Up until then, it had simply never occurred to me that one might legitimately be concerned with more than whether the point one was trying to make was true. At Bentley, however, there were entire departments for whom *what* was inextricably bound up with *how*, for whom the pursuit of truth necessarily implied a corporate rather than an individual undertaking. In time, disciplines like management and marketing became for me not only valid but even necessary areas of concern if the ideas I believed in were ever to attain more than personal significance.

My second discovery came after a long, smoldering discontent with traditional pedagogies led me to what I now recognize as service-learning. Service-learning is

> a credit-bearing educational experience in which students participate in an organized service activity that meets identified community needs and reflect on the service activity in such a way as to gain further understanding of the course content, a broader appreciation of the discipline, and an enhanced sense of civic responsibility. Unlike extracurricular voluntary service, service-learning is a course-based service experience that produces the best outcomes when meaningful service activities are related to the course material through reflection activities such as directed writings, small group discussions, and class presentations. Unlike practica and internships, the experiential activity in a service-learning course is not necessarily skill-based within the context of professional education (Bringle & Hatcher, 1996).

Having succeeded in launching a successful service-learning program at Bentley, I found myself increasingly called upon to share my organizational insights with others. However, as I discovered very quickly, what worked at Bentley worked precisely because it was tailored to the needs of that particular institution. While there certainly existed many lessons and insights I could usefully share with others, those lessons would have to be very carefully modified if they were to succeed in another institutional context.

*Successful Service-Learning Programs: New Models of Excellence in Higher Education* has grown out of the conviction that service-learning as an educational reform strategy cannot and will not succeed solely on the basis of its ideas and ideals, no matter how laudable. Instead, it must pay equal attention to the organizational cultures it seeks to engage—the cultures of specific educational institutions. One purpose, then, of this book is to provide concrete examples of how different kinds of institutions, facing different internal and external circumstances, have succeeded in making service-learning not just an institutional feature but an institutional asset.

Since, moreover, colleges and universities can be grouped by—and tend to see themselves in terms of—educational type, I have tried to include a broad spectrum of institutional models: private and public research universities, private and public comprehensive universities, sectarian and secular liberal arts colleges, a community college, an historically black institution, and even a business-oriented school. The institutions vary in size and experience in developing service-learning. Indeed, variety and comprehensiveness of institutional profile, as well as the success of the service-learning programs, have played a primary role in determining the schools to be included.

## OVERVIEW OF CONTENTS

Chapter One places service-learning in the broader context of a changing educational paradigm. It underscores service-learning's unique ability to contribute to the process of both pedagogical and institutional renewal. In doing so, it suggests that what is at stake here is less a discrete program type than a way of reconceptualizing the educational undertaking as a whole.

Chapters Two through Eleven profile ten successful service-learning programs. Although these chapters vary considerably in focus, each profile contains several common elements: a detailed history of the program's development, an overview of its basic internal operations, and a review of important community collaborations. In addition, each profile addresses either directly or implicitly a defining dimension of the program's identity; e.g., the relationship between service-learning and extracurricular volunteer work, development of a service major, service-learning in a research-oriented context, service-learning and comprehensive institutional reform, and service-learning and the liberal arts tradition. Thus, the ten profiles together constitute a discussion of some of the most common—and pressing—issues facing service-learning programs.

Of the ten programs included here, the Augsburg program is one of the oldest. Indeed, what makes this program especially interesting is not just the way in which it marks the latest chapter in the college's active

commitment to its founding vision, but also in the way in which its service-learning program has grown out of a larger commitment to experiential education. Furthermore, as a representative member of the Council
of Independent Colleges, Augsburg serves as an important model for a
large number of small to moderate-sized institutions.

Another liberal arts college, Bates, stands at the opposite end of the
spectrum when it comes to age of program. The success of the relatively
new Bates program raises many interesting questions about how service-
learning can be approached best in an institutional context where a more
traditional commitment to the liberal arts, as opposed to a special commitment to field-based learning, and an institutional emphasis on theory,
as opposed to engagement, sets the scene. Very much like Augsburg,
Bates speaks to a particular kind of institution, in this case, the highly
selective liberal arts college frequently associated with New England but
in fact to be found throughout the country.

Bentley College, my own home institution, represents an entirely different educational model. For unlike Augsburg and Bates, Bentley is a
business-oriented institution at which the liberal arts play an important
but not primary role. Thus, the Bentley program offers an opportunity to
look at some of the issues involved in developing service-learning in a
preprofessional context, a context where students are less interested in
intellectual exploration and personal development than they are in mar-
ketable skills and economic well-being. Furthermore, although relatively
few schools share Bentley's comprehensive business orientation, many
do find themselves with large concentrations of business majors. Since
many of these schools have had relatively little success enlisting either
business students or business faculty in their service-learning initiatives,
the Bentley essay may prove useful to more institutions than might at
first be apparent.

That the Brevard essay should prove useful to a very large number of
schools seems certain. For several years now, Brevard Community
College (BCC) has had one of the largest and most dynamic service-learning programs of any institution—two or four year—in the country.
Furthermore, as part of its operational plan for dealing with large numbers of students, faculty, and community partners, BCC has developed an
unusually comprehensive set of placement procedures and documents.
For this reason, it provides an excellent example of the way in which
community-college programs can have something important to teach not
just other community colleges but all institutions of higher learning.

A similar utility can be claimed for the program at North Carolina
Central University (NCCU). As one of the nation's Historically Black
Colleges and Universities (HBCU), NCCU can not only serve as a model
for this group (which has recently received considerable attention and
support for its service-learning efforts through the United Negro College

Fund), but can also help other non-HBCU institutions better appreciate the importance of including adequate minority representation in their program design. That there exists in the country significant and distinct traditions of service among Native Americans, Hispanic Americans, Asian Americans, and African Americans is a fact frequently overlooked by those otherwise eager to link service-learning with diversity concerns.

One important influence on NCCU as an urban institution has been the West Philadelphia Improvement Corps at the University of Pennsylvania (Penn). The power of Penn's program to serve as a model for certain kinds of urban institutions has also been demonstrated by foundation-funded replication efforts at three large universities. However, at least as important as these funded efforts has been Penn's importance in demonstrating how a highly selective, research-oriented university can make community-based programs an advantageous part of, rather than a distraction from, the research agenda of its faculty. If, as some have claimed, the research university exercises an importance out of all proportion to its actual numbers, Penn's example takes on even greater importance.

Portland State University (PSU) represents a very different kind of university in a very different kind of urban setting. With less of a research agenda and a healthier urban environment to work with, PSU nonetheless has had to face its own set of special challenges; namely, the necessity of dealing with what was perceived as an ineffective curriculum, while at the same time coping with severe budget constraints. The university's response to these challenges has been comprehensive institutional reform in which university-community collaboration has played a central role. Thus, of all the schools represented here, PSU may offer the best example of service-learning not as a discrete program but as a central feature of an institution's basic strategic plan. Perhaps for this reason, PSU has made more progress than most institutions in formally integrating community-based work into its faculty reward structure.

In sharp contrast to such comprehensive institutionalization stands the Feinstein Center for Public Service at Providence College (PC). Unlike all the other programs represented here, the PC program has had the luxury of not having to worry about financial support, having been founded on the basis of a generous grant. Ironically, however, this fiscal advantage has also resulted in one important parallel to developments at Portland State University: the creation of a program on the basis of comprehensive design, if not of comprehensive institutionalization. Thus, we find at PC the systematic elaboration of a major and minor in public and community service (i.e., a self-contained degree program capable of both complementing and competing with other concentrations).

It is, in part, toward such a curricular model that Santa Clara University's Eastside Project has also begun to evolve. However, what makes this program especially significant is the way in which it has been constructed to capture the very essence of its institution's guiding philosophy. In this regard, Santa Clara's program can be said to most closely resemble Augsburg's: Both explicitly reflect their school's commitment to Christian values, as seen from either a Lutheran (Augsburg) or a Jesuit (Santa Clara) perspective. Furthermore, what the Eastside Project refers to as a "preferential option for the poor" directly links its activities to a form of Catholic social activism that could, if similarly adopted elsewhere, redefine the meaning of Catholic higher education.

The last school to be included here is another research university, in this case a public institution, the University of Utah. As a representative example of a state flagship institution, Utah allows us to familiarize ourselves with another program model founded upon a secular, civic commitment to service. It also allows us to weigh the advantages and disadvantages of running a service-learning program out of the same center responsible for traditional, extracurricular community service. In this regard, the Utah model may be especially useful to those institutions where service-learning has been placed on the student affairs side of the house.

The book concludes with several appendices designed to supply practical documents related to service-learning institutionalization. In the first two of them (e.g., appendices A and B), I have included a variety of institutional models. In the others, arranged alphabetically by institution, I have chosen one outstanding example of a particular kind of document (e.g., Augsburg's faculty handbook and Brevard's student service forms).

## ACKNOWLEDGMENTS

I wish to thank, first of all, the ten authors who contributed to this volume. For all of them, developing a multifaceted essay on their institution's program represented a generous commitment of time and energy. I also wish to thank my friends at Anker Publishing Company both for their patience and for their commitment to quality as a first priority. A part of Chapter One was originally written for the *Journal of Public Service and Outreach*. I am grateful to the editors for their permission to use it here.

On a more personal note, I owe a special debt to Jeannette MacInnes, Coordinator of Student Programs at Bentley's Service-Learning Project, for her extensive help in preparing the final manuscript, and to my wife, Ellen Wolfe, for seeing me through still another project.

Edward Zlotkowski
*Bentley College*
*Waltham, Massachusetts*
*June 1997*

# 1

# A New Model
# of Excellence

**Edward Zlotkowski**

*Bentley College*

T he phrase, "a new model of excellence," like so much else in our way of thinking about higher education at the end of the 20th century, is Ernest Boyer's. In his now famous opinion piece published early in 1994 in *The Chronicle of Higher Education*, "Creating the New American College," Boyer issued a passionate call for American higher education to return to its "historic commitment to service . . . a commitment that was never more needed than it is today." Such a summons is hardly unique. However, what makes Boyer's words distinctive is their ability to rise above both censure and lament to sketch at least the broad outlines of what such a renewed commitment might look like—to see such a commitment in operational as well as philosophical terms.

What I'm describing might be called the "New American College," an institution that celebrates teaching and selectively supports research, while also taking special pride in its capacity to connect thought to action, theory to practice. This New American College would organize cross-disciplinary institutes around pressing social issues. Undergraduates at the college would participate in field projects, relating ideas to real life. Classrooms and laboratories would be extended to include health clinics, youth centers, schools, and government offices. Faculty members would build partners with practitioners who would, in turn, come to campus as lecturers and student advisers.

> The New American College, as a connected institution, would be committed to improving, in a very intentional way, the human condition. As clusters of such colleges formed, a new model of excellence in higher education would emerge, one that would enrich the campus, renew communities, and give new dignity and status to the scholarship of service.

This book can be viewed as an extended footnote to Boyer's vision, an attempt to explore some of the operational and philosophical ideas his essay references. I like to think he would be pleased, and perhaps not a little surprised, to see just how far the programs presented here have moved in the direction he sketched out. It has been my hope, since this project first began, to contribute to a shift in focus away from the academy's perceived failures to an exploration of its potential for self-renewal.

## A LANDSCAPE OF PERVASIVE CHANGE

That there exists a widespread perception that the academy is in the grip of some kind of crisis can hardly be contested. From iconoclasts like Page Smith (1990) to pillars of the establishment like Derek Bok (1982, 1990), from those primarily concerned with internal roles and functions (Lynton & Elman, 1987; Rice, 1991, 1996; Lynton 1995) to those primarily concerned with broad moral and social issues (Wilshire, 1990; Lampert, 1996), it is not difficult to assemble a rich bibliography of texts that articulate a need for fundamental change. So powerful has been this groundswell of internal criticism that many astute, seasoned observers have argued that, whether or not we choose to acknowledge it, "we may be experiencing the beginnings of [an educational] revolution no less significant than that which created the research university 100 years ago." So suggests Donald Kennedy (1995), former president of Stanford, while a continent away, Sheldon Hackney, former president of the University of Pennsylvania, has recourse to similar imagery in "calling for a great leap forward toward the radical reformation of the American university system" (1994).

Revolution, however, is but one of the key concepts being used to characterize the current wave of critiques, ideas, and proposals sweeping across the educational landscape. Another is "paradigm," as in Thomas Kuhn's "paradigm shift" (1962), and what is implied here is nothing less than the gradual replacement of our current model of education with a new one. Thus, Robert Barr and John Tagg (1995) talk about a necessary supplanting of the prevailing teaching paradigm by a new learning paradigm based on vastly different assumptions. Goodwin Liu, former Senior Program Officer for Higher Education at the Corporation for National Service, has written of the emergence of a new "knowledge paradigm"

(1995). William Hull, Provost at Samford University, has described a clash of organizational, functional, and "cultural assumptions . . . root[ed] in two very different paradigms" (1995).

## SERVICE-LEARNING'S EDUCATIONAL COORDINATES

Revolution, paradigm shift, and "the most significant transformation we will have seen in half a century—and perhaps half a millennium" (Plater, 1995)—can so many knowledgeable voices all be wrong? And if they are right, even if they are only partially right, where is such change taking us? As Ted Marchese, editor of *Change*, has noted (1995), "We have much clearer ideas about the need for change and the dysfunctions of the present system than we do what a new system might be like."

True. But our understanding of what a new model of excellence might look like may be clearer than is at first apparent. Although I do not believe there exists any single strategy capable of bringing about academic renewal, I do believe the educational paradigm latent in what has come to be called "service-learning"—meaningful community service that is linked to students' academic experience through related course materials and reflective activities—may represent a key to our moving successfully forward. Indeed, what makes service-learning—"a form of experiential education, deeply rooted in cognitive and developmental psychology, pragmatic philosophy, and democratic theory" (Morton & Troppe, 1996)—so fascinating is that it not only provides a way of grappling successfully with many of the dysfunctions referenced in critiques of the contemporary academy but also provides a way of organizing and coordinating some of the most exciting recent developments in pedagogical practice. In other words, service-learning can suggest a new ground of coherence, provide a template for the new organizing vision Marchese asks for. (For a more complete definition of service-learning, see Preface and Bringle & Hatcher, 1996.)

The reason for this is simple: Service-learning is positioned at that very point where two comprehensive sets of contemporary educational concerns intersect. On the one hand, it represents a pedagogy that extends our range of pedagogical resources beyond even such promising active learning strategies as cases, role playing, and simulations, and it does so by addressing directly those "problems of greatest human concern" that are "messy and confusing and incapable of technical solution" (Schon, 1995). Furthermore, far from denying the value of more traditional pedagogical strategies—including the basic lecture/discussion—it transforms and renews the educational enterprise as a whole. By linking the classroom to the world of praxis, it allows induction to complement deduction, personal discovery to challenge received truths, immediate experience to balance generalizations and abstract theory. In and through service-learning, students learn to engage in problem definition and problem solving in an authentic, powerful way.

On the other hand, service-learning works with a second, intersecting axis: From knowledge as self-interest and private good, it creates a bridge to knowledge as civic responsibility and public work (Boyte & Farr, 1997). Thus, it again exhibits important qualities of flexibility and inclusion. Just as knowledge as public work in no way denies the validity of knowledge as private good, knowledge as private good also should not exclude the former. Through service-learning, students can discover the possibility and the importance of simultaneously attending to their needs as individuals and as members of a community. By bringing public work into the very heart of the educational system—i.e., the curriculum—service-learning helps students avoid the schizophrenia of private advancement disassociated from public standards and public need. No longer does "doing well" hold center stage, while "doing good," if it exists at all, languishes somewhere off to the side.

Because it does rest at the intersection of these two primary axes—the traditional-active learning axis and the private-public axis—service-learning can draw upon and help connect an unusually large number of contemporary educational concerns and practices. Problem-based learning, collaborative learning, undergraduate research, critical thinking, multiculturalism and diversity, civic awareness, leadership skills, and professional and social responsibility—these are just a few items on the contemporary academic agenda that naturally ally themselves with service-learning programs.

When a writer like Sharon Parks (1986), exploring young adults' search for meaning, refers to the critical importance of "a tension between established meaning that is deeply rooted in both mind and heart—and new experience, which now stands in strong opposition over-against established meaning," she might well be describing what service-learning educators see when their students first make personal contact with disadvantaged communities (Ostrow, 1995). When Benjamin Barber (1989) characterizes learning as "a social activity that can take place only within a discursive community bringing together reflection and experience," he might well be pointing to the kind of learning community-based learning activities help effect. When Laura Resnick (1987) warns that deep discontinuities between "learning in school and out" turn contemporary education into "more a consumer good than a vehicle for increasing economic productivity," she might also be laying out the logic of service-learning's dialectic between theoretical paradigms and workplace/service site realities.

It is, in fact, impossible to scan even recent discipline-specific work on pedagogical reform without noticing how often the agenda put forth suggests the very same concerns and strategies modeled by service-learning practice at its best. Take, for example, the Accounting Education Change Commission's monograph *Intentional Learning: A Process for Learning to Learn in the Accounting Curriculum* (1995)—a publication that nowhere explicitly mentions service-learning. Here one finds a "Composite Profile of Capabilities Needed by Accounting Graduates," and in this profile such service-learning-related items as "awareness of personal and social values"; "ability to identify and solve unstructured problems in unfamiliar settings"; "ability to interact with culturally and intellectually diverse people"; and "knowledge of the activities of business, government, and nonprofit organizations, and of the environments in which they operate." If a discipline such as accounting—a discipline not usually associated with educational risk-taking—has proposed for itself a direction so thoroughly consonant with the aims and practices of service-learning, is it any surprise that disciplines like chemistry and composition, nursing and history have staked out similar agendas?

## A POTENTIAL FOR COHERENCE

But student- and discipline-oriented reforms are not the only concerns that service-learning helps organize and address. Of equal significance is its potential to promote far greater integration of faculty roles as well as far greater curricular coherence in general. Instead of faculty dividing their time between the conflicting demands of 1) publishable research, 2) undergraduate teaching, and 3) service defined in terms of administrative activities (institutional or disciplinary), service-learning facilitates linking undergraduate (and graduate) teaching directly to professional outreach activities, thereby providing opportunities both for what Boyer (1990) has called the scholarships of application, integration, and teaching, and also for significant institutional/disciplinary service in the form of academy-sponsored community assistance. As John Votruba (1996), Vice Provost for Outreach at Michigan State University, has noted:

> Traditionally, we have treated the academic trilogy of teaching, research, and service as if they were separate and conceptually distinct forms of professional activity. In times of limited resources, it is assumed that any attempt to strengthen one part of the trilogy must be done at the expense of the others. If outreach is to become a primary and fully integrated dimension of the overall academic mission, this "zero sum" mentality must be overcome.

Thus, the outreach agenda, including service-learning, necessarily drives a more organic approach to faculty responsibilities, and the appeal of such a development is reflected not only in the increasing attention it is attracting at gatherings such as the American Association for Higher Education's Forum on Faculty Roles and Rewards, but also in concrete initiatives such as Indiana Campus Compact's Faculty Fellows Program.

As for greater curricular coherence, one of the most interesting results of service-learning programming is the increased communication it promotes among faculty members. As many practitioners have discovered, service-learning activities tend to foster a sense of community not just with off-campus groups but also among on-campus units—faculty and student affairs staff, faculty and students, and faculty across departmental lines. This is due, in part, to the way in which service-learning rekindles a sense of educational idealism but also, in part, to the often noted fact that real problems simply don't fit into neat disciplinary compartments. Thus, collaboration develops quite naturally, as one aspect of a project (e.g., biology-based) gives rise to another (e.g., communication-based). At some institutions, such as my own, these natural connections have actually led to more formal arrangements whereby several courses simultaneously make use of the same service site, allowing students to concentrate their efforts and faculty to collaborate without abandoning their disciplinary bases or departmental responsibilities.

## IMPEDIMENTS

At this point, one might well ask: Why, if service-learning is so effective in facilitating reform on so many fronts, has it not already had more of an impact on the change process? The reasons for this are multiple, but three in particular deserve to be singled out.

1.  The ability of colleges and universities to resist change is proverbial. For all its potential, service-learning cannot eliminate traditional academic caution. Hence, it is especially important that it learn to ally itself with other reform agendas such as faculty professional service, reconfiguration of promotion and tenure criteria, technological innovation, and changes in graduate school education.

2.  Until fairly recently, the service-learning movement has shown considerable ambivalence about its relationship to the academy: Did it really want to move "from the margin to the mainstream," or did it see its outsider status as essential to its identity? (Zlotkowski, 1996). Given its commitment to constituencies the academy has all but ignored, academic alienation runs deep among many who have been most active in promoting service-learning. Hence, in many instances they have been either unwilling or unable to make the kinds of adjustments necessary to win a large academic constituency. By insisting on their own moral or social concerns rather than looking for entry points throughout the system, by inviting others to join

them rather than looking for ways to join others, they have, in effect, failed to leverage service-learning's strengths.

3. Even apart from the magnitude of the task and the ambivalence of some would-be reformers, service-learning only recently began to develop the intellectual resources it needs to demonstrate academic legitimacy. Such resources include, first and foremost, the kinds of outcomes assessment—cognitive and civic/personal—that have begun to appear in several quarters. For example, Alexander Astin (1996) recently reported preliminary findings from a study conducted by the Higher Education Research Institute at UCLA on the role of service (community service as well as service-learning) in higher education. According to Astin, these findings are "extremely encouraging" with "every one of the thirty-four outcome measures . . . positively affected by undergraduate participation in service-learning or volunteer service." The outcomes in question range from critical thinking to a commitment to promoting racial understanding. Other, less comprehensive studies have reported favorably on the comparative results of learning outcomes in two sections of the same class where one section included service-learning and the other did not (Markus et al., 1993; Boss, 1994). As more and more quantitative data become available to corroborate the vast amount of qualitative information already available, we can expect to find more and more faculty interest.

This will most certainly be the case if other simultaneous efforts to better document, evaluate, and recognize faculty outreach—whether in the form of service-learning or professional service—also continue to gain ground (Lynton & Elman, 1987; Lynton, 1996). Included in this volume is one concrete example of such an effort: a draft revision of promotion and tenure guidelines from Portland State University. (See appendix G.) Other institutions have launched similar explorations, either formally or informally, and the topic has generated strong interest among provosts and deans at conferences such as the American Association for Higher Education's Forum on Faculty Roles and Rewards.

Revision of promotion and tenure guidelines is, of course, closely related to opportunities for faculty to communicate and publish their work. Only in this way will the scholarships of application, integration, and teaching even begin to acquire the kind of legitimacy now claimed exclusively by the scholarship of discovery (Boyer, 1990). Increased recognition of and support for individual faculty members working in service-learning has been one important goal of the first national faculty organization, the Invisible College, founded in 1994 and now located at Portland State University. In both 1995 and 1996, the organization sponsored a national gathering to give service-learning faculty an opportunity to share and discuss their work.

It has also helped provide many of the editors and writers who have contributed to a new monograph series on service-learning and the individual academic disciplines. This series, first proposed by the Invisible College and now under the auspices of the American Association for Higher Education (AAHE), is currently planned to include 18 volumes. Since each of these volumes brings together theoretical essays, pedagogical models, and bibliographical resources appropriate to a specific discipline/interdisciplinary area, they should go a long way toward dispelling the misconceptions that service-learning is not really academic and that it may be academically appropriate, but only for a limited number of disciplines. By including in its ranks volumes on disciplines such as accounting, history, and biology, the series should help establish once and for all the universal applicability of service-learning.

New journals such as *The Michigan Journal of Community Service-Learning* and the *Journal of Public Service and Outreach*; readers such as Barber and Battistoni's *Community Service and Education for Democracy: A Teacher/Student Sourcebook* (1993); Watters and Ford's *Writing for Change: A Community Reader* (1995); and Albert's *Service-Learning Reader: Reflections and Perspectives on Service* (1994); recent studies such as Jacoby's *Service-Learning in Higher Education: Concepts and Practices* (1996) and Campus Compact's *Two Cases of Institutionalizing Service-Learning: How Campus Climate Affects the Change Process* (1996); discipline-specific monographs such as *Service-Learning and Undergraduate Sociology: Syllabi and Instructional Materials* (1996) and *Writing in the Public Interest: Service-Learning and the Writing Classroom* (1995); special editions of established journals (e.g., the January 1996 issue of *The Journal of Business Ethics* and the fall 1996 issue of *Metropolitan Universities*); the inclusion of service-learning in the national and regional programming of the Speech Communication Association, the American Psychological Association, the Academy of Management, and the American Accounting Association—all these developments help paint the picture of a movement building an ever stronger intellectual base. If such a trend continues, we should find service-learning not only well-established in the academy as we currently know it but, far more importantly, well-positioned to help lead a renewed academy into the 21st century.

## INSTITUTIONAL MODELS

*Successful Service-Learning Programs: New Models of Excellence in Higher Education* is intended to add to this growing body of intellectual resources. By bringing together essays on ten sometimes very different but comparably successful service-learning programs, it attempts to provide a spectrum of approaches to program design and development. In doing so, it both builds on and complements Campus Compact's multi-year Project on Integrating Service with Academic Study.

In a 1996 publication, *Two Cases of Institutionalizing Service-Learning: How Campus Climate Affects the Change Process,* Marie Troppe and Keith Morton, both key players in the Campus Compact project, present a valuable overview of what the organization has learned about the institutionalization process. Most of what they report—and recommend—is fully consonant with the experiences described in this volume. Since many of the schools profiled here were part of the Compact project, this coincidence is not surprising. However, several general points should be added to the Compact's findings.

Troppe and Morton note that the first step to successful institutionalization involves demonstrating "how service-learning aids the campus in achieving its mission. "Many of the programs included here do this in a very explicit way—from Augsburg's determination to live out its mission of "Education for Service" to Penn's "rededication to a tradition begun 250 years ago by its 'patron saint,' Benjamin Franklin." However, what makes such a move more than just a public relations ploy is its ability to draw upon the institution's own understanding of its fundamental mission. Thus, the success of service-learning at Portland State cannot be disassociated from the school's determination to find more effective ways to fulfill its role as Portland's urban university. The success of Bates's program must be seen in terms of what it contributes to the college's attempt to live out authentically its liberal arts tradition.

Highly successful service-learning programs learn not only to claim the mantle of their institution's mission, but also to exploit it. Bentley's program cannot run away from its business-education context; Brevard's must capitalize on its institution's closeness to the Brevard County community. Or, to make the same point in a different way, to the degree that a service-learning program is perceived to be extraneous to the primary concerns of its institution—either an exotic distraction or a generic add-on—to that degree it will struggle to put down roots. Despite its special endowment, the long-term prospects of a program like Providence College's Feinstein Institute very much depend on its success in getting the institution as a whole to "own" it, to see it as aiding the entire campus in achieving its mission.

A second, different kind of observation builds on Troppe and Morton's recommendation that "a team of faculty and administrators need to serve as a core group committed to service-learning and willing to advocate for it." All of the profiles in *Successful Service-Learning Programs: New Models of Excellence in Higher Education* confirm the accuracy of this suggestion. However, many also suggest that such a core group by itself may not be enough. What is also often needed is a specific leader, an individual willing and able to serve as program champion and program visionary. Such an individual commands wide respect, has considerable social skills—and has personally assumed responsibility for making the program successful. In one way or another, Carignan at Bates, Jones at North Carolina Central, Henry at Brevard, Fisher at Utah, and Harkavy at Penn have all played this role. Indeed, it is entirely appropriate that Hesser, himself a pivotal figure in the development of service-learning at Augsburg, should have chosen to call his essay "On the Shoulders of Giants: Building on a Tradition of Experiential Education at Augsburg College. "

Both the relationship between the service-learning program and the sponsoring institution, and the nature of program leadership reintroduce the critical issue of academic legitimacy. For the same reason, as Troppe and Morton point out, "nearly two-thirds of [the campuses participating in the Compact project] elected to house service-learning in academic, rather than student affairs." Even when this is not the case (e.g., Utah), successful program leaders have made every effort to win strong, public, faculty endorsement. Ultimately, what is at issue is not location per se but access—access to faculty trust and resources to support faculty work. If the programs presented here demonstrate anything, it is the critical importance of helping faculty see their work from a new perspective. Both parts of this formulation are essential: There must be no doubt that the work in question is indeed faculty work; i.e., work "concerned with the production and transmission of knowledge" (Benson & Harkavy, Chapter 7); but there must also be adequate opportunity for faculty to envisage "new pedagogical possibilities" (Driscoll, Chapter 8). This means, first, course development resources: mini-grants, release time, service conference funding, workshops, and opportunities to share with other service-learning practitioners (cf. Augsburg, North Carolina Central, Penn, Portland State, and Santa Clara). Second, it means logistical support: the development of support systems to help identify placements and partnerships, and provide assistance with transportation, communication, reflection, and record-keeping. To facilitate this second kind of support, many schools have developed special student assistant/student liaison positions, often supported with work-study funds (cf. Bentley, Providence, and Utah).

Why such extensive faculty support? One only need consider how little experience most faculty members have had working outside the classroom, let alone working with community partners. In other words, most faculty need to develop a new skills set—skills of designing, coaching, and helping students process fieldwork—to complement their traditional skills of lecturing and guiding text-based discussion. They also need an opportunity to develop new, more appropriate assessment techniques. That they can, in fact, do so, the pedagogical essays contained in the AAHE monograph series mentioned earlier—as well as the dozens of courses referenced in this volume—make abundantly clear.

## CONCLUSION

Institutional relevance, academic integrity, and adequate faculty support—these keys to successful institutionalization run like leitmotifs throughout the programs profiled here. However, there remains one final key to success that even many of these programs have not yet managed to make fully their own: formal recognition of service-learning within the promotion and tenure process. To be sure, all ten institutions encourage faculty to include appropriate community-based work on their activities reports and data sheets. At several of them, individual faculty members have even featured service-learning in successful promotion and/or tenure portfolios. Still, with the exception of Portland State, none of the schools represented here has comprehensively reviewed its faculty reward system with an eye toward both accommodating and facilitating service-learning excellence. But until this is done—and new as well as veteran faculty can see in black and white how service-learning achievements are officially evaluated, recognized, and rewarded—the process of institutionalization will necessarily remain incomplete.

I began this chapter by suggesting that the road to educational renewal may be closer than we think. Taken together, the programs featured in this volume provide powerful testimony to what already has been done. They also constitute a *de facto* guide to many practical issues concerning service-learning as a vehicle of such renewal. It is easy to relegate Boyer's New American College to a merely visionary place in our institutional imaginations. That need not be the case.

## REFERENCES

Albert, G., et al. (Eds.). (1994). *Reflections and perspectives on service.* Raleigh, NC: National Society for Experiential Education.

Astin, A. W. (1996, March/April). The role of service in higher education. *About Campus, 1* (1), 14-19.

Barber, B. R. (1989, Fall). The civic mission of the university. *Kettering Review,* 62–72.

Barber, B. R., & Battistoni, R. (1993). *Community service and education for democracy: A teacher/student sourcebook.* Dubuque, IA: Kendall-Hunt.

Barr, R. B., & Tagg, J. (1995, November/December). From teaching to learning—A new paradigm for undergraduate education. *Change, 27* (6), 12–25.

Bok, D. (1982). *Beyond the ivory tower: Social responsibilities of the modern university.* Cambridge, MA: Harvard University Press.

Bok, D. (1990). *Universities and the future of America.* Durham, NC: Duke University Press.

Boss, J. A. (1994). The effect of community service work on the moral development of college ethics students. *Journal of Moral Education, 23* (2), 183–198.

Boyer, E. L. (1990). *Scholarship reconsidered: Priorities of the professoriate.* Princeton, NJ: The Carnegie Foundation for the Advancement of Learning.

Boyer, E. (1994, March 9). Creating the new American college. *The Chronicle of Higher Education,* A48.

Boyte, H. C., & Farr, H. (1997). The work of citizenship and the problem of service-learning. In R. Battistoni & W. Hudson (Eds.), *Practicing democracy: Concepts and models of service-learning in political science.* Washington, DC: American Association for Higher Education.

Bringle, R. G., & Hatcher, J. A. (1996, March/April). Implementing service-learning in higher education. *Journal of Higher Education, 67* (2), 221–239.

Cooper, D. D., & Jenier, L. (Eds.). (1995). *Writing in the public interest: Service-learning and the writing classroom:* East Lansing, MI: The Writing Center at Michigan State University.

Ender, M.G., et al., (Eds.). (1996). *Service-learning and undergraduate sociology: Syllabi and instructional materials.* Washington, DC: American Sociological Association.

Francis, M. C., Mulder, T. C., & Stark, J. S. (1995). *Intentional learning: A process for learning to learn in the accounting curriculum.* Sarasota, FL: The Accounting Education Change Commission and the American Accounting Association.

Hackney, S. (1994, Fall-Winter). Reinventing the American university: Toward a university system for the twenty-first century. *Universities and community schools, 4* (1-2), 9–11.

Hull, W. E. (1995). The quality culture in academia and its implementation at Samford University. Paper commissioned for the 10th AAHE Conference on Assessment and Quality.

Jacoby, B., & Assoc. (1996). *Service-learning in higher education: Concepts and practices.* San Francisco, CA: Jossey-Bass.

Kennedy, D. (1995, May/June). Another century's end, another revolution for higher education. *Change, 27* (3), 8–15.

Kuhn, T. S. (1962). *The structure of scientific revolutions.* Chicago, IL: University of Chicago Press.

Lempert, D. H. (1996). *Escape from the ivory tower: Student adventures in democratic experiential education.* San Francisco, CA: Jossey-Bass.

Liu, G. (Fall 1995). Knowledge, foundations, and discourse: Philosophical support for service-learning. *Michigan Journal of Community Service-Learning,* 5–18.

Lynton, E. A. (1995). *Making the case for professional service.* Washington, DC: American Association for Higher Education.

Lynton, E. A., & Elman, S. E. (1987). *New priorities for the university.* San Francisco, CA: Jossey-Bass.

Marchese, T. (1995, May/June). It's the system, stupid. *Change, 27* (3), 4.

Markus, G. B., Howard, J. P. F., & King, D. C. (1993, Winter). Integrating community service and classroom instruction enhances learning: Results from an experiment. *Educational Evaluation and Policy Analysis, 15* (4), 410–419.

Morton, K., & Troppe, M. (1996, January). From the margin to the mainstream: Campus Compact's project on integrating service with academic study. *Journal of Business Ethics, 15* (1), 21–32.

Ostrow, J. M. (1995, Fall). Self-consciousness and social position: On college students changing their minds about the homeless. *Qualitative Sociology, 18* (3), 357–75.

Parks, S. (1986). *The critical years: Young adults and the search for meaning, faith, and commitment.* San Francisco, CA: Harper & Row.

Plater, W. M. (1995, May/June). Future work: Faculty time in the 21st century. *Change, 27* (3) 22–33.

Resnick, L. B. (1987, December). Learning in school and out. *Educational Researcher,* 13–20.

Rice, R. E. (1991, Spring). The new American scholar: Scholarship and the purposes of the university. *Metropolitan Universities, 1,* 7–18.

Rice, R. E. (1996). Making place for the new American scholar. Paper prepared for discussion at the AAHE Conference on Faculty Roles and Rewards.

Schon, D. A. (1995, November/December). Knowing-in-action: The new scholarship requires a new epistemology. *Change, 27* (6), 26–34.

Smith, P. (1990). *Killing the spirit: Higher education in America.* New York, NY: Penguin.

Troppe, M., & Morton, K. (1996). From the margin to the mainstream: Campus Compact's project on integrating service with academic study. In M. Troppe (Ed.), *Two cases of institutionalizing service-learning: How campus climate affects the change process.* Providence, RI: Campus Compact.

Votruba, J. C. (1996, Spring). Strengthening the university's alignment with society: Challenges and strategies. *Journal of Public Service and Outreach, 1* (1), 29–36.

Watters, A., & Ford, M. (1995). *Writing for change: A community reader.* New York, NY: McGraw-Hill.

Wilshire, B. (1990). *The moral collapse of the university: Professionalism, purity, and alienation.* Albany, NY: State University of New York Press.

Zlotkowski, E. (1996, January). Opportunity for all: Linking service-learning and business education. *Journal of Business Ethics, 15* (1), 5–19.

Zlotkowski, E. (1996, January ). A new voice at the table? Linking service-learning and the academy. *Change.*

# On the Shoulders of Giants: Building on a Tradition of Experiential Education at Augsburg College

Garry Hesser
*Augsburg College*

## INTRODUCTION

Augsburg College's original mission was that of a *Presteskole*, a ministerial training school for one of the Norwegian branches of the Lutheran church. It was founded in a small, rural setting in Marshall, Wisconsin, and relocated to Minneapolis when its founding president was evicted from a recycled school house, with 10 to 12 of the 20 students lodging in the president's home and all college activities conducted in an attic measuring ten by eighteen. This austere lifestyle continued when Augsburg relocated to Minneapolis, and the promised contributions of prominent civic leaders failed to materialize. The foundation of the first building was laid only after a young servant girl, Karen Danielson, loaned the school officials $60, which served as a catalyst for the delinquent pledges that eventually enabled the college to open its doors in its new, urban location in 1872. The founding fathers seemed to reflect the 19th century religious awakening in Norway which also emphasized the civic responsibilities of committed Christians and which called for full involvement in community life. For example, one of the earliest faculty members was elected to the Minneapolis Board of Education even before his final citizenship papers were received!

## VISION AND MISSION

With these humble origins and a focus on training preachers and teachers, Augsburg adopted a motto of "Education for Service" early in the 20th century. The president who allegedly coined that motto, Bernhard Christensen, attended Augsburg as a student and reinforced the Scandinavian traditions and social ethic of community involvement in a profound manner when he began teaching at Augsburg in 1930. Deeply influenced by these traditions and the example of Kagawa, a Japanese Christian who chose to live among the poorest in his society, Bernhard Christensen also chose to live in a deteriorating neighborhood in Minneapolis, turning his home into a hostel for people in need of a place to stay.

President Christensen was named by Mayor Hubert Humphrey to chair the first Human Relations Commission in Minneapolis, and Christensen actively supported students who initiated a controversial coffeehouse, a venue where Bob Dylan frequently played early in his career, as an alternative to the drug culture in a nearby neighborhood. It seems clear that Christensen's brand of nonsectarian Christianity continues to be reflected in the current mission statement of the college: "to develop future leaders of service to the world by providing high quality educational opportunities which are based in the liberal arts and shaped by the faith and values of the Christian church, by the context of a vital metropolitan setting, and by the intentionally diverse campus community."

Thus, the mission and vision of the service-learning program is built upon the scaffolding created by generations of those who embraced the community and saw Minneapolis as a place of opportunity and service.[1] Many of Augsburg's former students returned to serve on the faculty. They continued this rich tradition of "education for service," which was enhanced by their sophistication in their disciplines and involvement in the community, often including residency in adjacent neighborhoods.

## ORIGINS AND FOUNDATION: A LIBERAL ARTS COLLEGE IN THE MODERN METROPOLIS

In the 1940s the "education for service" theme forked in several directions. Joel Torstenson, an alumnus, became the visionary architect of many new academic ways to manifest the motto. Upon being named to chair the sociology department, he added courses in Intercultural Relations and Minority Problems, as well as Introduction to Social Work and Public Welfare. The department soon became the largest in the college, embracing the praxis between analysis and practice. In 1957, the department began to require field experience in a social agency as an integral part of the classroom course(s) in social work. While Torstenson continued to actively support the growth and eventually the independence of the social work program,[2] he emphasized that the primary objective of the sociology program was "to help students attain a better understanding of society . . . and [the] forces of social change, in the hope that departmental alumni would become effective agents of change" (Chrislock, 1969, p. 210).

Furthermore, Torstenson argued effectively that such an objective was consistent with the mission of a Christian liberal arts college. During the 1950s and 1960s, Torstenson and his colleagues expanded this educational philosophy to include a Social Science Research Center which engaged students and faculty in participatory action research; e.g., community studies for neighborhood groups, planning districts, and the emerging South Minneapolis Model Cities Program of the War on Poverty.

In addition to attracting new colleagues who shared his vision, Torstenson convinced the college to give him a year's sabbatical leave in 1965–66 in order to study what other urban colleges and universities were doing in the arena of urban and experiential education. He traveled widely, studying closely the ways in which urban colleges and universities were engaging themselves in their communities and milieu. The result was the formative document, "The Liberal Arts College in the Modern Metropolis," a paper presented to the Augsburg faculty on January 12, 1967, and adopted in principle as the faculty and administration increasingly began to refer to Augsburg as a college of the city. Torstenson argued that the college's location "at the heart of one of the fastest growing metropolitan areas in the United States gives it a strategic setting for deliberately developing an educational program responsive to the opportunities and challenges of such a community . . . [giving] careful attention to the forces at work in the modern metropolis. . . ." (Torstenson, 1967).

## Early Service-Learning Rationale and Programs

As a prophet ahead of his time, Torstenson (1967) identified a number of motifs of academic response to the metropolis. First, he posited the metropolis as a learning laboratory for liberal learning, including in his examples Johns Hopkins YMCA's extensive tutoring programs, where students became participant observers through volunteer or paid placements. Secondly, he saw the metropolis as a laboratory for research, including participatory action research. Thirdly, he identified the metropolis as an opportunity for community service for both students and faculty as members of communities "which not only need their help but also have some legitimate claim upon them." The fourth motif advanced by Torstenson and embraced by the faculty was the metropolis as an occasion for corporate academic responsibility. Here, in the best tradition of the liberal arts, he questioned individualistic perspectives and ethics that are inadequate for dealing with the question of what it means for colleges and universities, as well as businesses and corporations, to be colleagues and partners with their surrounding communities and the larger metropolitan area.

Torstenson emphasized the critical importance of "the interactive relationships between community and college/university as dynamic and adaptive social institutions responding to each other and the social forces within and beyond the local community" (1967). But equally importantly, his position paper and leadership led to the subsequent development of an Urban Concerns graduation requirement, the college-wide internship program, the urban studies program, an autonomous social work department, active involvement in the establishment of the Urban Corps in Minneapolis and St. Paul (for off-campus public and community service work-study internships), and the Higher Education Consortium for Urban Affairs (HECUA).

## Programmatic Developments in the 1960s and 1970s: Building on the Foundations

One response to Torstenson's position paper was the establishment of a task force on the college and metropolis. It initiated the development of an urban studies program and supportive courses, as well as the recruitment of faculty who were actively "interested in and concerned about the college's role in the modern city" (Torstenson, 1974). Of particular relevance to this chapter was the effort to "expand the field experience programs into areas beyond those developed for students enrolled in the courses in education and social work," as well as "an expanded student employment service . . . which takes more complete advantage of the urban setting . . . carefully consider[ing] the educative function of employment."[3]

During the late 1960s and early 1970s, Augsburg initiated a wide range of academically grounded experiential education programs that grew from this long tradition and history, and especially from the conceptual and organizational leadership of Professor Torstenson.

*Expansion of the Social Science Research Center (1964 and following).* Robert Clyde was hired to work closely with community groups and the newly established Model Cities Program. Efforts focused upon what would now be called participatory action research (PAR), involving the community residents, faculty, and students in data gathering and analysis that would be helpful in enabling the community to make decisions and press for changes and resources that would improve the quality of life of residents in the Model Cities neighborhoods. The center focused its participatory action research on the priorities and planning in urban neighborhoods, such as experimental schools, racism, and social cost accounting.

*Establishment of the Crisis Colony and the Higher Education Consortium for Urban Affairs (HECUA).* Torstenson's position paper was also grounded in the urban crises of the 1960s and the turbulence taking place in most U.S. cities. Following Martin Luther King, Jr.'s assassination, Ewald "Joe" Bash, an innovative pastor and educator, contacted Torstenson. Bash had already been developing immersion residency programs for high school students and seminarians on the north side of Minneapolis. Together they created and conducted a program in the summer of 1968. "It was an experiment with a 'live-in' learning program in which students . . . shared in the life and work of a ghetto community while studying the nature and dynamics of modern urban life for college credit" (Torstenson, 1974). Using a co-learning approach, ". . . ghetto 'street people,' indigenous leaders of local community organizations, and civil rights leaders were hired as 'adjunct professors' . . . [with] each student engaged in volunteer work in strategic agencies, organizations, or situations which would provide a sensitive 'participation-observer' situation" (Torstenson, 1974).

In addition to focusing on the societal crisis, Torstenson and Bash contended that there was an educational crisis that had been brewing all during the 1960s. Their work reflected the reemerging affirmation of the work of John Dewey and others who insisted upon a new epistemology and the relevance of experiential education. As Joe Bash put it, ". . . no longer was objectivity alone an adequate approach to learning. . . . Teaching and learning must happen in dynamics of experiential encounter" (Bash, 1969). Thus, at its core, the Crisis Colony was based upon an explicit experiential education epistemology. The powerful impact that it had on students and faculty alike led to its continuation the following year as a semester in the city program with students continuing to live in the community, engaging in community service internships and study that involved community-based instructors and college professors, as well as reading, critical analysis, and field study.

Other colleges and universities in Minnesota were impressed by what Bash and Torstenson had created. Hence, the Crisis Colony (renamed the Metropolitan Urban Studies Term) was opened to non-Augsburg students, and eventually evolved into a consortium of 18 colleges and universities in the upper Midwest. The Higher Education Consortium for Urban Affairs (HECUA) celebrated its 25th anniversary in 1996, honoring Joel Torstenson, Bob Clyde, Oscar Anderson, Gordon Nelson, and colleagues from the other colleges who joined with Augsburg in creating the consortium. Another indicator of Augsburg and Torstenson's commitment to experiential education was the housing of the consortium at Augsburg in its formative years with Torstenson serving HECUA as president and volunteer CEO during its early years.[4]

*Metro-Urban Studies Internship Program (MUSIP) and Urban Corps/Work-Study.*   In order to expand the opportunities for Augsburg students to engage in public and community service endeavors, a college-wide internship program was created in 1972. Since only a small percentage of students could participate in the full semester in the city programs, the faculty created internship options in every academic department, with the opportunity for students to take up to four of their 35 courses as internships. Most of those early internships focused upon connecting the students' major disciplines to the challenges facing the Twin Cities community, particularly in the central cities.

When Minneapolis and St. Paul established Urban Corps programs in the late 1960s, Augsburg allowed, even encouraged, students to use their work-study funding to engage in public and community service placements, with 10% of the work-study budget set aside for these off-campus opportunities. In addition, Herald Johnson, the financial aid director, sought out special federal and private funding for students to engage in extensive tutoring and literacy internships at the Curry Center, a settlement house in Augsburg's immediate neighborhood.

3President Oscar Anderson initiated a "Day in May" in 1968 in order for the whole college community to listen to the voices of desperation and revolt from the inner cities of Minneapolis and St. Paul. "The impact of that dramatic experience of students and faculty learning directly from its surrounding community about some of the deeply felt feelings of frustration and anger of hurting people in our cities was intense" (Torstenson, 1974).

William Youngdahl, producer of the film "Time for Burning," spent two years on campus exploring the establishment of a Center of Urban Care which involved a number of students and faculty. He became an important link between the college, the Urban Coalition, the Human Relations Commission, and other initiatives in the community. In addition, Youngdahl worked with students and faculty to develop new college responses to the challenges of minority education (Torstenson, 1974).

One other experiential educational strategy for connecting Augsburg with the community embraced the co-learning model in other ways. In the fall of 1969, a course in Crime and Society was initiated at the Minnesota Maximum Security Prison in Stillwater, located approximately 25 miles from the campus. The class was made up of 17 Augsburg students, 11 prison inmates, and four correctional officers. The basic readings were complemented by role playing and role reversals, with all students becoming the teachers as well as the learners. Professor Cal Appleby defined his role as that of an enabler. Subsequent co-learning courses were taught at Stillwater and expanded to the Women's Prison in Shakopee, the St. Cloud Reformatory, and Trevilla, a residence for physically and emotionally challenged adults.

Another by-product of this innovative experiential co-learning ironically eliminated a role for Augsburg students; namely, the establishment of funding for higher education opportunities at the above correctional institutions. One of the original inmates subsequently came to Augsburg and established the Center for the Education of Nontraditional Students (CENTS), with a wide range of programs serving the disabled and hearing impaired. This further led to a thorough physical renovation which made Augsburg the most fully accessible campus in the state. Vern Bloom continued to expand CHR (Conserving Human Resources), with courses offered in mental hospitals and rehabilitation centers, with each endeavor involving Augsburg students and residents in courses such as Mental Health and the Social Order.

Hence, since its founding as a *Presteskole* in 1869, Augsburg has had a growing emphasis on experience-based education, an appreciation for praxis and experiential learning. Long before the research of Pat Cross, Bill McKeachie, Zelda Gamson, Alexander Astin, and others that led to the Wingspread "Seven Principles for Good Practice in Undergraduate Education," Augsburg faculty and students had found that experiential principles are sound and fundamental to a liberal arts education in a modern metropolis. Augsburg did not participate in the University Year of Action efforts and was not connected to the founding of the Society for Field Experience Education or the National Center for Public Service Internships in the early 1970s (forerunners of the National Society for Experiential Education). But Augsburg was actively involved in the founding of the Minnesota Association for Field Experience Learning (MAFEL) in 1971 and the Minnesota State Internship Program, both of which brought together faculty, public, and community agency staff for the purpose of creating public and community service internships for college and university students.

## CONTINUING THE TRADITION: INSTITUTIONALIZING EXPERIENTIAL EDUCATION AND THE URBAN CONNECTION

### Handling the Succession

In 1977, a year before Joel Torstenson was to retire, he convinced the administration and his sociology colleagues that it was critical to find a successor who was committed to experiential, community-based educational programs and someone who had extensive experience in program development and urban studies. As a result, the college brought me to campus to work with Joel for a year before his retirement. I had been working with Steve Brooks and the GLCA Philadelphia urban program and directing the College of Wooster's Urban Studies Program, which had urban centers in Portland, San Diego, Cleveland, Detroit, and Columbus. Prior to and during my graduate work at Notre Dame, I also worked with OEO programs in South Bend and before that as an intern in public housing and public education programs in New York City in the early 1960s.

I came to Augsburg with a deep respect for what had already been created and a charge to build upon that base. This involved working with colleagues to expand the opportunities for Augsburg students, encouraging them to become further involved in a praxis relationship with the city and the challenges associated with urbanization. With the MUSIP and HECUA programs firmly in place, a colleague and I were able to build upon the community research emphasis. Our research involved six Augsburg students as research colleagues, as we interviewed over 500 Minneapolis residents with a focus on central city residents' perceptions and behavior regarding their neighborhoods and housing.

Another innovation involved our continuing relationship with Joe Bash, the co-founder of the Crisis Colony. Joe had also founded a community radio station, KMOJ-FM, in the middle of the Sumner Olson Public Housing project. The station's antenna sat on top of a senior citizen's high-rise apartment complex which was struggling to remain viable for older residents. As Augsburg's representative on the KMOJ board of directors, I was able to work with Joe, the Minneapolis Housing Authority, and eight students to pioneer an intergenerational living arrangement in the same neighborhood where the Crisis Colony was born. The students served on the residents' council and planned and co-facilitated social and educational activities both inside the building and at the nearby community center. The quality of life for all, including the students, was significantly enhanced over the four years before the program was phased out.

## External Funding in Difficult Times: Cooperative Education and Title VIII

The early 1980s were tight financial times at Augsburg. The staffing for MUSIP had already been eliminated in the 1970s due to funding cuts. All internships were now decentralized to each department, with increasing focus on career development and less emphasis on public and community service. In addition, the course credit that many faculty once received for sponsoring and directing internships was eliminated in early budget cuts. But, as so often happens, new doors opened.

Thanks to an unexpected opportunity to serve as the Associate Academic Dean in 1980–81, I was given responsibility for assessing the overall internship program and exploring what other colleges were doing. In the process, we discovered cooperative education and became acquainted with how other liberal arts colleges in Minnesota and elsewhere had used Title VIII funding to retool their internship programs and generate paid public and community service internships. We were able to use this funding to reestablish administrative and faculty support for experiential education. The timing was excellent, since even deeper cuts were made in the Augsburg budget during the 1982–83 academic year.

Hence, from 1984 through 1989, cooperative education funding provided administrative support that enabled me to devote all of my time, with the assistance of a staff, to experiential education. In addition, Title VIII funded faculty development in experiential education theory and practice and supported travel money to make possible Augsburg's full involvement in both the Cooperative Education Association (national, regional, and state) and the National Society for Internships and Experiential Education (NSIEE).

## The Ad Hoc Community Service Task Force and Notre Dame's Center for Social Concern

Of particular relevance to service-learning programming was our choice of consultants to help us in the first year of Title VIII funding. We were able to secure the services of Don McNeill, the Director of Notre Dame's Center for Social Concern (formerly the Center for Experiential Learning). More than 30 faculty attended his workshop on experiential education, which followed a morning convocation presentation concerning Notre Dame's newly renamed Center for Social Concern. Don showed an influential video which effectively portrayed community service in an experiential education context. In addition, he shared the podium with a recent Notre Dame alum who told of her life-changing experiences in their various urban-based community service-learning programs.

As we had hoped, faculty, staff, and students responded affirmatively to Don's workshop and his moving and articulate convocation connecting the liberal arts, Notre Dame's similar Christian mission and their version of education for service. The immediate result was the emergence of an ad hoc task force to explore programmatic alternatives and funding for the development of a community service program to be developed in conjunction with cooperative education and the existing internship programs. This group set about developing strategies to expand Augsburg's education for service.

## National Society for Internships and Experiential Education (NSIEE)

Cooperative education funding enabled me to attend the 1985 annual conference of the National Society for Internships and Experiential

Education (NSIEE) in Pittsburgh. There, I was greatly influenced by Cornell University's field study experiential workshop (led by Tim Stanton, Dwight Giles, et al.), the Service-Learning Special Interest Group, and Jane Kendall and her colleagues' FIPSE-funded Consultant Training program. Within the first two years of cooperative education funding, I found myself trained and active as a FIPSE-NSIEE consultant, as well as serving on the board of NSIEE and on the verge of becoming its president from 1987 to 1989 when NSIEE played a leading role in the reaffirmation of the value of combining service and learning.

As previously noted, it is ironic that all of this happened when the college was experiencing difficult financial times and cutbacks. However, cooperative education funding enabled me to travel and experience a full range of co-op education training, which included NSIEE. This, in turn, enabled me to become an active part of the initiatives and organizations that played a key role in the resurgence of interest in service-learning in the 1980s; i.e., the work of Jane Kendall, Bob Sigmon, Tim Stanton, Dwight Giles, John Duley, Sharon Rubin, Tom Little, Sally Migliore, and Dick Couto.

Needless to say, it was exciting and very rewarding to be able to serve as president of NSIEE (now NSEE) when its strategic planning directed and enabled the staff and membership to give highest priority to the theory and practice of service-learning. My work on the NSIEE board enabled me to be involved in the development of the ten Wingspread Principles of Combining Service and Learning and the Jane Kendall/ NSIEE 2-volume "bible," *Combining Service and Learning*. As a result of our involvement in NSEE, Augsburg was able to stay informed and connected with those leaders and institutions that were on the cutting edge of the reemergence of service-learning in higher education.

For example, from the mid–1980s, when NSIEE's FIPSE consultants authored the much used *Strengthening Experiential Education Within Your Institution*, Augsburg has been aware of and closely following the philosophy and practice espoused in that work by grounding our efforts in the following:

- The values and mission of the college

- Involving faculty at every point

- Integrating experiential education into the curriculum

- Giving attention to quality and assessment

- Establishing administrative structures that support the goals of experiential education and are congruent with the institution

- Integrating experiential education into the budget and financial system of the college

Some specific examples illustrate further how the NSIEE connection was of benefit to Augsburg. When Augsburg, HECUA, and MAFEL co-hosted the 1988 NSIEE Conference in Minneapolis, we were able to secure the services of the chair of the service-learning SIG, Janet Luce of Stanford University. She came to our campus and spent an afternoon with Trygve Nystuen, the president of the student senate and other students interested in creating a community service commission as part of the student government and activities program. That same 1988 conference included an all-day preconference workshop on service-learning led by Jon Wagner of the University of California system. This provided another catalyst for our efforts. In addition, because of my NSIEE involvement, I was invited to become a reader for the FIPSE community service grants and began to visit various campuses as an NSIEE-FIPSE consultant, learning even more about emerging programs.

## Student Initiatives and External Funding for Service-Learning
Meanwhile, the Augsburg Community Service Task Force was actively supporting Trygve Nystuen and his successful efforts to establish a new community service commission in student government. In addition, major attention was focused on finding funding for a community service coordinator. Thanks to information gained through involvement in cooperative education and NSIEE, I became aware of the shift of supplemental work-study funding to an emphasis on community service. Since our Community Service Task Force had been authorized by the president and his staff to seek funding, we were able to obtain $25,000 from the supplemental work-study money and use that grant to leverage another source of funding that had became available from the state of Minnesota in 1989. These were one-time grants of $12,500 to hire staff for service-learning programs if the college provided a matching cash grant of $12,500 or more. Had not the unexpected Federal Work-Study Supplemental grant been secured by Herald Johnson, there was little likelihood that any matching money would have been available.

In summary, it is critical to note that Augsburg's history and broadly based experiential education programs, in concert with the Cooperative Education Title VIII funding, made it possible for a faculty member to become actively engaged in the national dialogue on service-learning. This enabled Augsburg to take fuller advantage of new opportunities emerging in the field of service-learning. The college was already working actively with Mark Langseth and the staff of the National Youth Leadership Council to expand faculty involvement in service-learning.[5] Thus, the previous five years of groundwork by the task force all came to fruition in the form of the $37,500 from these two sources to hire a staff and add a service-learning and tutoring emphasis to our experiential education programs.[6]

# A NEW PHASE OF SERVICE-LEARNING: UNDERWRITING NEW STAFF

## Staffing Service-Learning

With funds in hand, a search committee was named by the task force. It included the two student co-chairs of the newly created Student Senate Commission (now named the LINK). Laura Elhardt and Krisi Miller joined the new chair of the task force, Nancy Guibeault, and two faculty members as the search committee.

After an extensive search which included interviewing seven candidates, the committee unanimously agreed upon Mary Laurel True. Her credentials included an MSW in community organizing and previous experience in organizing and staffing a health-related service-learning program in Worcester, Massachusetts. Mary knew the college well since she had been a participant in Augsburg's first global semester program in Mexico when she had been a student at St. Catherine's in St. Paul and had lived with Augsburg students after she returned to the U.S. In addition, since Mary had a young child, she chose to work part-time, making it possible for us to hire another part-time staff person as coordinator of tutoring and mentoring.

Along with the job description developed by the director of experiential education, to whom Mary would report, the task force had agreed that Wingspread's "Ten Principles for Combining Service and Learning" and "Seven Principles for Good Practice in Undergraduate Education" should guide our efforts. These two documents, along with NSIEE's *Strengthening Experiential Education Within Your Institution* (1986) formed the framework and principles for the building and expansion of the service-learning program. In addition, we had the benefit of having a collection of syllabi from courses that had incorporated service into the course content. These had come from NSIEE, COOL, and Campus Compact sources and were used in the syllabi sampling workshops referred to previously. Two faculty members, one in psychology and one in sociology, worked with Mary to incorporate a 15 to 20 hour service component into their courses as a trial run during the semester following her coming aboard.

## FIPSE Funding

As was the case with cooperative education, funding needed to be secured in order for the college to phase the staffing into permanent, hard-money positions. Hence, in addition to program development and supervision of the tutoring coordinator, Mary began right away to develop a proposal for FIPSE, continuing the initial efforts of the task force. With assistance from Carol Forbes, the newly hired Director of Corporate and Foundation Relations, and ideas from other FIPSE-funded programs,[7] Mary set to work, using feedback from the advisory committee and experiential education staff,[8] to meet the FIPSE deadline, framing the proposal in terms of experiential education and the college's specific context.

## Collaboration with the Faculty Development Program

The FIPSE proposal focused upon integrating service into specific courses with a faculty development focus to accomplish the long-term institutionalization of service-learning. This also led to the cultivation of new and continuing relationships with the community and community-based organizations. Immediately upon hearing that Augsburg would receive a two year FIPSE grant, Mary began to work with the director of faculty development to integrate all stipends and service-learning faculty development into the ongoing efforts and procedures of the faculty development program. The same proposal forms were used, and the FIPSE funds were channeled through faculty development and reviewed by their committee like any other request for funding to revise and/or develop a new course. It was decided that a stipend of $500 was appropriate for the revision of an existing course and consistent with funding for the creation of a new course; i.e., $1,500.

Mary and Lois Olson, the Coordinator of Internships and Cooperative Education, were invited by the director of faculty development to make a presentation at the summer faculty development workshop. The course revision stipends and Mary's availability to assist faculty in securing salient, quality placements for courses was announced and explained at that retreat. Faculty response was immediate and enthusiastic, with six faculty applying for grants during the fall term and an additional six the following term.

## PROGRAM STRUCTURE

In keeping with the long-standing tradition of having internships and cooperative education as a function of and a fundamental part of the academic program, the service-learning program is overseen by a faculty member who reports to the academic dean and vice president of academic affairs. In addition to being a part of the experiential education staff, the evolution of service-learning continued to have the benefit of a college-wide advisory committee which had evolved from the original task force. It consisted of the student LINK co-chairs, four faculty members, the assistant to the president for community affairs, and the chair from the student affairs division.

## Division of Labor and Reporting

While there is an integrated, collaborative relationship among all five members of the experiential education staff, there is also a clear division of labor. Mary Laurel True, Associate Director of Experiential Education, coordinates and promotes all aspects of service-learning, including the direct supervision of the tutoring-literacy coordinator.[9] Lois Olson, Associate Director of Experiential Education, coordinates and promotes the internship and cooperative education programs, including the direct supervision of the Placement and Employer Relations Coordinator. The entire staff meets regularly for planning and coordination, led by a tenured professor, who divides his time equally between teaching and administration. Each office uses student work-study assistants to carry out many of the day-to-day functions of the programs.[10]

In all aspects of the experiential education program, there is a concentrated effort to create reciprocal relationships and mutual benefits among the three constituents we seek to serve: our students, the community, and the faculty and academic programs they represent. To that end, each of the associate directors is responsible for creating continual feedback from these three sectors as we seek to serve their needs and interests synergistically and simultaneously. The experiential education staff team-teach an interim service-learning internship course as well as a general education City Seminar for students engaged in internships and community service.

Finally, to emphasize a point made earlier, the current president and vice president for academic affairs have been strong supporters of the experiential education program throughout their respective tenures, as were their predecessors before them. Of particular note is that President Anderson has served as the chair of the Minnesota Commission on National and Community Service since its founding. The commission coordinates all state and federal funding. President Anderson also belongs to the National and State Campus Compacts. The previous academic vice president participated in the 1992 Campus Compact Summer Institute in Boulder, co-authoring the rationale and strategic plan for service-learning along with four faculty members who attended with him.

## Role of Students

Students had been actively engaged in initiating community service projects well before there was a staff for service-learning or internships; e.g., Urban Corps involvement in public and community service internships, active participation in the Metropolitan Urban Studies Term semester programs, participation in a Freire-oriented Latin American program of the college, staffing a homeless shelter as part of campus ministry, developing a cross-generational community among residents of a senior citizen public housing project, staffing ESL programs at a settlement house near the campus.

Thus, it was a natural progression, in 1988, for the student government to create a community service commission with a budget and stipend for its chair(s). Beginning with the first two co-chairs, Laura Elhard and Krisi Miller, the commission chairs have worked collabora- tively, yet autonomously, with the coordinator of service-learning to pro- mote student involvement in community service. The coordinator of ser- vice-learning serves as the adviser to the LINK commissioner(s) as well.

Since its inception, LINK has planned and staffed annual Halloween and Christmas parties for neighborhood families in conjunction with the Marriott Food Service and the community service-learning staff. Every Wednesday evening, LINK provides mentors and volunteers as part of a program for children whose families attend a potluck dinner sponsored by Trinity Lutheran Congregation, the college, and Fairview Hospitals. The students plan and carry out an educational and recreational program for the children while the parents have time to talk and gain support from one another. This and other LINK programs are a collaboration with the Peace and Justice Commission of Campus Ministry.

Since 1988, LINK has recruited teams to participate in the Great American Clean-up every spring and, since 1995, LINK has planned and carried out spring break community service projects on the Mexican-U.S. border and in Appalachia working with Habitat for Humanity. Beginning in 1996, LINK and the service-learning staff have planned and carried out a multi-campus spring break program in the Twin Cities as well. In the summer of 1996, LINK, Campus Ministry, and the service- learning staff collaborated with Habitat and a nearby hospital to build a Habitat home in Augsburg's own neighborhood. In addition, Augsburg has had active chapters of MPIRG (Minnesota Public Interest Research Group), Amnesty International, and the Peace and Justice Commission in Campus Ministry.

## Sabo-Johnson-Torstenson Public and Community Service Scholars

Beginning in 1995, 12 students were awarded renewable $2,000 scholar- ships based on past involvement in public and community service. Each scholar then becomes a part of a leadership team that works closely with the coordinator of community service-learning and the director of experi- ential education to promote service-learning. The scholars have periodic retreats and meet regularly, framing their work around the social change model of leadership development along with Greenleaf's servant-leader- ship model.

Each scholar serves as a liaison between the college and one of Augsburg's core sites/organizations, with the latter defined as a key placement location for course-embedded service-learning and/or intern- ships and off-campus work-study placements. The scholars program endeavors to build student leadership which integrates LINK, MPIRG, and Campus Ministry, providing student leadership and collaboration in the ongoing effort to strengthen and expand public and community service at Augsburg. In addition, the scholar team has been consistently and intentionally representative of the diversity on and off campus.

The scholar program is funded by three endowment funds raised in honor of and by alumni of the college.[11] The largest endowment was raised in honor of alumnus Congressman Martin Sabo, who has served the public as a state legislator, Speaker of the Minnesota House of Representatives, and chair of the U.S. House Budget Committee. The other funding honors a 1931 graduate, Adeline Marie Rasmussen Johnson, and is provided by her family, who have been very involved in public and community service. The third endowment honors Joel and Fran Torstenson, whose example and leadership have been fundamental and foundational in the origins and educational philosophy of the service-learning program at Augsburg.

## STRATEGIES TO PROMOTE FACULTY INVOLVEMENT

As indicated in the preceding history, faculty have been the chief architects and supporters of experiential education, including service-learning, for at least three decades. This has firmly institutionalized experiential education throughout the curriculum through the college-wide internship, cooperative education, service-learning, and global education programs. With the advent of cooperative education funding, each academic department named a co-op education coordinator who was given a small annual stipend for participating in ongoing faculty development workshops and serving as a liaison for his/her respective department.

Similarly, and in conjunction with the faculty development program and outside funding, faculty have been provided with stipends to support their revision of courses to include a service-learning component. This has involved more than 25 faculty who now teach service-learning courses. A team of four faculty and the academic dean participated in the 1993 Campus Compact Summer Institute in Boulder. In addition, week-long service-learning summer institutes for faculty were held in 1994 and 1996 led by Augsburg faculty and the experiential education staff.

Indeed, the current director of faculty development, Victoria Littlefield, has played a key role in the expansion of service-learning. As a participant in the Campus Compact Summer Institute in 1993, she has been a co-planner with staff and has been instrumental in funding two Augsburg Summer Faculty Service-Learning Institutes (1994 and 1996). She serves on the Minnesota Campus Compact Advisory Council and has authored a faculty handbook for service-learning which focuses on incorporating community service into courses and has been widely circulated among other colleges and universities. Two Augsburg faculty members, Joe Erickson and I, have served as editors in the American Association for Higher Education's (AAHE) monograph project, *Service-Learning and the Academic Disciplines.*

Since 1990, more than 30 different Augsburg courses have been designed or redesigned to include a service-learning component. Cass Dalglish has developed an innovative journalism course in which each student has a beat and identifies an issue to research and write about. The issues grow out of service involvement in a wide range of placements; e.g., homelessness, literacy, domestic abuse, poverty, crime. The Sociology Research Methods course engages students and instructor in action research for a nonprofit or community organization such as Habitat for Humanity or the Neighborhood Revitalization Program.

In a Biblical Studies course, students serve in the community to deepen their understanding of the biblical concept of works of mercy. The professor who teaches Environment and Behavior assigns his students in pairs to serve in a variety of environmentally related organizations in order to ground and apply the concepts of the course. In the History of Social Movements, students serve in a wide range of social movement organizations in order to more fully understand how current issues relate to past struggles and the difficulties and obstacles which a social movement faces. In a course required for education majors, Human Relations, students interact with diverse populations in order to grow in their understanding of and ability to interact with persons of other races and cultures. In the Urban Sociology course, the students and professor provide service, including action research, to neighborhood organizations near the college in order for students to do participant observation and have a point of departure and frame of reference for the course objectives of learning how to read a community and how to understand communities as social systems which are being impacted by a global market economy.

Currently, a mathematics professor has received a Campus Compact grant under the Science, Engineering, Architecture, Mathematics, and Computer Science Program (SEAMS). She has integrated a service-learning component into Math 247, Mathematical Modeling and Differential Equations. Another faculty member in the MIS and Business Administration department assigns teams of students to community-based organizations and nonprofits to design and create MIS programs in conjunction with her Project Management class. The supportive structures of service-learning summer institutes, faculty development stipends, and ongoing peer support and coaching undergird the growing involvement of faculty in service-learning and experiential education in general.

## OTHER COMPONENTS AND ASPECTS OF THE COMMUNITY SERVICE-LEARNING PROGRAM

### First Year Experience (FYE) and Student Affairs

Every fall during new student orientation, each new student is assigned to a FYE group. All 300 first-year students participate. The faculty adviser and student orientation leader for each group work with Mary Laurel True and the service-learning staff to design a half-day service-learning experience in the community. Each year a quilt or collage is created, with each group contributing a square to the whole which is assembled and displayed at the opening convocation to mark and celebrate the centrality of service to the overall student experience at Augsburg. Convocation addresses always stress the education for service motto and the centrality of service to the academic program of the college.

In addition, the service-learning coordinator works with the residence hall coordinators and resident advisers (RA's) to create service-learning projects for each residence hall unit. All residence assistants arrange for at least one community service project for their floors each semester as part of their overall effort to enhance the quality of student life.

### Campus Ministry

As one of the early initiators of community service volunteer efforts, Campus Ministry continues to promote community and channel students into various service-learning endeavors. The service-learning staff and program works with the Peace and Justice Committee of Campus Ministry to jointly plan and promote community service projects.

Augsburg's Campus Minister, David Wold, has a long history of taking youth and adults to all parts of the world for service projects and increased global and cross-cultural understanding. His leadership and enthusiasm was instrumental in the creation of the initial Community Service-Learning Task Force in 1985 and the creation of a Peace and Justice Committee within Campus Ministry. Students, staff, and faculty active in community service are regularly invited to speak in chapel and promote the opportunities available in the wider community. Pastor Wold and a cadre of student volunteers have created a metropolitan-wide church basketball league which brings together thousands of boys and girls across race, class, and home neighborhood, making use of Augsburg's facilities to meet a community need.

### Community Participation and Key Community Partnerships

Augsburg's service-learning programs are built upon a long tradition of working with a wide range of community partners through a variety of academic programs, including internships, cooperative education, social work and education practica, as well as student teaching. More specifically, the service-learning program has identified a set of 12 to15 core sites determined by proximity to the campus, extent of need, and appropriateness of experiences for classes and student needs and interests. Most of these core sites have a Sabo-Johnson-Torstenson scholar who serves as a liaison between the organization/community and the college.

In recent years, the coordinator of service-learning has convened community leaders and agency staff to systematically identify community priorities and challenges with which the college and our experiential education programs can assist. All proposal and program development is done with the objective of achieving "reciprocity, collaboration and diversity" (Mintz & Hesser, 1996).

Beginning in 1994, community leaders and agency staff have been brought together to help in the identification of community assets and opportunities as part of an effort to write joint proposals for state funding of a tutoring and family support program for recent immigrant families who live in a community adjacent to the college. In addition, staff from the core sites are regularly consulted and convened to assist in the design and evaluation of the scholars program and the overall effectiveness of the service-learning program.

*Cedar Riverside Community School.* A very strong partnership has developed with a K–12 public charter school located in the most diverse and densely populated neighborhood in Minneapolis about four blocks from campus. In any given semester, there will be 40 to 60 Augsburg students serving in the classrooms, tutoring and assisting teachers and administrators in a variety of ways. A public and community service scholar works actively with the staff to coordinate and track student participation.

Several long-term collaborations have also developed. Augsburg's music department is assisting in the development of a music curriculum for the school. For example, piano pedagogy students teach charter school children piano, and music education majors teach percussion and are assisting in an effort to create and sustain a band program in a school which has no budget or resources for such a program. Studio arts majors offer computer design assistance for the school newspaper, and other art majors have developed a magazine project to enhance the writing and project development skills of students.

Students from an MIS project management class have assisted the administrative staff in the creation of programs to facilitate the writing of required reports and overall management of their record keeping. During the 1994–95 academic year, a comprehensive project involved a history class doing oral histories of seniors in the neighborhood high-rises, linking their stories with the children in the charter school who worked with an art class to create paintings and drawings depicting the seniors' stories. All of these were integrated into an art exhibit which was displayed at Augsburg and a local bank. The entire project culminated in a campus celebration involving the seniors, the K–12 students, college students, and faculty in conjunction with the opening of the art exhibit and inter-generational conversations among all the participants. Following that successful year-long collaboration, a "Kids Come to Campus Day" event was inaugurated in April of 1996. The day included a parade led by Heart of the Beast larger-than-life puppets from a local theater.

*Franklin Learning Center.* As an arm of the Minneapolis Public Library, the center provides free, flexible, self-paced instruction to adults who read, write, and compute at or below the 12th grade level. The special focus is upon those who do not have a high school diploma and the increasingly large numbers of community residents whose first language is not English. In any given semester, 30 to 50 Augsburg students complement the AmeriCorps volunteers and single staff member to provide ESL and GED instruction and tutoring to the approximately 400 learners from over 40 different countries. The center is located in the neighborhood adjacent to Augsburg, approximately ten blocks from campus in a historic Carnegie Library adjacent to the American Indian Center.

*Coyle Center.* This historic settlement house offers a full range of educational, social, and recreational activities in a newly constructed facility, located six blocks from campus in the highest density and most diverse neighborhood in the city. Augsburg's service-learning collaboration with Coyle extends back nearly 25 years, including extensive ESL and literacy tutoring on a large scale thanks to a targeted literacy work-study grant from the federal government. Augsburg has collaborated with the staff in the food shelves, job bank, ESL and tutoring projects, and in after-school sports programs. The collaborative and reciprocal nature of the relationship is illustrated by an ongoing project to develop a multi-ethnic cookbook in which a social work community organization class interviews residents and brings them on as the central players in the project. Then, a journalism class follows up to work with the community residents to write and help design the cookbook. All of this culminates in a community celebration of the over 40 national and ethnic groups served by the community. This is a joint project of the Coyle Center, the Franklin Learning Center, Augsburg, and community residents.[12]

## Evaluation

Each student who participates in a service-learning course completes an evaluation at the end of the semester with the results used to improve and promote the service-learning program. As Director of Experiential Education, and someone who has also taught courses in Program

Evaluation, I have undertaken formative evaluations on two different occasions, once in conjunction with a sabbatical leave. The results have been presented at NSEE, AAHE, CIC, and Campus Compact national meetings. They were published in the *Michigan Journal of Community Service Learning* (1995). Faculty and community feedback are sought on a regular basis, but primarily in a qualitative and case study approach which aids in the ongoing formative evaluation of our service-learning objectives.

## CONCLUSION

Based upon a history and motto of education for service, Augsburg College has built its service-learning program into and upon its nearly 30-year effort to fully institutionalize experiential education throughout the curriculum. The current vision statement and mission of the college emphasize the importance of experience in the development of future leaders of service to the world. The emergence of a clear educational rationale, developed by Joel Torstenson and the faculty in the 1960s became the base for expanding community connectedness as a liberal arts college in the modern metropolis. All the presidents since the 1930s have actively supported community partnerships and service. And the subsequent efforts by the academic dean, the faculty, and staff to clearly connect that rationale to service-learning have firmly established service-learning within the academic curriculum and as an essential part of the experiential education program. Our efforts have been continually enhanced by active involvement in national and regional experiential education and service-learning organizations like NSEE and Campus Compact, as well as the National Youth Leadership Council which is based in the Twin Cities.

In retrospect, one can see there has been a synergy operating at Augsburg in which the institutional culture has incubated and welcomed, indeed sought out, persons who would expand and deepen the college's commitment to education for service. Over the years, one could say that the motto has been enlarged to education through service, as well. In an earlier essay (1989), "Experiential Education as a Liberating Art," I concluded by suggesting that education was at its best when at least three entities were engaged in a collaborative "crucible of learning." When a student, a faculty member, and a community person are simultaneously engaged in mutually overlapping experiential learning cycles, there is the highest potential for learning that I can imagine. Augsburg's service-learning program has always endeavored to function in that way, as a partnership in which students, faculty, and community members seek to serve and learn, aided by the experiential education staff in this learning and serving enterprise.

From 1993–95, Augsburg played an active role in the Council of Independent Colleges initiatives to further the incorporation of service into the curriculum. Augsburg's efforts are captured in the "Serving to Learn . . . Learning to Serve" motif which CIC advanced. Our location, our tradition, and our commitment to growth and change continually challenge us to combine service and learning in ways that allow all of us learn from one another and serve one another as we serve to learn and learn to serve.

Are we there? Hardly. Have we learned from those giants, both within the Augsburg community and outside, upon whose shoulders we stand? Immensely. How will we know whether we are getting closer to the vision of our forefathers and foremothers and to the wisdom emerging from the field of service-learning and experiential education? Perhaps it will be when all of our work with students and the community takes the form of a partnership in which our practice mirrors collaboration, reciprocity, and diversity.

These meta-principles have driven our efforts over the years and continue to shape our service-learning journey. For these and countless other reasons, particularly the acknowledged, but often unheralded work of community partners, students, faculty, and administration colleagues who have paved and continue to pave the way with their passion and commitment, service-learning will continue to be deeply embedded in the mission, vision, and future of Augsburg College.

*For actual Augsburg College service-learning documents, see Appendix C: Timeline for Infusing Service-Learning into a Course*

## ENDNOTES

1. This positive assessment of the urban location has not always been unanimous. From the early part of the 20th century, organized efforts were made to move to the suburbs for "more room and fresh air . . . more desirable locations." Carl Chrislock's *From Fjord to Freeway*, a source for much of the pre-1970 detail of this chapter, traces this struggle with parochial and anti-urban tendencies, often among the faculty itself, noting that it was not until 1946 when a unanimous vote of the board of trustees (led by George Sverdrup Michaelsen, the grandson of one of the earliest presidents) committed the college to a long-range expansion within its historic inner city location (Chrislockh 1969).

2. Currently, an accredited B.S.W. and M.S.W. programs are among the largest undergraduate and the largest graduate programs of the college. These all grew out of Torstenson's effort to bring a series of talented social work faculty members to Augsburg, including Harold

and Merrilyn Belgum, Vern Bloom, Paul Steen, and Edwina Hertzberg. Not only did Torstenson see service-learning as fully compatible with the academic program, he was instrumental in creating majors and academic programs for students who wished to combine public and community service in careers, as well as in their citizenship role.

3. Several outcomes seem related to Torstenson's position paper, including Augsburg's leadership role in establishing the town meetings of the Twin Cities in collaboration with KTCA-TV (public TV) and a wide range of schools, agencies, adult educational organizations, and churches. This made the college's emerging urban orientation visible to many new audiences in the city. Further, when the college celebrated its centennial in 1969, the organizing theme was "The Challenge of the City," underscored by President Oscar Anderson's public statements and writings about the "unlimited laboratory," affirming the educational uses of the city. During the turbulent 1960s, there was a continued support for community service and good human relations which left its mark on the college curriculum as well as the college's relationship with the city (Torstenson, 1974). Finally, the 1970 *Academic Blueprint for Augsburg College* approved by faculty and regents, stresses that "Augsburg College should develop the greatest educational benefit from its urban location and should contribute to the enrichment of the life of the city . . . [directing] some of its energies to the needs of the city."

4. In 1973, Joel and Fran Torstenson took a group of students to Oslo, Norway, to learn how Scandinavians approach urban and social planning in contrast to what the U.S. does or does not do. The Scandinavian Urban Studies Term program continues as a program of HECUA. Subsequently, a former Peace Corps volunteer and his wife, Chip and Rosa Peterson, established a South American Urban Semester program in 1976 to enable students to learn about development and poverty in the southern hemisphere.

5. In 1989, Augsburg hosted the first Minnesota Faculty Gathering to discuss opportunities and developments relating to service-learning within classes and the curriculum. John Wallace, chair of the Board of the Campus Outreach Opportunity League (COOL) and a professor at the University of Minnesota, where COOL and NYLC were housed, and I had begun to present conference workshops at NYLC, COOL, and Bush Faculty Development conferences on "syllabus sampling." We were the faculty convenors at this initial Minnesota faculty gathering and were able to share what we had learned from across the country as regards the re-emerging curricular interests in service-learning.

6. In 1989, following the phasing out of Title VIII funding, the Internship and Cooperative Education Programs were fully integrated, with two full-time staff, and I returned to teaching a 3/7 load, with 4/7 time serving as Director of Experiential Education.

7. As a reader of FIPSE proposals, and a consultant with over 25 colleges and universities, I was able to ensure that our FIPSE proposal reflected the "Ten Principles of Combining Service and Learning" and was grounded in what was taking place nationally in service-learning.

8. The Experiential Education staff, in 1990, consisted of a Director, a Coordinator of Internships and Cooperative Education, a Coordinator of Placements and Employers, the Coordinator of Service-Learning, and the Coordinator of Tutoring and Mentoring.

9. This position has been further integrated into the teacher education placement process whereby the current holder of this position also works part-time in the education department, coordinating and placing practicum students in Minneapolis and St. Paul schools.

10. All of the staff positions and program budgets began with "soft money" from federal and state grants. Augsburg made a commitment to phase in those positions with regular college budget lines as the outside funding diminished. In every case that has been done, with four of the five positions fully funded by the operating budget, and the tutoring-literacy position partially funded by the operating budget and partially on "soft money" as of 1996. The director divides his time equally between teaching and administration.

11. Alumnus John Evans played a key role in raising funds for the endowment. As students and alums, John and his wife, Joan Moline, have served the community throughout the years.

12. In December 1996, Augsburg College, in its continual search for ways to deepen its commitment to service-learning, announced it would award scholarships of $5,000 a year to AmeriCorps volunteers who meet its entrance requirements. These awards—the first of their type in the nation—are renewable for four years, regardless of financial need. This unique expansion of service-learning grew out of Augsburg's long-standing collaboration with the Coyle Center and an idea proposed by Augsburg student Sheri Hixon. The idea was enthusiastically endorsed by First Lady Hillary Rodham Clinton's affirmation that Augsburg "sets an example for colleges and universities throughout the country and recognizes that national service is a vital investment in our future."

## REFERENCES

Bash, E. (1969). *A rationale for the 'crisis colony' approach to education.* Paper presented at a meeting of the American Lutheran Church Division of Higher Education, Minneapolis, MN.

Chickering, A., & Gamson, Z. (1987). *Seven principles of good practice in undergraduate education.* Racine, WI: The Johnson Foundation.

Chrislock, C. (1969). *From fjord to freeway: 100 years—Augsburg College.* Minneapolis, MN: Augsburg College.

Cross, P. (1994). The coming of age of experiential education. *NSEE Quarterly, 19* (3), 1, 22-24.

Cross, P. (1996). *Classroom research: Implementing the scholarship of teaching.* San Francisco, CA: Jossey-Bass.

Greenleaf, R. (1977). *Servant leadership.* New York, NY: Paulist Press.

Hesser, G. (1989). Experiential education as a liberating art. Raleigh, NC: National Society for Experiential Education.

Hesser, G. (1995). Faculty assessment of student learning: Outcomes attributed to service-learning and evidence of changes in faculty attitudes about experiential education. *Michigan Journal of Community Service Learning, 2,* 33–42.

Kendall, J., & Associates. (1990). *Combining service and learning: A resource book for community and public service.* Raleigh, NC: National Society for Internships and Experiential Education.

McKeachie, W. (1994). *Teaching tips: A guidebook for the beginning college teacher* (9th ed.). Lexington, MA: D.C. Heath.

McKeachie, W. (1996). What have we discovered about teaching and learning? Presentation at the annual conference of the American Association for Higher Education, Chicago, IL.

Mintz, S., & Hesser, G. (1996). Principles of good practice. In B. Jacoby (Ed.), *Service-learning in higher education.* San Francisco, CA: Jossey-Bass.

Torstenson, J. (1967). *The liberal arts college in the modern metropolis.* Unpublished position paper.

Torstenson, J. (1971, October). *Augsburg college as a developing urban center.* A report to the Board of College Education, American Lutheran Church.

Torstenson, J. (1974, October). *The church related college in the city.* Paper presented at the American Lutheran College Faculties Conference, Minneapolis, MN.

# Curriculum and Community Connection: The Center for Service-Learning at Bates College

James Carignan
*Bates College*

## INTRODUCTION

The Bates College Center for Service-Learning opened its doors in September of 1995, and in its first year of operation, 652 students participated in service-learning projects. Forty-two faculty members used service-learning in their courses with faculty involvement evenly spread across the ranks from senior to junior members. We estimate over 26,000 hours of student engagement in the community through service-learning. Students also engage in service activities through various extracurricular organizations under the aegis of the center.

By all standards, we have exceeded our expectations. Credit lies in the emergence of "Generation X," whose members are yearning for connection to others; while looking outward to their community, they are finding meaning in their lives. Surely, some of the activity also rests on the existence of a strong tradition of voluntary activity that it is entirely consistent with the historical goals of liberal learning at Bates—and by implication—to the traditions of liberal arts colleges across the nation.

The historic mission—the liberal arts focus on teaching, research, personal development, and nonpatronizing social responsibility—supports the steady and natural climb of service-learning on our campus.

## Service-Learning and Liberal Learning

All learning is rooted in place. The importance of community—the social and physical geography of place—is the real impetus for good town-gown relationships. The "town" is where the learning is grounded. The "other" as represented in the "places" where our teaching and learning occur is definitional in the dynamic that is liberal learning. Hence, community relations are much more significant than superficial concerns for a good public image. Service-learning connects teachers and students to place and contributes mightily to positive community relations essential to this dimension of learning.

First, to that sense of place, seminal to all teaching and learning, Bates College is a highly selective college of approximately 1,600 students and 150 faculty located in the post-industrial community of Lewiston-Auburn in central Maine. A classic example of a community that, prior to World War II, thrived economically on locally treasured and nationally touted textile and shoe manufacturing industries, it was, and is, a working class community with a proud Franco-American ethnic heritage and a strong work ethic.

Students at Bates come from all over the country to discover a culture that is marked by an egalitarian quality rooted in its founding by Freewill Baptists who supported the education of all, regardless of race and gender, although they were most concerned with the education of their own children. In spite of its distinctive elements, Bates is archetypical of a number of liberal arts colleges—often sectarian in root, but secular today—devoting all of their resources to undergraduate education and fulfilling a special American calling of raising up our best and brightest to positions of public leadership.

Lewiston-Auburn and Bates have a history of town-gown relationships that has been uneven through the years. Bates College students have variously labeled the community a mill town, working class, anti-intellectual, a cultural wasteland, economically depressed and blighted; i. e., the pits. Conversely, the college has been perceived by townsfolk as elitist, a party place, out of touch with reality, self-indulgent, ribald; i.e., a snobbish place where spoiled brats drink too much and don't understand life in the real world.

These exaggerated stereotypes have occurred in college communities across the country for most of our history. Indeed, as stereotypes they resonate remarkably well through the history of town-gown relationships throughout the western world. The residents of Bologna in Italy harbored similar views of students at the first western university. It was no accident that medieval universities were walled in the monastic tradition. The town was perceived with disdain, while everything about the routines of the university moved in the direction of separateness and disconnection. Many founders of American liberal artscolleges echoed the sentiment of the cleric who established a small midwestern college in a valley because the hills served as a natural separation from the world.

The rationale for separation was that the academy must draw back from the world in order to insulate itself from the passions of the day. To achieve perspective, it needs distance and time to puncture the particular and come to grips with the universal. Another related iteration has it that scholars must be freed from the day-to-day cares of the world in order to grapple with the fundamental issues of the human condition.

In spite of the strength of this position, there is a countervailing trend, especially in 20th century American education, perhaps reflective of our pragmatic orientation as a people. After all, Harvard, the oldest institution in the country, was established to provide ministers for the young colony. Ralph Waldo Emerson's message in his famous essay "The American Scholar," which he gave as an address to the 1837 Phi Beta Kappa graduates of Harvard, praised the work of scholarship that was followed by action. The American scholar, Emerson said, was connected to community through actions—a form of service.

Indeed, the pantheon of American thought is replete with those who saw learning linked to engagement in the community. None of these leaders were more significant than Jane Addams and John Dewey. Addams' Hull House was a remarkable intellectual movement, a place of learning, connected and rooted in community at its most problematic levels. And Dewey reminded us that the essence of democratic education was involvement with the community. Learning for Dewey was both active and reflective. It required engagement, hands-on activity. Such a concept of learning was central to his understanding of the democratic participatory ethic of American society.

In oversimplified, stark relief, then, there are these two traditions in the history and philosophy of American higher education in liberal arts institutions. One leads in the direction of the academy as a place of retreat from society, a refuge that is free from distraction by the diversions of the contemporary world. The other is connected to community and links learning to reflective engagement. To the latter, the academy is both in and of the community. It is this thread of the education fabric that helps to connect colleges like Bates to place; it roots us in community. That rootedness is enhanced by the Center for Service-Learning at Bates.

But we must be clear about the tension between engagement and disconnection. We must respect both traditions here at Bates and in liberal arts colleges in general. Indeed, it is possible to argue that the creative energy emerging from this discordance has helped to shape some of the distinguishing characteristics of Bates and liberal arts colleges in general.

Liberal learning is not applied learning. Liberal arts and science colleges do not train engineers or accountants. Our subject, broadly speaking, is the human condition and the natural world. We seek answers to the eternal questions of beauty, truth, the nature of the good life, and the secrets of the natural world. We develop intellectual skills which place a premium on precision of language, reason, logic, analysis, and articulation—habits of mind necessary to all callings and to living a life of quality. Much of that enterprise traditionally leads in the direction of abstraction and theory. But we are also, at our best, attentive to our duty (an old-fashioned word that still resonates at colleges like this one) to prepare young people to lead and serve in the larger world. It continues to be our responsibility to encourage habits of engagement with others. In that sense, our mission is also fundamentally rooted in the community.

Liberal learning has always had at its heart the concept of service. There is a strong tradition that the liberally educated have a responsibility to serve society. Prior to World War II and the movement toward the democratization of education in this country, there was more than a touch of elitism in the *noblesse oblige* quality of that vision. But it was, nevertheless, a palpable commitment to linking liberal learning to the commonweal. A quick review of liberal arts college catalogs throughout the century reveals this theme as a constant. It is a tradition that continues to influence these colleges, but in these more democratic times in higher education it takes on less elitist, condescending characteristics.

## SERVICE-LEARNING AT BATES

Bates shares this historic commitment to encouraging its graduates to become a part of the civic life of the nation. The sense of contributing to what Robert Putnam of Harvard calls social capital—the social connectedness that mediates between the individual and the state—has always been at the center of a Bates education. In the short time of one year, the Center for Service-Learning became increasingly perceived as one of the most effective ways of assisting in this core function of liberal arts education at Bates. Service-learning encourages connection. To borrow Robert Bellah's phrase, it inculcates those "habits of the heart" that characterize the engaged citizen. Bates students, who serve in the schools or the soup kitchen in Lewiston, learn the importance and significance of that kind of engagement to a democratic structure and a civic society.

This historic connection to community is deeply rooted in the traditions of Bates, but it has not always flowed from principle; sometimes

economic necessity has been the motivation. In the early years, Bates' academic calendar was adjusted to allow our students to teach part of the
year in Maine's rural schools in order to earn funds to pay tuition bills.
Sometimes the sectarian foundational impulses which encouraged "good
acts of charity" were the source of student engagement in the community.
Such a motive is probably behind the phrase, "they helped every one his
neighbor," that is chiseled into the archway over the main entry of the
early 20th century building at Bates which serves as a student union. The
epitaph reminds students of their responsibilities to others in the community each time they enter Chase Hall for meals and student activities. The
presence of this tradition at Bates created a welcoming context for the
Center for Service-Learning.

A central part of the Bates mission (and we are typical of liberal arts
colleges) gives weight to personal development. Service-learning transforms this goal into reality. Self-development and self-understanding are,
in major ways, the product of encounters with others. Students who cook
and eat dinner with guests in a homeless shelter learn not only about the
face of poverty amidst plenty, but they also confront and discover self.
Such encounters quicken the sense of the necessity of engagement with
others in order to attend to the task of personal development. They help
to take selfishness out of the process of self-actualization.

Service-learning thus adds to the pedagogical arsenal of the faculty at
Bates where there is a very heavy emphasis on good teaching. Service-
learning represents a forceful pedagogy for effective, innovative teaching.
Properly integrated in a syllabus, it provides a vibrant connection
between the theoretical and practical. The abstract is more penetrable,
and the practical is more nuanced. Students themselves embody this connection between the theoretical and practical, while the pedagogy deepens understanding on both levels. The hands-on experience deepens the
understanding of the conceptual, and the ideas discussed in the classroom enrich the practical experience.

Service-learning is also be considered an avenue for conducting
research—in studies that produce results that also benefit community
groups. In this regard, service-learning is akin to the laboratory research
conducted in the natural sciences. The most dramatic manner in which
this has developed at Bates is in an action-research course offered by
Professors Georgia Nigro and Stanton Wortham. Teachers or social service agency staff in the community identify issues or problems of importance to them, and with the assistance of students, frame critical questions, develop appropriate research models and structures, and execute
the needed studies. Thus, students are the driving part of a research team.
Such an action-research project led to significant data that helped the
Montello School guidance counseling staff develop programs significantly different than originally planned thanks to a clearer understanding

of the issues. Student empowerment and a more sophisticated understanding of issues of social scientific research and methodology were made possible by the real-world context of the work.

For Bates and other liberal arts colleges, the world of the mind—ideas—is vitally important. However, given the practical bent of our culture and a habit of anti-intellectualism that frequently characterizes it, ideas and the institutions that deal in them are often regarded as simply out of touch. For students to experience the direct relevance of ideas to the real world represents an important means of validating something we seek to inculcate as a lifelong passion—taking ideas seriously.

Through service-learning, students can connect ideas to public policy. Working in public administration as part of a short-term course in that area, Bates students have brought ideas directly from the classroom into the practical arena, helping shape the development of public policy. Thus, while studying ideas, students simultaneously live the connection of those ideas to the practical world. In this way they learn that ideas—the fundamental currency of liberal arts colleges—do indeed make a difference.

## FOUNDING OF THE BATES CENTER FOR SERVICE-LEARNING

It was into some version of the bifurcated foundational tradition of liberal learning described earlier—a tradition that moves simultaneously in the direction of separation and connection—that service-learning entered the scene at Bates. When Don Harward became president of the college in 1989, he emphasized the importance of service, engagement, and connection to the community in our educational discourse. In his 1991 fall convocation, President Harward underscored the significance of a strong connection to community in this institution's history and future. The tradition of volunteerism at the college had recently been given added support with the 1990 appointment of a volunteer coordinator who helped students interested in community service become engaged with a minimum of logistical hassles. In December 1994, President Harward asked me, as Dean of the College, to consider establishing a center for service-learning at Bates. He asked me to articulate a mission and a plan of operation. Several conversations later, the president authorized the establishment of a center for service-learning which opened its doors in September 1995.

Before discussing in detail the process that led to the development of the center, it is instructive to reflect on a revealing service-learning story that captures the connection between liberal learning and service-learning. It is the story of a dynamic connection between Bates and the Lewiston-Auburn community that demonstrates how the tensions revealed in the philosophical and historical traditions of American education can be creatively reconciled in a manner that serves students, faculty, and community well while simultaneously remaining faithful to the sometimes conflicting pull of our own twin traditions of withdrawal and engagement.

In December 1994, as part of a series of five presidential breakfasts for members of the community (ca. 120 regularly attend), the topic was municipal government. A panel of presenters, including the mayors of the twin cities which border the Androscoggin River, were addressing the question of municipal structure, including the nature of institutional cooperation between the cities of Lewiston and Auburn. One of the panelists asked President Harward if Bates College would be willing to facilitate study and conversations between the two municipalities as they considered ways in which they might operate more cooperatively even to the point of merger. The president readily agreed.

President Harward then convened a group of community leaders, along with myself, the director of the office of college relations, and other college officials; the mayors, city administrators, and city planners of both cities; the associate editor of the local newspaper; and the head of the chamber of commerce. This steering committee planned a series of activities to study various forms of collaboration, including merger, and to create opportunities for informed conversations in the community on the desirability and form of future cooperation.

The college hosted a series of dinners and invited community leaders to share their views. The college's Muskie Archives, which annually sponsors public affairs programs designed to complement the curriculum, sponsored a lecture series focusing on issues of municipal government, especially collaborative forms ranging from regional agreements to mergers.

As the steering committee was developing its plan for a year-long consideration of this topic, the college was simultaneously laying plans for inaugurating a center for service-learning. In December 1994, the president asked me to develop a proposal for a center which would operate under his administrative aegis.

As these two projects—facilitation of the consideration of collaborative models for the cities of Lewiston and Auburn and development of plans for a center for service-learning—proceeded apace, it seemed clear that there was an opportunity to make service-learning serve the college's facilitative role in the community.

I approached Professor Douglas Hodgkin, a member of the political science department, who was scheduled to teach courses in municipal government and public opinion polling, to ask if he thought it might be possible for his students to be involved in the collaboration project. Hodgkin agreed to talk with the Community Steering Committee, and he was promptly installed as a member of the committee.

As a result of the considerable expertise that he brought to the deliberations of the steering committee, two clear needs emerged. First was a need to review the informal, historical instances of collaboration that had occurred between the two cities to assess their standing and evaluate them against other national models. Second, the steering committee needed to discover how the citizens of the two communities felt about cooperative ventures and what they wanted to occur in the future.

Professor Hodgkin put his students in the municipal government course to work on a review of current collaborative activity and other models extant in the county. Students did research papers on examples from across the country, and they interviewed local participants in cooperative ventures to determine their relative success and point out areas where additional cooperation might be desirable.

The class on public opinion polling learned the theory of public opinion polling by actually developing, administering, and interpreting the results of a poll for Lewiston-Auburn residents. They learned the processes of sampling, question construction, written and telephone polling, and data analysis by doing them. Instead of interpreting fictitious data, they analyzed real data that they had generated themselves.

Each class developed a formal report on the results of their analyses. These reports were attractively bound and formally presented to the mayors, city councilors, and administrative officers of both communities at a luncheon. The results were telling and formed the basis for the appointment of a blue-ribbon commission to make recommendations for expanded cooperative organizational activity. Much of the commission's work is based on the analyses and reports from Professor Hodgkin's classes.

Everyone learned from this enterprise. Students directly felt the significance of their theoretical considerations as their research grounded them in the real issues of their community. It was enormously empowering for them that their work helped determine the direction of public policy in the two cities. The connection of the theoretical to the practical energized their understanding of the conceptual course material. I will never forget one student from Texas passionately presenting his interpretation of the polling data to a skeptical city councilor—it was as if he were talking about his hometown. And, he got the better part of the discussion.

The communities learned as well. They came to understand the progressive nature of the informal cooperative arrangements they had developed over the years. The political leadership got a better handle on the positions of the citizens on a variety of collaborative issues. The next steps in public policy were much clearer as a result of this student work. And the results of the study continue to drive much of the decision-making of the blue-ribbon commission, which I now co-chair and on which Professor Hodgkin serves as a prominent member.

Professor Hodgkin learned too. He came to appreciate the power of service-learning as a pedagogical and research tool. His students were more alive to the issues than they had been in previous iterations of his courses. Not by accident, enrollment in his courses increased significantly, and this fall one of his courses is doing statewide polling work for public television for a critical referendum issue before the voters.

All involved were served. The students were provided with a connection to a real-world situation which gave concrete and direct meaning to their theoretical concerns. They were connected to the community. They personally experienced the linkage between the theoretical and the practical. The community received information that it needed before it could make decisions and move forward. Professor Hodgkin gained more community connections for future hands-on work in his area of teaching and scholarship.

All involved also taught. Students were informed by police chiefs, fire captains, economic developers, and scores of citizens how these issues were viewed—beyond the confines of an academic context. The community was taught some things about itself that students discovered and shared with them. Professor Hodgkin taught in a mode and manner new and invigorating to his pedagogy. It was win-win across the board.

Finally, research emerged. Professor Hodgkin has since delivered a paper on municipal collaboration at the northeast meeting of the American Political Science Association. The paper drew heavily on the work done by the students in his courses.

This story has been recounted in some detail because it illustrates key qualities of service-learning as we have experienced them at Bates. Service-learning works best, is most meaningful, when it is directly connected to the curriculum. It has enormous potential to revitalize traditional pedagogies—both for faculty and for students. Most importantly, when effectively integrated into the context of a course, it deepens and enriches the theoretical and conceptual side of learning— always central to liberal arts education. Contrary to the claims of critics who argue that it takes time away from traditional texts and classroom deliberation, it actually enhances the meaning of those texts and the quality of those deliberations. It also provides living testimony to the relevance of knowledge. It makes clear that connecting reflection and thought to action—a quality long ago espoused by Emerson in his "The American Scholar"—is not only possible, but highly desirable.

Thus, the seemingly contradictory traditions of separation and engagement that lie at the heart of the history and philosophy of liberal learning can indeed be reconciled. Service-learning can connect those traditions in a way that enlivens both so that they can interact in a complementary, mutually reinforcing manner. While the theoretical and the conceptual are deepened by engagement, the practical is enhanced by reflective comprehension.

## PROGRAM STRUCTURE

### Core Positions

The Center for Service-Learning is located in a lovely, inviting house situated among a number of Victorian homes that serve as much sought-after student residences. The center operates under the aegis of the dean of the college who also serves as director of the program. At Bates, the dean/director is a hands-on participant in the program, as well as having administrative responsibility for its organization.

The director is ably assisted by an associate director, who is responsible for working with students, faculty, and the community to structure effective service-learning partnerships. As such, she is often the communications conduit among faculty, students, and community organizations. The associate director is very much on the front lines of service-learning at Bates.

The director and associate director often prod faculty by bringing to their attention projects or partnerships that might significantly enhance teaching and learning in their courses. For example, the center suggested a service-learning component for a literature course on storytelling. As a result of that initiative, the students worked with individuals who had lived all their lives along the Androscoggin River to produce a documentary of their stories of life along the river. The documentary is now part of the Androscoggin Greenways Project committed to the environmental reclamation of the Androscoggin and the land immediately adjacent to it. Similarly, a group of students enrolled in an economics course on the Great Depression interviewed and filmed volunteers in the community about their recollections of the impact of the Depression on the community. They produced a video documentary of the residents' recollections of that traumatic time in America's past. The documentary is now a permanent part of the Androscoggin Historical Society's collection and the public library's holdings. A highlight of that undertaking was a special celebratory moment when students and residents gathered for a reception and showing of the documentary on campus. At that event, it was clear that all participants had experienced both service and learning.

The director and associate director often respond to student interest in becoming more involved in the community. A not uncommon occurrence is the student who has worked in a volunteer capacity with a local agency who wishes to fashion a curricular program around that work. The trust and interest that have developed in the volunteer program pique the interest of the student and the agency in moving to a more structured relationship. The student will seek to upscale his/her work, infusing it with a significantly increased reflective component and structuring it to produce a project that adds value to the agency. Brokering that set of interests into an independent study course with sufficient academic input is often the responsibility of the center staff. It requires knowing faculty interests and inclinations and understanding the importance of encouraging students to incorporate into their projected plans sufficient academic content to warrant faculty support and endorsement. It also requires encouraging faculty to accord service-learning students full parity with traditional students when their work justifies it. While students and faculty must, in concert with community agencies, own their own partnerships, center staff facilitate that process by establishing the communication, providing logistical support (e.g., transportation), and administering a contract that students, faculty, and community supervisor(s) execute to ensure clarity of responsibility for all participants.

Much of our work in the center is ably assisted by a secretary. Sensitive to the nuances of the relationships necessary for effective partnerships, he can be counted on to handle programmatic logistical details diplomatically and efficiently. Every successful service-learning program needs front desk personnel who are dedicated, tactful, and sensitive to the duality of the liberal arts heritage discussed above.

In order to ensure a regular review of the center by critical friends as well as a steady flow of new ideas, an advisory committee was established at the very outset. This committee, which numbers 16—eight faculty, four students, and four community members—functions very much like a board of trustees. Although it has no administrative responsibilities, it advises the center staff on a variety of issues. The committee meets twice a year, usually over dinner, when its agenda normally consists of reporting on activities and brainstorming new approaches to effective programming. The advisory committee played an important role in lending legitimacy to the center during its gestational stage.

## Faculty Relations

The cornerstone of the Bates program is our relationship with faculty. We facilitate this relationship in a variety of ways. Faculty members of the advisory committee are carefully chosen for their commitment to service-learning and for the respect they enjoy as faculty leaders.

Our other faculty relationships are similarly personal. The center staff talks with new faculty each year about service-learning. We propose service components to courses on a regular basis but are careful to do so in a respectful, supportive, non-intrusive manner. We find that faculty are responsive to good service-learning ideas that help them achieve their goals in the classroom. Service-learning dressed in appropriate academic clothing gets genuine attention, but faculty are quick to identify a masquerade. Suggestions that enliven a course's pedagogy, expand research possibilities, or engage students more fully with content are usually well received.

The way in which we approach faculty is extremely important. Our usual strategy is to insinuate a service-learning possibility in a non-bureaucratic way. A phone call, a personal letter, or best of all, a lunch meeting, allow us to tell the service-learning story most effectively. Just as it is important to know when to introduce the idea, so it is equally important to know when to stop pushing the idea. We also make a point of avoiding poorly conceived suggestions that don't serve the educational agenda of the faculty member involved.

Another important part of the relationship we seek to develop with faculty is to assist them in professional development. We do this in a variety of ways. First, a small fund made available to the center by the president supports faculty efforts to develop service-learning components in their courses. Faculty can use these funds to support student assistants, to attend conferences, to develop solid foundations for community partnerships, or to cover other costs related to curriculum development. This incentive has enticed a number of faculty to consider ways in which they can imaginatively incorporate service-learning into their courses and departmental programs.

We also assist faculty by laying the foundation for effective community partnerships. We have assisted faculty in psychology and education, for example, by sponsoring a conference for local teachers and nonprofit support agencies interested in participating in action-research projects involving their practice or agency. Experienced action researchers from other parts of New England have come to campus to discuss methodology, successful approaches, and pitfalls.

Annually the center sponsors a series of faculty luncheon seminars on service-learning. We provide a free buffet lunch while faculty from Bates or other institutions describe the way in which service-learning has worked for them. A philosopher from Swarthmore discussed the significance of a partnership he had formed with a public housing project for his courses in the philosophy of poverty. A geologist from Bates discussed his partnership with the local water authority which puts his students in the field learning geology by doing projects that affect policy decisions. Occasionally, students tell their own powerful stories so that faculty can understand the pedagogical or research potential of service-learning for their students.

A professional development component is central to our effort. We work very hard to be supportive of faculty interested in experimenting with service-learning in their courses. We believe that service-learning does not work effectively as a mere add-on to courses, but should be completely integrated. Complete integration based on relevance and a theory of learning is essential to successful efforts. Students should not walk away from service-learning courses feeling they have merely provided some free community service; they should experience service as integral to the understanding of the content of the course. The center must be trusted by faculty in order to achieve this sometimes elusive goal. Likewise, we must respect faculty who do not wish to incorporate service-learning. It is not a panacea that works well everywhere in the curriculum.

## Student Involvement

Student engagement with the center is as important as faculty alignment. We seek to be accessible in a variety of ways. First, students serve on our advisory committee. In addition to seeking their advice in formal meetings of the committee, we convene students intermittently for counsel and suggestions on particular programs or projects as these emerge. A recent session resulted in plans for a roundtable among students and faculty participating in service-learning in order to deepen their understanding of its pedagogical potential.

We also employ student assistants who carry out tasks ranging from research activities to logistical support. One of our student assistants, for example, edits the center newsletter, *Service-Learning at Bates*, which we distribute three or four times a year. The purpose of the newsletter is to try to influence faculty and student culture by giving service-learning a regular campus presence. It includes messages from the director, program announcements, and testimonies by faculty and staff. Most importantly, it invites students and faculty to be players in the service-learning story at Bates.

Working with extracurricular student organizations is another way in which we seek to develop projects. For example, a small grant from Maine Campus Compact funded the initial year of a mentoring/tutoring program that paired Bates student-athletes with aspiring student-athletes at the local middle school. A special focus was at-risk students. The program now continues under full center funding. Similarly, Amandla!, the Bates African-American society, sponsors a mentoring program for local African-American youth. Lewiston-Auburn is a very white community; the opportunity for African-American youth to associate with other African-Americans of college age has the potential to reinforce cultural and racial identities that are difficult to maintain in overwhelmingly white communities. The center supports these programs by offering reflective opportunities for participants, as well as functional support in initiating and structuring the programs. The center also provides workshop training in mentoring strategies.

As a residential college, we make a special effort to imbed service-learning in that side of campus life. We work with resident coordinators and junior advisers, upper-class students with residential leadership responsibilities, to entice dormitories and houses to undertake community projects which we support logistically and with reflective practices. We are currently lobbying the office of the dean of students to establish a service-learning house next academic year. At Bates, 95+% of the student body lives on campus. We often fail to realize the full educational potential inherent in that circumstance. The Center for Service-Learning strives to maximize this potential resource for connecting students to community "others."

The center administers two small student grant programs. The Croft Awards offer up to $300 to assist students engaged in service-learning projects that are related to course work. This money is often awarded in connection with senior thesis research projects or independent study courses. The funds support travel, material needs, and other incidental expenses. We are able to make approximately 15 awards annually at three different times in the academic year. A second grant program, the Mulford Awards, support more extensive projects, usually in the summer months. These are often ambitious research-rooted undertakings that result in senior honors theses or other substantial studies or projects, some of which find their way to publication.

We place a high priority on direct, personal interaction with students. Indeed, we expend the majority of our time with students in personal interaction. There is really no replacement for the teacher/educator at one end of the log and the student at the other (though a computer probably needs to join that picture today). There is no substitute for such labor-intensive, direct interaction as we support student efforts to increase the service-learning component in their individual educational agendas.

## Other Relationships

Our relationships with key administrative offices in the college are cordial and supportive, and they need to be. The dean of the faculty is clear with her colleagues about her support for service-learning. She has consistently supported initiatives to move service-learning into the mainstream of the curriculum. The center is currently working with the committee that oversees the American cultural studies and African-American studies majors to establish an off-campus semester program with a service component as the central characteristic. This requires flexibility for faculty and a willingness to rotate faculty participating in the program. The support we receive from the dean of the faculty will be critical to our success in this effort.

Similarly, our work with the dean of students' office is cordial. We are hoping to have its support for a dedicated service-learning residence. Our relationship with the volunteer coordinator's office, which is part of the dean of students' structure, is mutually supportive. At the outset we had urged that the volunteer coordinator work out of the center, thereby administratively coordinating all community service programs. However, because of other responsibilities associated with the volunteer coordinator's office that are particularly germane to the dean of students' office, we have not been able to accomplish that goal. In its place, we coordinated our efforts to ensure minimal duplication. For example, the center and the volunteer coordinator's office co-sponsor an early "in-the-community" program. First-year students come to campus four days early to participate in projects in the community. This is an effective way to introduce the community, the center, and the volunteer programs to new students, and it helps point students toward the community from the very beginning of their undergraduate careers.

College vans are available for service-learning activities. Students working in a bilingual program for immigrant workers use the vans regularly to travel 20 miles to the egg farm on which the program operates. Incidentally, transportation is a big issue for the service-learning program. We are working to develop an arrangement with the office of the dean of students whereby the Center for Service-Learning receives priority access to college vans for center-sanctioned projects.

Crucial to the success we have enjoyed thus far has been the support of President Donald W. Harward. His vision was the initial inspiration for the establishment of the center, and he has been generous with the college's resources in providing us with comfortable and inviting space on campus. His budget largesse supported staff additions and included a reasonable allocation for programmatic development—professional development, travel, materials, etc.

Most importantly, President Harward has been a tireless proponent of the central concept that liberal learning is connected at its very core to the concept of service—not service in a condescending, patronizing *noblesse oblige* sense, but service rooted in the very meaning of liberal learning. He has factored this notion into public addresses at occasions such as all-college convocations and in annual reports that highlight the significance of service-learning to the mission of the college. The president has also ensured that the work of a special multiconstituent committee—Goals 2005, a blue ribbon group preparing a report on the direction the college should pursue as it prepares for the sesquicentennial celebration of its founding—gives careful consideration to the role of service in liberal learning. Early drafts of the Goals 2005 report clearly place the concept of service and the Center for Service-Learning among the distinctive features that will identify Bates in the next century.

Service-learning can be successful only if it has clear, forthright support from the president's office. President Harward's decision to make it the direct responsibility of a senior administrative officer, the dean of the college, and to ensure that its activities are directly reported to him has made an enormous difference. Service-learning at Bates is not "buried" in student affairs, chaplaincy, or other such predictable places. Such status makes an enormous difference in our ability to function proactively with all constituencies in the college community. The president's careful organizational structuring of the center, his financial support, and his "bully pulpit" promotion of service-learning have made it possible for our new center to lay claim to Bates' campus culture.

## THE COMMUNITY

In spite of all of this, the center cannot survive without a willing and cooperative community. Bates is blessed in this regard. Lewiston-Auburn is a community whose size (population ca. 65,000) means that it experiences many of the issues and problems associated with urban areas but on a scale that is accessible to faculty and students. Thanks in part to President Harward's efforts to tear down the walls around Bates and enter into more supportive, neighborly relationships with the surrounding community, there is now much greater acceptance of the college's presence in the community.

The center's staff works hard to know the agencies and their leaders in the public/nonprofit sector. This is important. We can talk directly to the district attorney and arrange a service project for a sociology or psychology student interested in studying the "deadbeat dad" issue. We can call up the city administrator and develop a project for a student in public administration that the city needs done.

In addition to the labor-intensive task of knowing the people and projects in the community in a personal way, we try to work systematically with them. Each year the college sponsors a community-action fair when all nonprofit agencies in the area are welcomed to the campus. Students swarm to the fair to learn of opportunities to become involved. Similarly, we make a big effort to show our appreciation to community partners. We sponsor an annual celebratory reception to which we invite all of them. We also try to end major projects with a celebratory event to express our gratitude.

A combination of personal interaction and structural access is essential for effective community interaction. We need to respect the concept of partnership—community agencies cannot become dumping grounds for eager, but poorly supervised undergraduates. The service must be a two-way, mutually beneficial arrangement, and we try to ensure that agencies are not cast in the role of taking on the burden of an undergraduate with no real value added to the agency. To ensure that that doesn't happen means constant work at keeping the lines of communication open.

The strength in the center's relationship with the community lies in our personal approach. Both the director and the associate director are heavily invested in community activities. The director works regularly with the municipal governments, as well as with the educational communities of both Lewiston and Auburn. The associate director is very active in the community, especially with schools. As a member of the Lewiston School Committee and a leader in the Maine State School Board Association, she personally knows a majority of the teachers and all of the administrators in the twin-city area.

Not all service-learning centers need to have staff with those particular credentials, but in an urban community of our size, the personal relationships open up rich possibilities. We know what is going on in many of our 60-plus partner agencies and have personal relationships with the key agency personnel. We can pick up the phone, talk with the individuals who make decisions, arrange interviews for students, and wrap up the details of a project in a short period of time. All of this is significant in making the partnerships relatively nonbureaucratic.

If a personal approach is an integral part of our strategy, so is a habit of involving the community in the structuring and implementation of projects. We need to ensure that the activity is owned by the community as much as by the student or faculty person. The center must be very accessible to community partners. We encourage and welcome requests from community agencies, and although we are quite candid about our incapacity to respond immediately in many cases, or sometimes not at all, we try to be responsive. It is essential that the center encourage the community in every way possible.

Since community partners need to be engaged up front in the design of projects, the center needs to work especially carefully with faculty and students to help them understand and respect this facet of our partnering strategy. Students, and sometimes faculty, may well begin by thinking of the community as a laboratory for experimentation or a passive recipient of the college's expertise and generosity. It is our responsibility to disabuse them of this notion. We work systematically to foster real working partnerships.

We also highlight the value of community participants by encouraging their inclusion in reflection activities. Often community members will come into the classroom to participate in discussions or make presentations. Sometimes they will join a reflection dinner at which students involved in a variety of reflection activities participate. We plan to sponsor a series of pizza suppers at the dean's home to which we will invite community partners and faculty sponsors for discussion.

The center insists that programs and projects produce real results for local partners. When a project is over, there must be value added for the local partner. That is only fair given the important teaching role such partners play in our students' education. Still another way in which we seek to empower our community partners is by encouraging them to recognize and appreciate their teaching role in their partnerships with us.

## Conclusion

The Bates story in service-learning is replicable precisely because it emerges from an understanding of the philosophy and history of American education and builds on those traditions. It is sensitive to the academic thrust of the college: It is attached to the faculty and the curriculum—the driving forces in the life of the institution—and the center pays careful attention to the needs, biases, and hopes of faculty. We work with faculty members to help them understand the pedagogical strength of service-learning: how it helps to strengthen student understanding of course content. We make connections, wherever possible, to the research tradition and agenda of the college and its faculty.

To be sure, some aspects of our program still need significant development. Our evaluative efforts, for example, are still in an embryonic stage. We ask all students directly assisted by the center to complete a questionnaire evaluating their experience. Likewise, we ask supervisors to complete a questionnaire at the end of a project. These are helpful, but we recognize that they constitute only a beginning in what can and should be done in this important area.

We are confident we will succeed and that our service-learning program will flourish. Given the support of the president and relevant administrative offices, and the willingness of the community to work with us, we will continue to build a context for students and faculty to establish ever more satisfactory community partnerships. Bates College is a personal place. Labor-intensive, one-on-one work has been and will continue to be at the heart of our enterprise.

*For actual Bates College service-learning documents, see Appendix D: President's Corner: Directions in Learning*

## References

Addams, J. (1990). *Twenty years at Hull House*. Chicago, IL: University of Illinois Press.

Bellah, R., et al. (1985). *Habits of the heart: Individualism and commitment in American life*. Berkeley, CA: University of California Press.

Dewey, John. (1966). *Democracy and education: An introduction to the philosophy of education*. New York, NY: Free Press.

Emerson, R. W. (1941). The American scholar today. In G. Haight (Ed.), *The best of Ralph Waldo Emerson*. New York, NY: Walter J. Black.

Putnam, R. D. (1995, January). Bowling alone: America's declining social capital. *Journal of Democracy, 6* (1), 65–78.

Putnam, R. D. (1996, Winter). The strange disappearance of civic America. *The American Prospect, 24*.

# 4

# Redrawing the Bottom Line: The Bentley Service-Learning Project

**Edward Zlotkowski**
*Bentley College*

## INTRODUCTION

At a time of increasing social fragmentation, Bentley College, "New England's largest institute of higher learning specializing in professional business education" (1996–97 catalog), has embarked upon an unusual but potentially significant educational venture. Since the fall of 1989, Bentley instructors have deliberately sought to introduce service-learning into the college's curriculum. By the fall of 1996, approximately 25% of the college's 200-plus full-time faculty—representing all 15 of its undergraduate departments—had at some time participated in this undertaking. Indeed, during the college's 75th anniversary celebration, service-learning was singled out as one of the institution's flagship programs. Reflecting this special focus, Bentley's mission statement has been rewritten and now concludes with the phrase "making responsible contributions to society at large" (1996–97 catalog).

None of this is in and of itself very remarkable. Nowadays, many colleges and universities can boast widespread faculty participation in

59

service-learning. Furthermore, genuflecting to social responsibility is so common a feature of college mission statements that its absence would be more remarkable than its presence! But this was not the case back in 1989. At that time, the closest the college's mission statement came to an expression of social responsibility was the declaration that its "primary purpose ... [was] to produce the liberally educated business professional," capable of "achieving personal fulfillment and meeting the rapidly changing needs of the larger community" (1991–92 catalog). In the replacement of "meeting the rapidly changing needs of the larger community" with "making responsible contributions to society at large" lies the story of the Bentley Service-Learning Project (BSLP).

## PROGRAM HISTORY

The BSLP, or as it was first called, the Bentley Homelessness Project, did not begin as a service-learning program. Its origins lay in the simple fact that most of the college's students clearly had had limited social experience with underprivileged members of the larger community. As a professor of English, more or less convinced I had a role to play in helping my students develop a humanistic framework within which they could operate, I had become increasingly skeptical that traditional liberal arts courses could, in and of themselves, equip those students to become either responsible business leaders or informed citizens. Since, moreover, the college itself had formally recognized the importance of nonbusiness disciplines by requiring that they constitute approximately 50% of every undergraduate's course of studies, I felt I had implicit institutional sanction to make what I taught as dynamic as possible.

The first steps toward what would eventually become known as the Bentley Homelessness Project were taken in the summer of 1989 when, in my capacity as an instructor in the interdisciplinary course Values and Choices, I contacted the Pine Street Inn, Boston's best known shelter for the homeless, to see if I could arrange for those students taking the evening section of the course in the fall to make service visits there. Having already experienced the difficulty of trying to discuss social issues to which the students brought all but impermeable stereotypes, I decided my only course of action was to jolt them into a more critical mindset by involving them in face-to-face contact with those they preferred not to see.

Hence, in October of 1989, approximately 20 students—most of them business professionals in their late 20s—made a series of service visits to the Pine Street Inn in the context of a discussion of economic stereotypes. Their visits were preceded by an orientation session with the Pine Street's director of volunteers and readings in Jonathan Kozol's *Rachel and Her*

*Children: Homeless Families in America.* Despite strong initial skepticism—not to mention disbelief that I would have the nerve to send tuition-paying students to a shelter—the service visits went well and the unit in general was a clear success. Most students reported major learning experiences, not just about a social group they had previously ignored but also about themselves—their values, responsibilities, assumptions, and priorities. In many cases, the energy generated by this experience even spilled over into other course units, the net result being one of the most exciting classes I had ever taught.

The success of this first experiment encouraged me to design a similar unit for the day section of the course the following spring. Since, however, the day section consisted of younger, for the most part residential students, I decided I should look for service opportunities closer to the campus. I began meeting with representatives of a shelter in Waltham, Bentley's hometown. Again, the same multifaceted course unit (orientation, visits, reading, written assignments) was implemented. Again, the unit proved to be educationally powerful, its results comparable to those obtained in the fall. My curiosity about what was happening grew intense. Would the kind of intellectual and moral stretching I was seeing in my students also occur in classes where a concern with values and choices was not part of the actual course agenda?

I decided I would try to find out. In the spring of 1990, I applied for and received a modest summer grant to investigate the possibility of incorporating service-learning into other courses. My initial goal was to work with three or four instructors representing a range of disciplines. By late June, I had found the colleagues I needed: in business communication, sociology, philosophy, and management. During the summer, we met several times to discuss both placement ideas/needs and my contacts/resources. As immediately became clear, the academic logic governing the students' service work would vary not only with each discipline but also with each instructor's willingness to take risks. Basically, all four instructors worked with some modification of the core learning unit I had designed for Values and Choices. However, for some, the service was required; for others, an option. While one instructor expected a significant time commitment and a major report, another chose to use the service work as a short-term spur to in-class discussion.

As these four projects started taking shape, other instructors began to inquire about the possibility of introducing similar assignments in their classes. By December 1990, when the fall semester ended, nine instructors and approximately 250 students had been involved in service projects of some kind. And with every single instructor expressing satisfaction with the results of his/her experiment—despite a variety of logistical snafus—it had by now become clear that the college had received a good return on its investment. Indeed, despite my desire to take a semester's break from placement assistance, faculty interest continued throughout the spring.

However, while the homelessness project continued much as it had before, other events were taking place that would fundamentally change the scope of what I now understood was service-learning. In July 1990, the college hired a new provost, Dr. Philip Friedman, and by early fall it was clear the new chief academic officer did not need to be sold on the value of service. Indeed, it was he who eventually suggested the name Bentley Homelessness Project be changed to Bentley Service-Learning Project so as to reflect better the project's potential scope. Thanks to his support, as well as the past year's record of success, I felt encouraged to apply for a major in-house grant that would, for the first time, give me some real resources to work with to begin developing a truly college-wide program.

The grant was awarded, and in the summer of 1991 I set to work doing precisely that. Two tasks called out for immediate attention. First, we needed to expand and solidify our ties with the community. Even the limited number of courses participating in the Homelessness Project had stretched service opportunities at the local shelter and soup kitchen to the maximum. If the number of courses participating were now to grow even larger, more service placements would have to be identified at once. Hence, a questionnaire was prepared and mailed to approximately 50 human service agencies in the greater Boston area asking them to identify kinds of assistance they might need. I then spent the better part of the summer visiting these sites, talking to their directors and coordinators, taking notes, and following leads.

At the same time, it was important that more of the campus community be brought on board and that some kind of structure be established to deal with the proliferating tasks and opportunities. Even before my grant was officially awarded, I had begun identifying those faculty and staff members who seemed to have more than a casual interest in developing a full-fledged service-learning program. These included, above all, Jim Ostrow, a sociologist whose research interests included the relationship between experience and social position, and Ed Wondoloski of the management department, with whom I had already team-taught a variety of courses and whose commitment to socially responsible business was unqualified. At that time Ed was serving as director of the management department's internship program, and thus represented an especially valuable ally. Other people were also key early allies:

- Gary Kelly and Chris Palumbo, Student Activities: During a number of meetings I had with the staff of the vice president for student and administrative services, Gary and Chris emerged as their division's primary advocates in the community-service area. During the

1991–92 academic year, they assumed major responsibility for planning and implementing events during the college's first Service-Learning Week.

- Mary Louise Pauli, Office of Sponsored Programs and Chris Danelski, Development Office: Throughout the summer of 1991, Mary Louise and Chris met with me on a regular basis to plan a strategy to obtain outside funding and to create the document package that would support such a strategy.

- Elliott Levy, Center for Excellence in Teaching: Ever since fall 1989, Elliott had closely followed and supported the growth of service activities. He met regularly with me, Mary Louise, and Chris Danelski to plan our first college-wide faculty event. He also helped plan and implement several other faculty functions. Under his leadership the center provided crucial support and recognition for individuals working on service-learning projects.

- Mark Pecenik, Public Affairs: Having covered several early service events for the faculty-staff newsletter, Mark eventually emerged as one of the program's primary publicists/writers. In September 1991, he drafted the copy for its first informational brochure.

- Amy Kenworthy, student, class of 1992: Having already been active in service-learning activities during AY 1990–91, Amy became, in September 1991, by far the program's most articulate and persuasive student spokesperson. She assumed a leadership role in providing orientation for service-learning classes and in organizing a new student-community partnership program.

I have written elsewhere of the organizational strategy that guided this group's early efforts (Zlotkowski, 1993). However, even more interesting than the particulars of that strategy was the fact that we had any organizational strategy at all, and it is difficult for me not to see this fact as a direct reflection of the business-college culture within which we operated. Unlike many, perhaps most, other initiatives of this kind, the program that would come to be known as the Bentley Service-Learning Project managed to thrive in an initially unlikely context not because of its institution's underlying charter or guiding vision, not because of the college's need to deal with the social distress at its doorstep, but because it deliberately developed a comprehensive strategy for getting where it wanted to go. To be sure, the support, first, of a new provost and then, a year later, of a new president, were invaluable. So also was the receipt, at the most opportune time possible, of two prestigious grants. Nonetheless, none of these factors in and of themselves would have allowed the program to take root the way it did were it not for our constant and conscious effort to leverage every advantage for its maximum impact.

There is, perhaps, no better example of such leveraging than the way in which the program's founders set about creating an infrastructure that would support faculty-sponsored service projects. As the number of stakeholders both on and off campus grew, the need for such an infrastructure quickly became the program's most pressing problem. On the one hand, most faculty who had expressed a willingness to sponsor service projects had only done so in the belief that I would be available to find and set up their students' placements as well as to deal with whatever logistical difficulties and/or complaints arose. On the other hand, the number of participating faculty had already exceeded my own ability to perform these functions in any but the most cursory manner.

Much to my relief, the Office of Student Affairs, in response to what seemed to be a one-sided faculty effort, decided the time had come for the college to have its first genuine student-based volunteer center, and this new center (founded in the spring of 1991) quickly began providing placement services. Since, however, many of our potentially most exciting projects required a degree of attention the volunteer center was not equipped to provide, the situation still remained tenuous. It was at this point that Amy Kenworthy agreed to help with some of the more academically demanding arrangements—first as a work-study student, later a part of her business communication senior internship. Since her internship required a concrete product if it were to be academically acceptable, I also suggested that she develop for the program a project manager's manual; i.e., a document that, drawing upon her two-semester experience facilitating course-based projects, would explain to other students, step-by-step, how they could do the same.

Between Amy's unusual competence and the resources of the new volunteer center, the program managed to handle its logistical responsibilities reasonably well during AY 1991–92. So well, in fact, that by the end of the fall semester, the provost decided the time had come to make official what had already happened in fact. In February 1992, the Bentley Service-Learning Project was formally constituted as a college-wide program, and I was appointed its first director. We now had a faculty-led service-learning program as well as a separate but complementary student volunteer center, a de facto managing board made up of the key supporters identified above, several promising community partnerships, and both a president and a provost who genuinely believed in the value of our work. Our primary ongoing problem continued to be that, as the program became ever more successful, its very success would continue to demand an increasing amount of logistical support. If only we could clone Amy and make her a permanent part of the program!

So that, in effect, is exactly what we did. With the high school graduate pool as well as the number of students majoring in business decreasing annually, we had no hope whatsoever of winning any more new resources than we already had won. Hiring additional staff was completely out of the question. And yet, without adequate logistical support, faculty participation would wither in a matter of months. But Amy's example provided a way out. Suppose, the provost suggested, we were to take a part of our financial aid budget and out of it create a special service scholarship program. We could then target market this program to high school seniors who had already demonstrated leadership in community service. Such a group could become the nucleus of a student service team, willing and able to serve as liaisons between the faculty and the community. Amy's project manager's manual could serve as their guide.

In retrospect, it seems incredible we could have been as naive as we were about the effort it would take to train and manage our new service team. However, as luck would have it, several big breaks fell our way. First, and perhaps most importantly, Amy decided to stay on at Bentley to get an MBA. That meant she would continue to be available to us—now in the guise of a graduate assistant. Second, a FIPSE community service grant for which we had applied came through, providing funds that would allow me to devote more of my time to setting up the new program. In this way, the FIPSE grant made it possible for us to work in a much more deliberate, thoughtful manner than would otherwise have been the case. It even led us to design an entirely new position, program evaluator, a position that provided course release time for Jim Ostrow—and thus helped involve him ever more deeply in program development. Thanks to Jim, the program would have a quality control mechanism built into it almost from the start.

Finally, as if these two breaks were not enough, in June we learned we had also won a grant from the newly funded Corporation for National and Community Service. This grant, in contrast to the FIPSE grant, had an emphatically external focus; namely, the creation of a partnership involving the resources and needs of a suburban, largely business-oriented college (Bentley) and the resources and needs of an urban multiservice agency, primarily devoted to support services for the homeless (Project Place). What made this particular collaboration especially exciting was the opportunity it gave us not only to enter into our most substantive community collaboration to date, but also to strengthen our ties with various business departments. Since the agency's goal—breaking the cycle of homelessness—called for the creation of a new in-house economic development unit, the grant would support our linking management, marketing, and business communication faculty directly with this effort. Grant monies would also be available to help Ed Wondoloski develop a new service-based internship option.

One other event needs to be referenced to complete this sketch of the BSLP's founding. In July 1992, Bentley was invited to send a team to participate in Campus Compact's second annual Summer Institute on Integrating Service with Academic Study. This invitation was significant for several reasons. Up until the end of AY 1991–92, the only substantive contact anyone in the program had had with the national service-learning movement was Amy's and my participation in two annual conferences of the Partnership for Service-Learning. While the Partnership was—and still is—one of the most thoughtful, idealistic service-learning programs in the country, its membership is relatively small and its focus is international. The Compact institute offered several of our core leaders a chance to learn much more about the theory and practice of domestic service-learning.

Second, the invitation made it necessary for us not only to take stock of all we had accomplished thus far, but also to formulate explicitly where we hoped to go next. Thus, it served as a powerful planning tool. It also served as that year's final stamp of outside legitimization, additional proof, if any was needed, that the BSLP was indeed capable of playing a leadership role in the national service-learning movement. What had begun as a rather serendipitous experiment had developed, in less than three years, into a program in which more than two dozen faculty from a wide variety of disciplines had participated. We now had our own director and our own campus space. We were officially on a level with such established programs as the Center for Excellence in Teaching and had won in the last six months more grant money than any other program on campus, with the possible exception of International Studies. We had become part of the college's admissions and financial aid thinking and had become well-known throughout the greater Boston human service community. Slowly—or perhaps not so slowly—we had started to impact the very ethos of the institution that sponsored us. From this point on, though many things would occur that would further strengthen our position, our institutional place was more or less secure. Before I move on to the program as it exists today, it might be useful to summarize the key factors and strategies that had made this achievement possible.

The story of the BSLP is atypical in that the program's creation was driven neither by community needs nor by institutional culture. From the very first, its logic and its thrust were pedagogical. Thus, if it had to contend with the absence of any real tradition of service on which to build, it did not have to contend with the perception that it was a transplant from student affairs. Furthermore, because it was faculty-driven, it always demonstrated great sensitivity to faculty language and faculty concerns. This may well account for the speed with which it won faculty participants.

Less atypical, perhaps, but equally characteristic, was its opportunism. Rarely did the program's leaders fail to take advantage of openings or perceived openings. When a new provost was hired in the summer of 1990, and a new president in 1991, service-learning was on the newcomer's second day's agenda. When the BSLP team returned from the 1992 Campus Compact Summer Institute, its report was linked to a request for written recognition of the academic value of the program. A similar kind of opportunism can be seen in the fact that the program made sure it responded to the Corporation for National and Community Service's very first RFP—a year before the new funding source had attracted widespread attention. The creation of a new scholarship program out of preexisting funds, assumption of responsibility for the 5% of work-study students placed in the community (thus creating a new resource to broker faculty-community collaborations), the use of already established resources like the faculty development luncheon series and in-house grants, co-sponsorship of events and internal publicity—all these point in the same direction.

But perhaps the single most important strategic move the program made was to embrace rather than run away from the college's own sense of its identity. Everywhere and always the BSLP was put forward as the program of a business-oriented institution. If Bentley was known for business, then it was business education the program would champion. Thus, it resisted all suggestions of a discrete major or minor—even suggestions of a nonprofit management program. Since most Bentley students were preparing themselves to work in corporate America, it was their preparation for that work that would constitute our primary concern: as the provost liked to put it, "capitalism with a human face," or "doing good and doing well." By participating in service-learning, faculty could not only help their students take with them into the corporate world the names, faces, and stories of those whose interests are all but invisible to the affluent; they could also help those students begin to apply business skills in real organizational settings. In short, the BSLP was there not to replace but to enhance, not to compete but to assist. All we wanted to do was to help the college better achieve its own potential.

In July 1995, I went on sabbatical, and Jim Ostrow, Associate Professor of Sociology and up until then Principal Program Researcher, stepped in to take my place. Although Jim was only appointed to serve as acting director in my absence, the entire managing board was in agreement that this change represented too important a learning opportunity for us simply to rest with the status quo. Indeed, the provost's office had suggested some time ago that it would like to help us review our operational efficiency, and AY 1995–96 seemed like a good time to do that. Hence, while Jim began his tenure as director with no set agenda for change, the possibility of change was present from the start.

Such change is precisely what has come about. With the assistance of Moira Ounjian, Special Assistant to the Provost, major adjustments were made in staff responsibilities. Since Jim was now serving as director, his responsibility for program evaluation was passed on to a graduate assistant working under his supervision. Even more importantly, Amy Kenworthy's decision to go on to get a Ph.D. meant that she also would have to be replaced. Her replacement, Terry Robinson, though initially hired to assume Amy's responsibilities as general coordinator in charge of both community placements and the scholarship program (Amy's graduate assistantship had evolved into a full-time position), soon found her hands full with the tasks of strengthening our partnerships while familiarizing herself with our faculty. Hence, toward the end of AY 1995–96, the managing board, with Moira's concurrence, proposed that Terry's job be redefined to allow her to concentrate solely on course placements and community partnerships while Jeannette MacInnes, up until then our administrative assistant, became a second coordinator, responsible for supervising special student programs as well as student office help. In assuming these new responsibilities, Jeannette would be supported by an assistant coordinator drawn from the ranks of the scholarship students.

Such a reorganization has worked extremely well. Terry's community organization background and Jeannette's long history with the BSLP have prepared them perfectly for their newly designed positions. Business faculty participation has increased both in quantity and in quality while students in all of our special programs feel they now have someone capable of giving them sustained guidance. The fact that such a major change has gone so smoothly is a tribute not only to the maturity and commitment of BSLP staff but also to the underlying correctness of the new fit.

Thanks in part to Jim's skill in facilitating this important development, as well as his success both in launching our long-awaited corporate advisory board and in establishing for the first time a secure service-learning base in accounting (Bentley's oldest and most prestigious department), I felt comfortable in asking him to continue to serve as acting director while I wrapped up several projects begun during my sabbatical year. Even more recently, I have decided to hand over to him the directorship on a permanent basis. As will be explained, the learning organization model has been of critical importance for us. In moving from one director's skills to another's, the service-learning project has reinvented—and renewed—itself in unexpected ways.

## PROGRAM VISION AND MISSION

Much of what has just been chronicled is reflected in the BSLP's first mission statement (1992) and in the vision it represents today. According to the former, the very first goal of the program was "To make Bentley a national model for a new kind of business education—one that combines traditional academic excellence with social service." Relatedly, the last goal articulated in this early document was "To provide a vehicle for enlisting the support of non-Bentley individuals and institutions—corporate, educational, political, and social—to participate in this work." The priority given to the corporate community in this list of possible off-campus auxiliaries was not accidental. For despite its many similarities to other service-learning programs, one distinctive feature it has insisted on from the very start is its special mission—and opportunity—to pioneer creative ways of making business-oriented education, especially on the undergraduate level, more responsive to the needs of the larger community.

Such a sense of mission helps explain many strategic decisions. For example, it was the driving force behind our first substantive community partnership—our multiyear alliance with Project Place—an alliance created to promote economic development and business expertise. It was also the driving force behind our seeking collaborative relationships with such professional service organizations as the Support Center of Massachusetts, Accounting Assistance Project, and Business Volunteers for the Arts, Boston. It has led to the establishment of a corporate advisory board whose primary purpose, unlike that of many other such boards, is neither to raise money nor to oversee general operations but to help develop a variety of triangular relationships among Bentley students, community partners, and socially responsive business professionals.

This sense of mission stamps all of the many documents we have created both for students and for faculty. For example, the latest version of the BSLP's primary informational brochure begins with the assertion: "The relationship between business and the community has never been more complex or more important." Its faculty overview immediately identifies hands-on experience and ability to function better as business professionals as two of the initiative's primary goals. Not that we are unmindful of the importance of the arts and sciences both in our students' general education and in their ability to discharge their social responsibilities. We have attempted to provide as many service opportunities for the humanities, social sciences, and natural sciences as for the business disciplines. Nonetheless, it is for business education that most of our students have chosen to come to Bentley, and it is, therefore, business education that must lie at the center of our work.

## PROGRAM STRUCTURE AND OPERATIONS

Throughout its brief history, the BSLP has been unusually self-conscious and deliberate about organizational matters. Of particular importance in this regard is the work of Peter Senge, whose book *The Fifth Discipline: The*

*Art and Practice of the Learning Organization* (1992) has provided the general model that has guided our thinking (Zlotkowski, 1993). As a would-be learning organization, we have consistently emphasized effective process over functional boundaries, reassessment over stability, participant ownership over program standardization. Such priorities have resulted in a relatively flat organization in which faculty and staff work as equals while students are included in deliberative processes in a wide variety of ways. Representatives of the community, while not involved in routine operational matters, do nonetheless play a shaping role in decisions regarding the direction of the program in general as well as activities related to specific community interests.

The program director reports directly to the provost/vice president for academic affairs. And although the program, as a faculty-based initiative, has always been located on the academic side of the house, it was only over time that we succeeded in placing it directly under the provost. Thus, at least formally, its director is now on the same level as the deans of the undergraduate, graduate, and continuing education divisions, sharing this distinction with only two other flagship programs.

Parallel to this rise in the organizational status of the director's position has been the evolution of an ever more iependent and comprehensive budget. This budget, which in AY 1995–1996 totaled approximately $145,000 exclusive of service scholarship funds (also approximately $145,000), has been almost completely institutionalized. Thus, while the program actively seeks grant funding to support and develop its programs, it is not dependent on them. This independence makes possible stable long-term planning.

The director, who is a full-time, tenured faculty member, continues to teach one course per semester. In this regard, his position is equivalent to that of the chairs of large departments. Aside from general oversight of all BSLP activities, the director is responsible for the annual budget and takes a leadership role in establishing strategic priorities. He also serves as the program's primary representative to national educational organizations, pro bono business groups, foundations, and other institutions of higher learning. The director supervises both the coordinator of student programs and the coordinator of academic programs, and receives reports from other key personnel such as the service internship coordinator.

Despite his leadership responsibilities, the director serves on a more or less equal footing with other key BSLP personnel on what has come to be called the managing board. This board, which meets approximately every two weeks, is responsible for facilitating the work of the service-learning project as a whole. Its regular members include

- The Coordinator of Academic Programs: Responsible for the design, implementation, and monitoring of course projects, the academic coordinator serves as the primary logistical link between the faculty and the community. Terry Robinson, who currently holds this position, brings to it extensive experience working in and with community organizations. She also coordinates special events and projects, marketing and recruitment efforts, and works with the director to ensure ongoing program evaluation.

- The Coordinator of Student Programs: This coordinator supervises all service scholarship and Community Work Program (CWP) students. She designs, establishes, and monitors their community site placements and evaluates their performance in these programs. Jeannette MacInnes, who holds this position, has been with the program since its beginning, and thus brings to her job over five years of counseling and organizational experience. Other responsibilities of this position include coordination of special student events (retreats, workshops, administrative meetings) and general BSLP office management (coordinating office procedures, supervising work-study students, managing the monthly budget, managing grant-related student funding).

- The Assistant Coordinator of Student Programs: First created in the fall of 1996, this position has been designed for an experienced community scholar (service scholarship student). Its purpose is to help strengthen lines of communication between faculty/professional staff and student service leaders (service scholarship, CWP, and service internship students). Currently, the position is filled by Heather Maugeri, a senior who has experience in several service areas and possesses excellent interpersonal skills. The assistant coordinator of student programs not only represents students on the managing board, she also helps plan and facilitate student-run meetings and events.

- The Service Internship Coordinator: Overseeing all service internships, this coordinator works closely with both a wide variety of human service agencies and departmental representatives to ensure proper student placement and supervision. Since the person who holds this position, Ed Wondoloski, Professor of Management, has had extensive experience running several businesses as well as his own department's internship program, he brings to this position an ideal background. Ed also serves as an employment resource, identifying nonprofit job opportunities for both current students and alumni. As the staff member with the most hands-on business experience, Ed spearheads almost all initiatives having to do with community economic development.

- The Volunteer Center Coordinator: Responsible for the supervision and training of the students who staff the extracurricular volunteer center, the official name for this position is student-life coordinator for orientation, the volunteer center and Greek advising. As the only regular managing board member who does not report to the BSLP director, Madeline Powell, the current student-life coordinator, serves as a living link between the BSLP and Student Affairs. As such, she helps the program achieve greater visibility in residence halls, student organizations, and the first-year orientation program.

In addition to the positions identified above, managing board meetings are frequently attended by representatives from the Provost's Office, the Development Office, Public Relations, and/or Enrollment Management.

As important as these positions are to an understanding of BSLP operations, no less important are the different kinds of student participation the program provides (see appendix). With regard to program mission, the most important of these is, of course, student participation in curriculum-based service-activities, for it was such participation that the program was created to facilitate. However, with regard to program operations, pride of place must go to the BSLP's community scholars. This group, ranging from between 24 and 28 individuals, consists of students who during either their high school years or their early years at Bentley have demonstrated a combination of scholastic excellence and community leadership. Successful applicants each receive a renewable $5,000 per year scholarship and are obliged, in return, to play leading roles on the college's service-learning team. The BSLP's financial aid brochure describes this program as follows:

> The scholarship program allows incoming freshmen with a demonstrated interest in community service to develop their community awareness, leadership, and interpersonal skills over a four-year period. Additional scholarships are available for upperclass students.
>
> Students work approximately ten hours per week at one of the many nonprofit agencies affiliated with the BSLP in the Greater Waltham and Boston areas. . . . They also participate in workshops that explore time management, communication, reflection, and diversity issues, among other topics.
>
> As students move through the program, they take on greater leadership roles on campus and within the community. Students work closely with faculty and serve as project managers and course coordinators, facilitating the progress of specific service-learning assignments. They may also attend . . . conferences as representatives of the BSLP; make presentations to students, faculty and staff; and lead reflection sessions. Students are strongly encouraged to develop their own service-learning initiatives.

It would not be an exaggeration to say that it was the scholarship program around which and upon which the BSLP was built. Because students who are accepted into the program have already developed considerable leadership skills, they are capable of assuming responsibilities that would be difficult for other students their age. Scholarship students have addressed plenary faculty sessions, participated in departmental meetings, and created community-based programs of their own. Because many of them spend several years at the same community site, they receive extensive on-site training, become trusted and valued members of their off-campus communities, and develop an expertise that allows them to serve as knowledgeable resources to faculty and other students alike.

CWP students also play a special role. Like the community scholars, CWP students must apply to be accepted into the program, though the process is less formal. This second group of students, which typically averages just under 40 each semester, earn work-study and Bentley work position funds by committing to BSLP-community collaborations as well as regular training and reflection meetings. The same brochure cited above describes the CWP program in this way:

> Students who qualify for federal work-study or Bentley work program funds, and have an interest in community issues, are eligible for semester-long community service assignments. . . .
>
> Once a student has been awarded an assignment, his or her work schedule is arranged on an individual basis. During the regular academic year . . . students new to the program can work up to 12 hours per week; all other students can work up to 15 hours per week. Travel time to the work site is taken into account.

The purpose of the CWP program, from a BSLP perspective, is to make available to key partners and affiliates additional personnel resources, resources that will strengthen their ability and willingness to work productively with the college. Thus, CWP students, though typically not asked to play the critical liaison role played by scholarship students and not as extensively trained, do nevertheless report to the same BSLP coordinator as do the scholarship students. In this way, the activities of the two groups can be coordinated to maximum community and college advantage. Incidentally, it is not at all unusual for outstanding CWP students to be invited to apply for upperclass scholarships when the latter become available.

Two final groups of student participants need to be briefly described. Service interns are almost always juniors and seniors, devote at least 15 to 20 hours per week to significant projects, and undertake some of the BSLP's most demanding community work. Service interns are designated "ID" or interdisciplinary but frequently retain the disciplinary identities of the departments students come from. Whenever feasible and useful, such students are grouped together in cross-disciplinary teams in order to increase both their community impact and their ability to learn from each other. Such teams were responsible for most of the technical assistance Bentley students contributed to the Project Place partnership. Internships may be paid or unpaid and are designed to meet all the criteria of other academic service-learning projects; e.g., equality and mutual respect among all stakeholders, opportunities for guided reflection, a heightened understanding of community needs and assets. Service scholars are all required to do a service internship in their third or fourth year.

The final group of students to be discussed are the graduate assistants assigned to the service-learning project. Every year at least three full-time graduate assistants (a minimum of 12 hours per week) have been assigned to the director and the coordinators. What these students do is very much a function of the priorities at hand, but one is always assigned to work at least part-time on program evaluation. This means evaluation in four areas: community impact and satisfaction, faculty satisfaction, course-based student satisfaction, and core program operations. Other graduate assistant tasks typically include oversight of specific area programs (e.g., the Accounting Assistance Program, the high school collaboration program) and information management, especially as this pertains to the BSLP's participation in national and regional initiatives.

## Important Community Collaborations

Unlike institutions that find proximity a powerful factor in shaping the direction of their community outreach efforts, Bentley's location has helped de-emphasize the importance of immediate proximity. Located on a self-contained campus in a suburban section of a small city some seven miles from downtown Boston, Bentley students must travel to their community sites, even if that only means using a local shuttle bus. Practical and psychological stimuli to work with specific neighborhoods and/or social groups are simply not a part of the college's context.

This factor, taken together with the school's business priorities, has led to a rather eclectic group of primary partners—a homeless resource center in Boston's South End, a high school in Somerville, a theater in Boston's Back Bay, even a shelter in Quincy, some 15 miles distant. To be sure, the BSLP has had and continues to have placements all over the greater Waltham area, and some of these—like its work with the local Boys' and Girls' Club—have blossomed into significant, long-term partnerships. Still, resource concentration has more typically followed the prospect of tapping our students' specific business orientation.

Certainly the clearest and most dramatic instance of this was the multiyear partnership formed with Boston's Project Place. Because the underlying logic of this relationship rested on 1) the economic development interests of Project Place staff and clients, and 2) the opportunity those interests afforded our students to work on projects that simultaneously expanded both their social awareness and their technical expertise, this collaboration was unusually rich, drawing upon students and faculty from several business disciplines as well as different levels of participation and commitment (e.g., minor and major class projects, internships, scholarship students). Still another factor that made this alliance in many ways paradigmatic was its eventual inclusion of a private sector participant (the Pepsi Cola Company), thus realizing the BSLP's stated aim of trying to tie the resources of the private sector into community-based work whenever appropriate and feasible.

Other key relationships have exhibited many of the same characteristics. The Quincy Interfaith Sheltering Coalition is not only sufficiently proactive to seek employment and housing opportunities for its clients; it is also sufficiently well-managed to achieve tangible results. Thus, service-learning projects do not represent merely well-intentioned efforts; they also have the potential to facilitate real change, a circumstance that enhances their value to the college as well as to the agency.

Even collaborations that do not inherently invite a business dimension often wind up doing so. For several years the BSLP has worked with a number of the local public schools. Tutoring in math, computers, and reading have all been part of this initiative. However, what has proven to be probably the single most reliable delivery vehicle for Bentley student involvement has been Junior Achievement—a business-sponsored program that the BSLP has succeeded in adapting to its own ends. Or, to take another, very different example, of the six area high schools with which the program entered into a service-learning collaboration two years ago, perhaps the most promising today is the one that sees Bentley's business orientation as a potentially powerful way to draw academically undermotivated teenagers back into a serious learning track.

Other examples of business-related collaborations involving the theater, museums, and even church-affiliated efforts in the inner city could be adduced, but they would, in the end, only demonstrate the range of interests with which the BSLP's primary focus can be and has been linked. Whether the collaboration in question is a one-time placement intended to meet a specific need or a complex partnership sustained by many objectives and many kinds of stakeholders, it is likely that business skills will at some point enter the picture in an explicit way. And this distinctive feature of the Bentley program is as likely to be stressed by the community as by the college.

## SERVICE-LEARNING AT A SPECIAL-FOCUS INSTITUTION

Service-learning at an institution like Bentley, while recognizably of the same species as service-learning in general, nevertheless has features that bear the unmistakable stamp of its environment. Our ability to build upon and through that environment—to see it as an asset rather than as something to ignore or even to fight—has been key to our success.

When we first began trying to develop a service-learning initiative here, many suggested our undertaking would have very little chance of success precisely because of the institution's special environment. When these skeptics thought of a program like the one we had in mind, they immediately thought of politically aware, socially engaged students— students with strong intellectual interests and a sense of the importance of public action. Clearly, the average Bentley student does not fit this pro- file. As a January 1995 report pointed out, "Bentley freshmen . . . com- pared with [freshmen in] all four-year colleges and four-year private institutions . . . list the same five reasons as their top reasons for attending a college. . . . However, the order of the reasons varies by type of school."

| Bentley | Four-Year Colleges | Private Colleges |
|---|---|---|
| *Make more money* | *Get a better job* | *Learn more about things* |
| *Get a better job* | *Learn more about things* | *Get a better job* |
| *Learn more about things* | *Make more money* | *Gain general education* |
| *Prepare for grad school* | *Gain general education* | *Make more money* |
| *Gain general education* | *Prepare for grad school* | *Prepare for grad school* |

According to this survey, Bentley freshmen are not only more inter- ested in making money than most of their non-Bentley peers; they are also less interested than those same peers in gaining a general education. Other indicators point in the same direction. When asked to assess their own strengths and weakness, Bentley freshmen characterize themselves as stronger than average in their competitiveness and drive to achieve but weaker than average in artistic ability and creativity. Relatedly, they are not only more likely to work for pay more than 16 hours per week (43% vs. 31%) but also more likely to do no volunteer work of any kind (45% vs. 33%). What makes these results even more significant is the fact that many faculty, staff, and students would also maintain that Bentley undergraduates tend to become more rather than less narrowly focused as they go on.

One can, therefore, hardly blame those who predicted little success for a Bentley service-learning initiative. However, such a student profile can also be read strategically rather than pessimistically. If the typical Bentley student is not likely to clamor for service opportunities and social engagement, one can focus all the more intensively on mechanisms that pair public service with private advantage; e.g., provide a wide range of opportunities to embed service in a credit-bearing context. One can also find ways to create and maintain a special corps of role models; i.e., students for whom service is important. Hence the scholarship and community work programs.

One can also try to harness students' self-described interest in achievement and competition. If the typical Bentley student is less motivated than his/her peers elsewhere by a general desire to learn, he/she may very well be more motivated by the challenge of bringing about concrete results. In short, it is by no means clear that a strong interest in personal advantage is any more an obstacle to effective public work than a strong penchant for theorizing and political abstractions. In fact, most community groups with which our students have worked have explicitly noted their refreshing lack of intellectual arrogance and academic pretense.

A similar kind of contextual adjustment can be made with the faculty—at least with the business faculty. For the most part, service-learning programs have reported little luck in generating enthusiastic business faculty participation. Given the fact that most of the people running service-learning programs come themselves from humanistic or social science backgrounds, this is not surprising. As I have noted elsewhere (Rama & Zlotkowski, 1996), the service-learning movement, as a movement, has been articulated largely in terms of concepts and models foreign to the business disciplines. When business educators (and students) are confronted with an ideological environment in which all things associated with business, corporations, and personal gain are mentioned with disapproval, one can well understand why they feel out of place and hesitate to become involved.

To make business faculty feel more welcome and appreciated, the BSLP has employed several strategies, most of which have already been referred to. For example, in describing the benefits of service work, we have most heavily stressed its 1) hands-on nature and 2) its value in helping students develop a sense of professional responsibility. The importance of gaining practical experience is something most business faculty will readily admit while an emphasis on professional responsibility speaks more directly to their interests than does a more general emphasis on civic responsibility. Furthermore, we have tried to strengthen the case for both kinds of benefits by establishing working relationships with community-minded practitioners. As I have already noted, this was the logic behind both our forming a corporate advisory board and our alliances with the Support Center of Massachusetts, Accounting Assistance Project, and Business Volunteers for the Arts, Boston.

We have also tried to make participation in service-learning more attractive by providing services that speak to business faculty reservations. Thus, in addition to the placement and logistics help we routinely offer, we have also stressed our willingness to help create effective reflective units—whether that entailed bringing in outside facilitators or having BSLP staff lead such sessions themselves. Since most of our business faculty have had little direct experience working with the small non-profits that typically serve community groups, they already have to make significant adjustments in the way in which they think about course projects. Our ability to facilitate this transition by assuming responsibility for other challenges (e.g., finding an appropriate site, monitoring off-campus work, leading nontechnical reflection), may well spell the difference between their willingness to give service-learning a try and a sense of too many risks for personal comfort.

Still a third way in which we have worked to develop a specifically business-friendly environment is in our cultivation of community partners. To be sure, the BSLP, like most programs at other schools, has developed important ties with neighborhood schools, youth groups, shelters, and agencies serving a variety of marginalized populations. However, in addition to these, it has also established ties with organizations like the Virtually Wired Educational Foundation, Inc., a "downtown experiment in bringing the world of telecommunications to the community of Boston" (corporate advisory board document, 1996) and the Christian Economic Coalition, an effort to introduce inner-city residents, "without regard to faith, to the business world, [provide] them with a basic knowledge of business practices, and [enroll] their businesses in a strong, mutually supportive economic network" (corporate advisory board document, 1996). By working with organizations such as these—organizations that see their mission as helping provide the community with critically needed technical expertise—the BSLP can demonstrate to students and faculty alike that community involvement does not belong only to the humanities and social sciences. Indeed, one can argue, as I myself have argued elsewhere (Zlotkowski, 1996), that unless we succeed in enlisting the special kinds of assistance business students and faculty can provide, it will be difficult for all of us to succeed in the larger task of helping to revitalize America's communities.

## CONCLUSION

If the benefits of business-oriented service-learning are clear from a general community perspective, they are no less clear from a general educational perspective. I refer here not so much to the ways in which such projects can improve student learning, be it technical or ethical/social, but to the ways in which they can help business education become a more integrated part of higher education as a whole. By sponsoring service-learning projects and recognizing the importance of every business student's becoming what David Schon (1984, 1988) has called a reflective practitioner, business programs can make their pedagogy as current as their technology. By sponsoring work at sites that naturally lend themselves to a broad range of discipline-specific activities, they increase the likelihood that students will be able to construct conceptual and practical bridges between business and nonbusiness courses. At Bentley, such integration has long been a conscious goal. Thus, for example, while a shelter or youth program may initially approach us for assistance with a business plan, marketing research, or cash flow questions, in all likelihood it will also offer opportunities for tutoring (English and math) and other kinds of client-related services (psychology, sociology, nutrition, etc.). Students who become familiar with the site from one disciplinary perspective will be in an even stronger position to contribute to its work from a second perspective.

Indeed, as business and nonbusiness disciplines learn to work more effectively together, it is likely that the two will also begin cross fertilizing: While business courses become less vehicles for information transfer and more vehicles for complex problem solving, arts and sciences courses will lose some of their self-referential insularity and become instead opportunities for a dialectic between classroom theory and real world practice. In this way, the primary locus of business education will move deeper inside the student, allowing him/her to become more aware of process, more comfortable with uncertainty, and better prepared for lifelong learning. As Robert Hogner, Associate Professor in Business Environment, has written of his own institution's community-based business initiative:

> The community service in management education enterprises underway at Florida International University's College of Business Administration and elsewhere are . . . truly boundaryless education. They are enterprises of education not training, of experience not fact absorption, of process not object, and of value-recognition not value-neutrality/value-rejection (Hogner, 1996).

If the reforms envisioned by documents such as the Accounting Education Change Commission's *Intentional Learning: A Process for Learning to Learn in the Accounting Curriculum* (1996) and the American Assembly of Collegiate Schools of Business's *Management Education and Development: Drift or Thrust into the 21st Century?* (1988) are to stand any chance of success, they will have to build upon the kinds of conceptual repositioning that service-learning promotes.

On many campuses, the business disciplines (including administration, management, marketing, business communication, accounting, and finance) still constitute one of largest concentrations of majors. Neither the service-learning movement nor the country in general can afford to overlook the potential these majors represent. By positioning itself as a program that aims not to steer business students into nonprofit management, let alone the social sciences, but instead to deepen their appreciation of the contribution contemporary business professionals can—and must make—to the well being of our communities, the Bentley Service-Learning Project hopes to help close the gap between corporate practice and private benevolence that many business practitioners experience. It is our belief that, unless that gap is closed, the current disjuncture that exists between those whose primary concern is questions of resource development and those whose primary concern is questions of resource distribution—in other words, between those who manage wealth and those who nurture people—will only grow worse. We invite other institutions with business programs to join us in this work.

*For actual Bentley College service-learning documents, see*
   *Appendix B: Categories of Student Positions*
   *Appendix E: Selected Service-Learning Projects in Business*

## REFERENCES

*Bentley College catalog, 1991–92*: (1991). Waltham, MA: Bentley College.

*Bentley College catalog, 1996–97*: (1996). Waltham, MA: Bentley College.

Hogner, R. H. (1996, January). Speaking in poetry: Community service-based business education. *Journal of Business Ethics, 15* (1), 33-43.

Rama, D. V., & Zlotkowski, E. (1996, Summer). Service-learning and business education: Creating conceptual bridges. *NSEE Quarterly, 21* (4), 10-11, 26-27.

Schon, D. (1983). *The reflective practitioner.* New York, NY: Basic Books.

Schon, D. (1987). *Educating the reflective practitioner.* San Francisco, CA: Jossey-Bass.

Senge, P. (1992). *The fifth discipline: The art and practice of the learning organization.* New York, NY: Doubleday.

Zlotkowski, E. (1993). Service-learning as campus culture. In T. Y. Kupiec (Ed.), *Rethinking tradition: Integrating service with academic study on college campuses.* Providence, RI: Campus Compact.

Zlotkowski, E. (1996). Opportunity for all: Linking service-learning and business education. *Journal of Business Ethics, 15* (1), 5–19.

# 5

# Community College and Service-Learning: A Natural at Brevard Community College

Roger K. Henry

*Brevard Community College*

## INTRODUCTION

**B**revard Community College (BCC), like many community colleges, is inextricably interwoven into the fabric of the community, providing a wealth of community services to its surrounding populace. The college has for years had a commitment to community service, but there was no formal institutional support until 1986, when the college joined Campus Compact, the Project for Public and Community Service. In 1988, the college established its own Campus Compact Project, which in 1990 became the Center for Service-Learning (CSL). The Center for Service-Learning, the beacon of the college's public and community service-learning program, has involved over 12,000 students who have served over 393,000 hours in over 240 community organizations and programs. Community service is embedded throughout the culture of the institution, including the curriculum, which has over 90 instructors who integrate service with over 125 courses and about 275 course sections. The college offers service as a part of its general education program and enrolls over 400 students annually in stand-alone service-learning courses. Over 2,500 students participate annually in service-learning and volunteer service/activities.

The service-learning program has significant administrative and financial support (over $190,000 annually from the college's general fund). Today, all student service-learning hours are recorded on students' academic transcripts, and the number of cocurricular service projects has proliferated. The college provides a diversified framework for student involvement and supports student service-learners with meticulous organization from the Center for Service-Learning, which is composed of four full-time staff, two part-time staff, and six student workers. The college's service-learning program has become a model for community colleges, universities, and colleges throughout the nation. Its resources and publications are used by hundreds of institutions and organizations.

## PROGRAM VISION

The vision for the college's service-learning program emanates from four key sources which uniquely shape BCC's comprehensive initiative:

1. The theory and practice of human relations at Kent State University

2. Lessons learned from service-learning experiences of the 1970s and 1980s

3. Key principles and good practices of service-learning

4. The community college's closeness to its community and the leadership of its president, Dr. Maxwell C. King

### Human Relations at Kent State University

BCC's service-learning program has its historical and philosophical origins in the Kent State University volunteer and community service program founded in 1968. The student protests against racism and the Vietnam War and the participation of human relations department staff in conflict resolution efforts produced many important learnings which underlay programmatic efforts. One such effort produced the Center for Human Understanding which housed and joined the Center for Peaceful Change, International Student Services, Handicapped Student Services, Minority Relations, the Upward Bound program, and the Office of Volunteer and Community Services which later became the Office for Service-Learning. All of these offices and programs stressed the value of the human being and the right of all human beings to develop to their full potential for their own sakes and for the good of society.

The Center for Human Understanding and the human relations department emphasized the recognition, understanding, and appreciation of the impact of differences—culture, race, class, age, gender, sexual orientation, religion, and physical ability. This emphasis on understanding difference and on broadening horizons shaped the volunteer and community services program at Kent State University and impacted me as its coordinator of 14 years.

## History Lessons

Lessons learned from the 1970s and 1980s community service movement had a prodigious effect on how BCC's service-learning program operates today. Most programs were not integrated into the central missions and goals of higher educational institutions and became expendable when volunteer or community service was not "in." The service experience did not ensure that significant learning or effective service would occur. Doing good to the community did not work for most programs and communities. There was little reciprocity in service-learning programs (Kendall, 1986). Also, with few exceptions, top administrative support was notably absent. College and university presidents usually were not involved in proactively supporting service programs. A lack of sharing and networking among higher educational institutions caused long start-up times for many programs and missed windows of opportunity for others. Lastly, significant numbers of faculty were not involved in using service-learning as a pedagogy. Since many programs were housed in student services, they lacked the clout and credibility to link service and the curriculum.

## Principles and Good Practices of Service-Learning

Three service-learning principles first promulgated by Robert Sigmon in *Synergist,* Spring 1979, provide the parameters for our program.

1. Those being served control the services provided.

2. Those being served become better able to serve and be served by their own actions.

3. Those who serve are also learners and have significant control over what is expected to be learned.

The above principles are rooted in the belief that all persons are of unique worth and have gifts to share with others. An important guiding document for service-learning at BCC is the *Principles of Good Practice in Combining Service and Learning* (Johnson Foundation, Inc., 1989).

## The College as Community

As a community college, Brevard accepts community as a part of its mission, goals, and service delivery system. Brevard Community College serves 50% of the residents of Brevard County and works closely with human services agencies, businesses and industries, the school system, NASA, and the government. Our students are both of and in the community.

President Maxwell C. King's belief that community service is an important way to prepare BCC students for their role as responsible citizens provides the visionary leadership needed to sustain a model service-learning program. Because of his leadership and longtime belief in the value of public service, the college has developed an infrastructure to support a comprehensive service-learning program.

## MISSION STATEMENT AND FIT

According to BCC's 1996–97 catalog:

> Brevard Community College is a comprehensive, public, two-year community college. College programs and services provide accessible, affordable, high quality postsecondary education that prepares students to enter the job market, allows them to transfer to senior colleges and universities, helps them meet their civic responsibilities, or assists them in achieving their professional and personal goals. Through its programs, service, and diverse delivery modes, the college offers higher education opportunities to our students and promotes the economic growth of the region.
>
> The purpose of Brevard Community College is to produce a climate conducive to personal, professional, cultural and economic growth of Brevard County and to provide a broad range of service on an ongoing basis including, but not limited to, undergraduate academic studies, two-year technical programs, vocational programs, remedial education, advisement, cultural activities, student activities, intercollegiate athletics, community education, service-learning, and continuing education programs.

Since the center's staff had input in rewriting the college's mission statement, it is hardly surprising that the service-learning program is so congruent with that mission. The center's own mission stated needs as follows:

> The Center for Service-Learning strives to make service an integral part of students' education at the college, creating an expectation of service as an intentional part of the collegiate experience.
>
> Importantly the center provides a diversified framework for student involvement to make these reciprocally beneficial (for student and community) service-learning opportunities available to as many students as possible. All students should be eligible for community service and learning.

The college provides a continuum of service and learning experiences which is inclusionary: cocurricular community service and episodic, short duration projects; class-related observational assignments; volunteer service; fourth credit options; service pay experiences; introductory service courses; service-learning course;, and in-depth internship experiences.

At the center of the continuum is service-learning (75% of all students who participate in service activities at BCC do service-learning options or take service-learning courses), but all service opportunities are important to suffuse service throughout the institution. Many of the service opportunities are developmental, intentionally leading to other, more involved, and educational service-learning experiences.

The main goals of the Center for Service-Learning encompass faculty, students, and community:

- Recruiting and placing students in meaningful and educational community service positions

- Providing service to Brevard County agencies and organizations

- Supporting students who are involved in service-learning activities

- Integrating and linking service and academic study

- Involving and supporting faculty who use service-learning as a pedagogy

## PROGRAM HISTORY

Even before 1986, when service-learning was officially implemented, BCC had a history of community service. BCC was extensively involved in adult literacy outreach and adult and community education, and Dr. Maxwell C. King, the college's president since 1968, was committed to the concept of public service and civic engagement. However, the first formal act of institutional support for a service-learning program began when BCC joined Campus Compact in 1986. During 1986–87, the college participated in two Campus Compact initiatives: the Robinson Student Humanitarian Award and the Peace Corps internship program.

### The 1980s

In 1987, Bette Singer, Dean for Adult Education, hired me to work with a thriving adult literacy program on the Melbourne and Cocoa campuses. She introduced me to the college's Campus Compact Coordinator and the Dean for Administrative Services. At the request of BCC President King, Dean Lawton invited me to address the president's cabinet in January 1987. This allowed key administrators to receive important background information on service-learning while my work with the adult literacy program enabled me to develop key community contacts. In February 1987, I directed a 15-week project to explore formalizing a service program. This small financial investment yielded huge dividends. Meetings were held with key administrators, experiential educators, students, potential service site personnel, and faculty. A survey of existent

practices and attitudes about public and community service was distributed to faculty and staff college-wide. The results indicated interest in
increasing the capacity for such a program and called for existing practitioners' support. During this period, the president also provided me with
the opportunity to speak before a plethora of academic divisions, academic departments, the management club, the board of trustees, and at student affairs staff meetings. Concurrently, the president was weighing the
promise and benefits of a service program.

In March 1988, the college applied for an Action Student Community
Service grant, which was approved in July. The three-year grant gave us
monetary support to augment college resources as well as three years to
demonstrate the worth of such a program. The grant guidelines forced us
to carefully delineate an action plan with goals, objectives, activities, and
a workable budget which concretized our rudimentary frameworks for a
full-blown program.

We moved quickly to establish a physical presence and location
under the provost of the Open Campus who reported to the president. In
early August 1988, the president invited me to speak at his annual
Leadership Conference attended by administrators, staff, faculty, and student leaders. During this key event, a humanities instructor asked me to
help her incorporate service into her five humanities classes for fall 1988.
An advisory committee composed of community representatives, students, faculty, and key administrators was formed to give direction to the
project.

Next, the tangible tools of a program were developed; i.e., program
brochures, posters, student application forms, placement process guidelines, a fact sheet, and a directory of service opportunities. During
1987–90, I worked closely with the volunteer community: volunteer coordinators, agency administrators, and human services staff. Because of our
working relationship, volunteerism was improved countywide which, in
turn, helped create more niches for students. The CSL helped to create the
Brevard Association of Volunteer Management (BAVM) and the Brevard
Volunteer Center. Formal requests for participation were sent to agencies,
faculty, and student groups. The community response was overwhelming. Over 50 organizations requested student volunteers.

In August 1988, Dr. King and Dean Lawton decided to fund with college monies the full-time position of a Campus Compact director. The following October, over 100 humanities students were recruited and placed
by project staff, the director, and two student volunteers. Two priorities
for our initial efforts were to 1) develop a continuum of service opportunities which included both short- and long-term student experiences, volunteer efforts, and service-learning courses, and 2) document as quickly
as possible constituent benefits, especially for students, and to market
those successes widely.

Marketing and publicity were essential during this period of program infancy. So, also, was developing an effective support system for students. Meticulous and energetic support for students once they had been recruited became a trademark and strength of the program.

By 1989, the college started to gain a reputation as a leader in community service and service-learning. The president was chosen to speak about service-learning at the American Association of Community and Junior Colleges' national conference in Seattle. The college was featured in several statewide and national publications. The program received support from a local Exceptional Education Network organization and was able to hire a part-time secretary. Perhaps most importantly, the program became a part of several official documents at the college including the policy manual, the college catalog, and the annual report. The office was moved from the administration building to the student center, and operations spread to the Melbourne and Titusville campuses in spring 1989. This gave us more visibility with students and a presence on two new campuses.

During the fall semester of 1989, three one-credit service-learning courses (Human Service Experience I, II, and III) were implemented and placed in the social sciences division. These courses gave students an additional service-learning option and generated full-time equivalent student (FTE) monies for the college and the program. The program now had its own course section called Community Service-Learning in the schedule of classes. Finally, our first Teaching for Service seminar attracted ten instructors, three of whom are among the best we have today at incorporating service-learning into their classes.

## The 1990s

A pivotal year for the program was 1990. Two additional sources of operating funds were secured, a two-year Student Literacy Corps grant and college work-study/service-learning reallocation funds. Staffing increased dramatically to three full-time and two part-time staff supplemented by five student workers. This was critical because the Action Student Community Service grant was now in its last year of funding. The name of the program was changed to the Center for Service-Learning and was placed under the academic umbrella, reporting to the provost and dean for instruction at the Cocoa campus. At the same time, a three-credit course, Community Involvement, was approved and became a capstone service-learning course with a 32-hour service component and extensive class work.

In 1990 two BCC students were awarded Campus Compact's Student Humanitarian Award, the first community college students ever to win this prestigious national award. Although the college experienced severe financial cutbacks, the CSL was maintained. Indeed, students, faculty, and service site participation increased dramatically, with the number of students participating increasing from 203 to 650, the number of faculty using a service-learning pedagogy increasing from 6 to 20, and the number of service sites expanding to 100.

The next year was also critical for the center. Although the action grant ended, staff and program development funds were used to augment staff support positions. The director's position now became funded completely through college general operating monies. Again, the college was experiencing serious financial cutbacks, but the CSL was not adversely affected because of top administrative support and the CSL's outstanding performance record. In addition, two external events further elevated the CSL's fortunes. BCC was chosen as the first community college to attend Campus Compact's Summer Institute on Integrating Service with Academic Study. It was also chosen to house and administer the Florida Campus Compact. During this year, 1,100 students served 32,500 hours in the community, 35 instructors used the service-learning pedagogy, and 315 students enrolled in our service-learning courses.

During years three through five, I spent much more time networking statewide and nationally and administering the program college-wide. Selling the program and using political acumen were very important in spreading and stabilizing service-learning across the institution. Other service-learning staff worked more with students and agencies during these critical years. Meanwhile, the president convened a service-learning task force to implement the action plan developed by BCC's Summer Institute team. In 1992 the CSL formed the Student Action Leadership Team whose charge was to enlist students to serve as liaisons between the CSL and student service sites. Funded by a small state grant, this project attempted to develop a student leadership component for our program.

During 1992, the CSL awarded its first Outstanding Student Humanitarian Scholarship, a tuition award for significant humanitarian service to the community. It also established a service-learning training and technical assistance clearinghouse which enabled us to gather hundreds of resources for distribution and use by the center. The CSL staff created a set of packets and publications which were sold and used across the country. Service-learning now expanded to the Palm Bay campus and our College Center at Patrick Air Force Base.

Nineteen ninety-two was also a good year for recognition. The governor of Florida visited one of our best programs, the Hacienda Girls' Ranch, a residential facility for abused girls. The director of the federal government's Student Literacy Corps program visited our program, and the staff was awarded the Davis Productivity Award sponsored by Taxwatch of Florida. The CSL also convened several successful workshops and conferences. Lyvier Conss, director of the Campus Compact Center for Community Colleges, addressed the college's board of trustees, and at the president's administrative staff meeting stated that BCC was "light years ahead of other institutions in service-learning."

During 1993, over 1,500 students and 70 faculty members participated in CSL projects. Stand-alone community service-learning courses enrolled 450 students, an all-time high. Over 170 course sections contained service-learning components. Student-initiated service projects expanded to include Rotaract, Partners in Community, and Phi Theta Kappa, the community college honor society which has a requirement of monthly service. The Terraphile Club, an environmental club on the Cocoa Campus, increased its conservation efforts, and student organizations brought to the forefront such important social issues as AIDS, the environment, and homelessness/hunger.

Visibility and outreach also continued to grow. Twelve statewide or national publications highlighted our program. Fourteen institutions received hands-on training at the CSL, and our resources were distributed to over 200 universities and colleges. Staff members presented at several state and national conferences.

The CSL record was not without setbacks. In 1992–93, two critical attempts to further saturate the college with service-learning failed. During that academic year, the CSL proposed a flexible service-learning requirement, and in 1994 proposed a service-learning course for inclusion in the general education core. Although both proposals had support, they did not come to fruition. However, these efforts still played an important role for the CSL in that they increased college-wide awareness of service-learning. Also, they taught the staff important lessons about academic territoriality.

During the 1994–96 period, a major CSL priority was to involve more faculty in service-learning. Using our staff and program development office and the president's support, the CSL received from $2,000 to $10,000 annually to support faculty in a number of service-learning endeavors:

- Faculty research and comparative studies on the effects of service-learning on students

- Mini-grants for service-learning course development, especially in less well-represented disciplines such as math, art, the sciences, technology, and English

- K–14 collaboration to establish service-learning in the school system

- Faculty workshops on reflection and service-learning course development

- An international service-learning pilot project in India

- Faculty authored service-learning publications

- Faculty travel to statewide and national conferences for workshop presentations and professional development activities

- BCC Southeast Regional Institute Team support for service-learning staff, administrators, and faculty

These initiatives served as incentives to develop faculty ownership of the service-learning program and as means to support our first campus faculty coordinators who recruited and assisted other instructors on their respective campuses.

During 1994–95, BCC's Institute Team developed two action plans to guide the college's service-learning priorities for the next two years: increased student reflection opportunities and more faculty incentives. Thus, in 1995 a decision was made to place the CSL under the vice president for academic affairs and student development, a district-wide position. This assignment was close to the top of the college's district-wide administrative structure.

Also at this time, office space increased dramatically to support additional staff and an abundance of service-learning students. The CSL promulgated individualized plans to improve service-learning on all of the college's campuses, and entered into an official partnership with the public school system to increase service-learning at selected high schools. Over 1,800 BCC students served almost 75,000 hours in the community. Ninety-three courses and 220 course sections contained service-learning options. Over 80 faculty members used service-learning.

In 1996, we gained institutional support. The president approved a new position, service-learning coordinator, which enabled the CSL to increase its capacity on less active campuses. Staff and program development funds (over $8,000) became a part of the CSL's regular budget during the 1997–98 fiscal year. Developments in other areas include: A fourth credit option was created to enable students to earn an additional service-learning credit in selected regular classes; a project called Service Hours in Academic Transcript (SHOAT) will allow all student service hours to be documented on students' academic transcripts; a portfolio folder was created to help students organize their service documentation forms and reflection materials. Most importantly, as of May 1996, Community Involvement, SOW 2054, became a social science elective meeting the general education requirements. This development moves service-learning into an even more central place in the curriculum.

## PROGRAM STRUCTURE

The college's service-learning program features an extensive infrastructure which includes a center for service-learning staff, student support, faculty involvement, an advisory committee, and ad hoc special service-learning task forces or teams. Its director reports to the vice president for academic affairs and student development, who reports directly to the president of the college.

## Relationship with Administration

One of the most defining characteristics of the Center for Service-Learning has been the staff's ability to work closely with key administrators at the college as well as faculty and students. The program has needed the support of all of these constituencies. At Brevard, top administrative support helped to start the service-learning program when the college became a member of Campus Compact.

The multicampus structure of the college was another important factor to take into account. The relationship of the service-learning program with individual campus administrators varied considerably. However, we soon learned that we did not need the support of all administrators, only that of key administrators, including the district president, the college-wide vice president of finance, the dean of staff and program development, the associate vice president of college relations, and the campus provosts. We also discovered that in many community colleges the decision-making process is more centralized than at a large university or a big research institution. Although BCC has much campus-based autonomy and authority, district-wide support is vital.

We customized our marketing efforts to our various constituents. Volunteerism was more valued than service-learning by some administrators, while service-learning was more valued by some faculty. CSL staff marketed the program to an array of people on campus including the board of trustees, district-wide task forces, the Strategic Planning Committee, and disciplinary departments. Although our program was mainly "service-learning," it took approximately two years for the concept to be recognized across the institution.

In 1989 our cooperative education program director wanted the CSL to join cooperative education to form an experiential learning office. However, for various reasons, cooperative education was not at that time a strong program. In retrospect, carving out our own identity of service and service-learning represented an important strategy for our survival and growth. I decided then that it would be best for the CSL to grow autonomously because of our uniqueness—and because of the priority given to the program by key administrators.

Locating the program, both in the institutional hierarchy and geographically, was important but tricky. We wanted to operate under the academic umbrella, but to be located in the student services offices to give us proximity to advisers, students, and student affairs staff.

We learned not to overlook the importance of any unit. The Accounting Department mattered because we had grants and concomitant needs to effectively budget our program. We worked closely with our staff and program development dean because she had faculty and office support funds available for curriculum development and new program needs. Certain administrators knew the pulse of the institution and were invaluable in providing both feedback and administrative know how on logistical or delicate policy matters. Astute CSL staff could assess the perception of service-learning's institutional value by listening to well-placed inside staff. Also, getting the ear of administrative office support staff paid big dividends.

Knowledge of how to negotiate territoriality was a survival skill. The more people, departments, and courses impacted, the more likely opposition will appear—overtly or covertly. Political finesse and astuteness take time and hard work but were essential in our securing more space and equipment as well as in maneuvering service-learning courses into the curriculum.

Working closely with the administration at BCC has always been a priority for the CSL. The program was fortunate in having a president who really valued service initiatives and provided the resources needed to establish a CSL. Cultivating and nurturing good relations with the administration has not been just important, it has been vital for the long-term success of our program.

## Faculty Involvement

Enlisting the support of a sufficient number of faculty is necessary for any service-learning program to be successful. At Brevard, over 90 instructors in 43 disciplines use service-learning in about 125 courses and 275 course sections. Faculty play several critical roles in service-learning. They incorporate service into their courses in very creative ways, either for extra credit or in lieu of other course requirements. Usually from 5% to 40% of a course grade is related to service-learning activities. Many instructors provide tremendous incentives for BCC students to get involved. For example, an algebra instructor ties 15% of a student's grade for the course to its service-learning component. The only way a student can replace a test score is to successfully document 20 hours of service tutoring in a local high school or on campus, and to write a journal relating that work to course concepts. A developmental psychology instructor automatically increases a student's grade one letter if he/she does 20 hours of service and writes a journal and final essay on the service experience. Service-learning options are offered in world religions, English, honors, psychology, education, art, theater, college success skills, marketing, business, statistics, legal assisting, hospitality management, air conditioning, social science, sociology, philosophy, government, biology, anatomy and physiology, speech, physics, and others.

Despite this success, some departments either are not represented or are clearly underrepresented. While a major strength of BCC's program is its central coordination, this strength is also a weakness because faculty frequently depend on the CSL for too much. Some instructors do not have or make the time to be involved outside of their regular courses. Developing more inroads for faculty ownership and leadership has been a priority since 1994 as has working consistently with department chairs on the various campuses.

## Task Forces, Teams, and Faculty Work Groups

The center uses experienced service-learning instructors to initiate and assist with curriculum matters. A core of faculty works closely with the director in recruiting and training other faculty to effectively use the service-learning pedagogy. This key group gives seminars on service-learning and reflection; participates or presents in supervisor as educator workshops with community organization staff; helps organize and implement new initiatives (e.g., international service-learning, research projects, new service-learning course approval, service-learning publications); and advises the director on faculty concerns, issues, and satisfaction with the program. These instructors may receive mini-grants, contract supplements, and travel to conferences/workshops, but often they perform these duties without any formal compensation.

The CSL has used task forces and teams to give direction to the service-learning program. Appointed by the district president or convened by the director, these special work groups have strengthened the service-learning program at critical times. One such task force (1991) was appointed to implement Brevard's action plan devised at Campus Compact's Summer Institute on Integrating Service with Academic Study.

A second active working group (1994–96) helped to implement the action plans developed at three Florida Campus Compact Institutes on Integrating Service with Academic Study. Both working groups provided important strategic support for key decision-makers at the college and helped more instructors become involved in college-wide service-learning activities.

## Overview of Faculty Operations

1. The CSL provides instructors with technical resources on how to incorporate service into their classes. This allows faculty to incorporate service-learning options into their courses without undue hardship or an excessive amount of time.

2. The CSL does many of the routine tasks (recruitment, placement, and support) to free faculty for the assessment of student learning in the service-learning experience.

3. The CSL continually recognizes outstanding faculty contributions to service-learning. We recognize faculty at our Annual Recognition Event and recognize faculty efforts daily through newspaper articles, thank you letters from the district president or director, and pats on the back.

4. Staff and program development funds (from $2,000 to $10,000 annually) serve as a major catalyst for faculty service-learning involvement. Mini-grants are an excellent way to get faculty to try service-learning. A mini-grant involves a contract with specified steps for instructors. Faculty meet with the director, implement a service-learning option in their classes, and complete a written assessment of the option. Supplemental contracts for faculty to devise reflection components, teach service-learning seminars, do research projects, and author or edit service-learning publications are also successful.

5. The CSL provides many services to faculty. We tailor student placements to course content and requirements. CSL staff present overviews of service-learning in hundreds of classes every semester. These presentations orient faculty to service-learning and help the CSL to recruit the majority of its students. CSL staff also facilitate in-class debriefing and reflection sessions and consistently communicate feedback to and from faculty. The CSL staff and the director of college employee relations are promoting service-learning and community service venues for faculty to receive continuing contract credits for tenure consideration. Faculty can receive such credits for substantially revising their courses to include service-learning.

6. From the beginning, the CSL has worked to make service-learning options and our separate service-learning courses (Community Involvement and Human Service Experience I, II, and III) academically credible.

7. Although we follow the principles of good practice, we also give faculty much autonomy in incorporating service into their courses. The CSL promulgates basic guidelines and minimum standards to ensure an academic-community balance, but instructors are free to make their own individual adjustments.

## Working with Students

The CSL is known for its extensive support system for students; Indeed, its efforts in this area distinguish BCC's service-learning program.

Our intricate student application process is clearly delineated and contains several built-in access points for staff to interact with students. The application and interviews match student interests and qualifications with community needs. Students are given service and learning materials to help with service documentation and reflection needs. Documentation forms, i.e., placement confirmations, service hour logs, and performance evaluations are included. When possible, an appointment is arranged between the student and agency while the student is still at the CSL office. All students are given a referral card to present to agency or organization staff when they go to the service site for an interview or orientation. This card contains the agency name, contact person, address, telephone number, and CSL staff referral person.

All students are given a file in the office which contains a contact log of every one of their CSL activities, their original application, copies of service documentation forms, and, if applicable, references written for them by CSL staff.

During the application and placement process, student applications are categorized in the following way:

*Pending.*      Unsure of placement; waiting for call-back about placement status

*Referred.*     Appointment set or will attend orientation

*Placed.*       Actually doing community work; placement confirmation form has been turned in to CSL

*Canceled.*     Did not ever start service assignment

*Closed.*       Started service assignment, but did not complete service hour obligation

*Completed.*  Finished service commitment

The placement status categories help CSL staff to set priorities for helping students and trigger staff actions within the CSL (e.g., copy application, send thank-you notes, type labels, make call-backs, give application to director for action, and provide follow- up letters).

During the application/service period, a CSL staff person or student worker calls each student. In fact, a student may receive several calls from staff:

- In response to a CSL recruitment form distributed by an instructor after a CSL staff member has spoken in the instructor's classes

- To check the student's application status if pending or referred

- In response to a particular problem with the placement or service-learning course

- To thank the new service-learner after he/she has been placed

- In response to a CSL service-learning status form from faculty concerning student placement status and satisfaction with assignment

- For feedback on how a service assignment is progressing (monitored every 4–6 weeks)

- To alert a student to deadlines or special events which may be sponsored by the CSL

The CSL also uses written correspondence to further personalize the student service-learning experience. Every student service-learner receives a personally signed thank you from CSL staff, holiday cards, and mailings about upcoming CSL events, service-learning courses, and scholarship opportunities. Finally, all service-learners receive regular day-to-day recognition and certificates of appreciation after the completion of their service-learning projects. Many are also invited to our Annual Recognition Event and receive special awards for outstanding service contributions.

Some other services CSL provides to students include the following:

- Providing service-learning course textbooks

- Providing supplemental liability and accident insurance for volunteers

- Documenting service hours on academic transcripts

- Writing recommendations for students who are known by staff

- Mediating service-related conflicts or problems

- Providing for periodic on-site visits

- Providing information on public service careers and national service or internship opportunities

- Providing alternative placement(s) if original assignment needs to be abrogated

- Advising students on programmatic, personal, or job matters

- Referring students to job openings at community organizations

## Student Role

Since the Center for Service-Learning's inception in 1988, students have provided programmatic leadership in several capacities. They have touched every aspect of the CSL's activities and operations. Initially students were the CSL support staff in the office. We employ six or seven students who work 12 hours weekly to recruit, interview, place, and do follow-up for student service-learners. Student CSL workers provide office coverage and help to support special events such as workshops or recruitment fairs. Students are also used as ambassadors to recruit other students. They speak in classes and to student organizations, participate on radio and television shows, and devise new CSL publicity and recruitment methods. They have been used to coordinate important projects such as the Student Literacy Corps project and the Student Action Leadership Team.

Students also assist faculty with research projects, recruit faculty into the service-learning arena, and champion community causes. Some students initiate new CSL projects because they are already involved in leadership capacities in community organizations; they are a rich source of service site development. Our diverse student population has always served on the CSL's advisory committee and has played an important role in evaluating and advising the center on how to improve its delivery system for students. Frequently, students have supported and implemented campus-based service initiatives through student organizations. BCC students have organized and implemented voter registration drives, environmental projects, food and hunger campaigns, hurricane relief expeditions, high school and middle school collaborations, Rotary-related activities, a Chernobyl Clinic Project, human rights programs, and AIDS education and action forums. Through our service-learning college work-study program, students work 12 hours weekly in important community organizations such as the March of Dimes, the Melbourne Police Department, and the Epilepsy Association.

Since service-learning provides rich leadership development opportunities for students, the CSL works with student affairs' staff in related activities (e.g., the President's Leadership Conference which brings students, faculty, staff, and administrators together to examine the BCC community, leadership, and student concerns). It also recognizes the outstanding service efforts of student organizations and frequently gives information to students and student groups about service or service-learning awards and scholarships. Providing service-learning course credit information to student service organizations is an invaluable method to gain the support of student groups.

## Evaluation Procedures

Evaluation is an ongoing and important part of CSL's efforts. Both qualitative and quantitative instruments are used to measure the impacts of service-learning on students, the community, and the curriculum. The results are disseminated widely to demonstrate the worth of the program and to educate significant decision-makers on the powerful effects of service-learning and CSL productivity. The following instruments are routinely used and can be incorporated into the design of a comprehensive program evaluation.

*Project evaluation.*    Completed at the end of each academic year by agency service-learning coordinators. Used to evaluate CSL performance, objectives, accomplishments, and community needs.

*Agency student evaluation.*     Completed each semester by direct agency supervisors of students. Used to assess service progress and performance of students and to document quality and quantity of service delivery to community. Placement confirmation form, service hour report, midterm and final performance evaluations are given to the instructor, the CSL, and the student.

*Annual, semester, and special reports.*     Planning tools used to regularly document what CSL has done and intends to do. Distributed to administration, key faculty, and staff depending on type of report.

*Outside research.*     Formal studies or surveys conducted periodically by faculty to assess the overall efficacy of the program.

*Unstructured faculty/staff/agency feedback.*     Derived periodically from interviews or correspondence.

*Office management tools.*     Updated annually as aids to program planning and evaluation. Distributed to key administrators and staff.

*Interaction chart.*     Periodically updated to document number of college units worked with, interdependencies, nature of interactions, and major contacts outside of the institution.

*First impressions card.*     Rates student's initial visit with CSL, usually after the application and placement process.

*Student separation card.*     Sent to students who terminate assignment, have trouble with assignment, or are difficult to contact about placement status.

*Service-learning questionnaire.*     Open-ended and closed-ended questions used to derive information on students and their service-learning experiences. Students rate the value of service-learning experience; effects on major/career; performance of CSL, faculty, and service site; effects of service-learning on retention, academic performance, civic and personal growth, college satisfaction, and career/occupation. Form also includes information on the demographics and motivation of the student. Completed by student service-learners at the end of each semester. Results are distributed widely to faculty, staff, administrators, students, community organizations, and presented at workshops, institutes, and conferences.

*Reflective learning tools.*     Journals, essays, service-learning plans and contracts, research reports. Used to enhance student learning. Excerpts or exemplary journals are copied and used in reports or given to other students as examples.

*Needs assessment.*     Surveys (e.g., applicant profiles, grade point averages, alumni questionnaires) conducted periodically to monitor changing student needs.

*Research survey.*     Instrument used to compare service-learners versus non-service-learners in same academic courses. Also used to compare service-learning option students with students in stand-alone service-learning courses. Measures impacts on students, college, community, career/occupation, academic, personal, and civic development.

*Course evaluations.* Standard end-of-term course evaluations providing basis to compare service-learning courses to other college courses.

*Faculty surveys.* Short open-ended or closed-ended surveys to rate faculty satisfaction and needs in service-learning. One such survey asks faculty about incentives needed to increase commitment to service-learning or to get involved in using the service-learning pedagogy.

*Client evaluations.* Essay or closed-ended questionnaires periodically used to obtain feedback directly from agency clients served by student service-learners. Usually tied to grant requirement (e.g., Student Literacy Corps project).

*Service site report form.* Analysis of on-site agency visit by CSL staff person. Form provides insights on changing agency needs, logistics, and job descriptions. Used by CSL staff for project improvement.

*Staff evaluations.* Official evaluation of director, project coordinator, coordinator, project assistants, secretary, and student workers. Conducted annually for staff performance and each semester for student workers.

*CSL special events evaluations.* Short evaluations used during workshops, institutes, conferences, supervisor as educator forums, etc. Measure effectiveness of CSL-sponsored events and individual speaker or staff performance.

## COMMUNITY ROLE AND PARTNERSHIPS

As a community college, Brevard works with myriad human service agencies, government offices, businesses, and other organizations. Involvement and partnership with its community is reflected in the mission and educational delivery system of the college and in the nature and diversity of our students. The students are the community and feel ownership for and responsibility to that community.

Since the inception of service-learning at Brevard, the community has determined the needs to be met through student involvement. Regularly, the CSL requests written job descriptions from agencies, organizations, or community groups. The organizations develop the job descriptions for their needs. They determine the number of service-learning slots, the roles students play, and the duration of student service commitments. Community representatives participate on the CSL's advisory committee and are key members in providing direction to the center and its programs.

Community and state funding for specific societal needs yields new community projects which include student service; i.e., literacy, child care, safety, drug prevention, and mentoring. For example, $190,000 was awarded by the State Attorney General's office for a collaboration involving the school system, the Police Athletic League, the Youth Services Center, and Brevard Community College. The CSL played a key role in developing service positions for at-risk ninth graders to do service-learning with BCC students at local human service organizations. College students also tutored the ninth graders, and CSL staff developed service-learning curricula for the high school.

Agency or organization personnel who supervise students are truly educators. They create the service tasks for students and orient, train, supervise, and evaluate their service performances. They speak in BCC classes to educate and recruit students; make presentations at health-related, environmental, and political forums or events; and attend CSL workshops with students, faculty, and CSL staff. Several organizations hold orientation or training sessions on campus and/or in the service setting. Many recommend outstanding students for scholarships and service-learning recognition awards. Supervisors provide ongoing feedback to students and participate in reflection or class sessions at the college.

Community organizations validate the CSL's importance to the community in many ways. They appear with students and staff on radio and television shows, send thank-you letters for CSL support to key decision-makers at the college, and publicize our program in newspapers, newsletters, and at formal recognition events. Many offer BCC students paid positions within their organizations. Agencies regularly evaluate the CSL and service-learning program and get feedback from clients to further codify CSL's impact on the community.

Because of logistical, philosophical, and/or resource factors, not all organizations can adapt to the needs of a service-learning program. The CSL considers the following variables in developing or maintaining a service site: safety, importance of community need, student service site feedback, learning potential despite obstacles, and future change possibilities. Many organizations significantly adapt their volunteer programs to accommodate students once they have realized the benefits of service-learning.

## Service Site Activities

The CSL works with over 240 community organizations, agencies, and projects. Many are placement sites, some are partners with the CSL, and a few are collaborators. The number and kinds of relationships change according to community needs, agency resources, funding priorities, personnel turnover, and ability to work with students effectively.

The CSL maintains the following program areas for students: animal care, the arts, child care, community development, crisis care, drug prevention/rehabilitation, education, environment, family services, government and political involvement, health care, historical sites, justice system, media-related work, mental health, physically challenged populations, recreation, senior services, special children/adults, subsistence services, and youth services.

Since 1985, the CSL has also worked with community partners on several special projects. The Student Literacy Corps project matched hundreds of BCC students with adults and youth to help improve their basic literacy skills. Currently, a far-reaching African-American history project involves faculty, students, key administrators, significant community leaders, and the NAACP in interviewing senior citizens and collecting and codifying memorabilia and artifacts.

Scores of students have served as role models and tutors at Hacienda Girls' Ranch, a residential facility for abused girls. In 1992, some of the girls from Hacienda enrolled at BCC for the first time. Although their education at BCC is completely financed by Hacienda, no resident had ever attended BCC until BCC students became active role models in 1989.

The county government's volunteer program has become a formidable ally and partner. Students are active in many diverse areas: the social work, probation/parole, architecture, and engineering departments; board of elections; alternative services division; hazardous materials and waste division; medical examiner's office; family and children's services; and emergency management. Students serve in these areas as volunteers, service-learners, work-study community service placements, and interns. Many technical, vocational, and associate of arts degree students participate in this continuum of service opportunities. But perhaps the best example of a dynamic collaboration involves the CSL's work with the Brevard County school system.

## Public School Collaborations

The college and school district have a rich history of cooperation including early admission/dual enrollment programs, literacy education, and college student volunteers who have served for years in countywide schools. The major catalyst for our present collaboration was the creation and development of CSL. Annually, the CSL places in the school system over 350 students who tutor, mentor, assist teachers, and work in diverse capacities.

The Brevard County School Board, through its volunteer program, the Apple Corps, has been an effective conduit for the placement and support of BCC students. Thanks to the college's commitment to service-learning and the school board's willingness to use college students, we have been able to establish a framework for significant collaboration. The college established key relationships with several school personnel including the district Apple Corps Coordinator, assistant principals, counselors, and exceptional education program administrators.

A small but important mini-grant coauthored in 1989 by BCC service-learning and Johnson Junior High School staff allowed BCC students to tutor and mentor about 20 at-risk students at the school. Successful implementation of the grant demonstrated the college's intent and capacity to provide students as resources to help in the schools. Simultaneously, college students documented, through evaluations and journals, the positive learning experiences they received through working in the schools. Indeed, many decided to make teaching a career. The CSL shared these testimonials with key school district administrators.

Periodically, service-learning staff spoke with teachers and administrators about the benefits of service-learning. Several key resource mailers were sent to the school district staff. One of the most critical ingredients for further development of the partnership emerged right in the middle of the college's operations: Scores of high school students, who were early admission or dual enrolled, began doing service-learning in their regular college classes for partial or extra credit. Some of these students became service-learning ambassadors in their own high schools.

Three other factors contributed to a model service-learning partnership:

1. The state established the Florida Academic Scholars Program which required high school students to do 75 hours of community service as one of the criteria to receive the scholarship.

2. BCC submitted a service-learning grant to the federal government's Fund to Improve Post-Secondary Education (FIPSE). Although the proposal was not funded, the college and school both supported and authored the grant application. This effort planted fertile seeds for the future.

3. The Florida K–12 Learn and Serve program provided service-learning grants to individual schools in Brevard County, and teachers began to seek information from the college on how to conceptualize and utilize service-learning.

School reform initiatives nationally (Blueprint 2000) and statewide (Florida Scholars) placed service-learning on the table of educational possibilities. The college, through its staff and program development funds, launched a pilot project in the fall of 1994. Reflection and Incorporating Service and Education (RISE) demonstrated that high schools could effectively incorporate service-learning into regular classes. At the same time, the school district designated the Resource Teacher for Accelerated Programs and Equity as its contact with the CSL. For the first time, district-wide support was evident.

The provost and dean for instruction on our Cocoa campus enthusi-astically endorsed and supported our blossoming efforts. The provost encouraged the inclusion of BCC's service-learning course, Community Involvement, in dual enrollment course offerings with the school system. Additionally, the provost authorized and championed a part-time K–12 coordinator position which significantly increased the breadth and depth of our partnership. The CSL director, district resource teacher, and K–12 coordinator could now work as a team to coordinate and implement new service-learning curriculum initiatives.

During 1995–96 several initiatives came to fruition:

*Service-learning infrastructure building in selected schools.* Service-learning staff work with individual school staff to support teach-ers and students.

*Co-authoring of a Learn and Serve grant.* This yielded an official school district commitment to enter into partnership with BCC.

*Development and scheduling of a dual enrollment service-learn-ing course, SOW 2054, Community Involvement, at one high school.* Ten students enrolled in this initial service-learning course. This led to the scheduling of courses at three other high schools for the fall of 1996 (enrollment 65 students).

*Initiation of ongoing teacher training.* In-service teacher training workshops are held each semester. The initial workshop enrolled over 20 teachers who received four hours of training in the service-learning ped-agogy. A recertification course consisting of 16 hours of seminars and 32 hours of service attracted ten teachers in its initial offering. The course, SOW 2054, Community Involvement, provides opportunities for teachers to build competence in service-learning through personal participation in service and reflection. During fall semester 1996, a second course was developed for certification, EDG 2020, Applications of Service-Learning. This course is open to elementary, middle school, high school, and adult education teachers in any discipline.

*Collaboration with Cocoa High School on an at-risk youth program.* In this program funded by a grant from the Florida Attorney General's office, teachers and students were taught service-learning, and a service mentor program pairing college students with at-risk high school students at service site locations was implemented.

*CSL and school board administrative and curriculum collaborations.* BCC service-learning staff are infusing service-learn-ing into several curricular frameworks. Staff work closely with the dis-trict's grant coordinator to provide technical assistance to teachers and schools who seek service-learning grants. CSL staff speak at various school and district-wide meetings such as curriculum contact and teacher meetings.

## CUSTOMIZING FOR DIVERSE CONSTITUENCIES

Brevard Community College comprises four campuses that serve similar but varied communities and have different campus environments. The diverse nature of our campuses and communities poses interesting opportunities and challenges for a service-learning program. What overall program structure best meets the needs of such diversity? What are some important strategies that can be used to maximize service-learning on each campus and in each surrounding community?

We decided early on to develop a centrally organized office structure with individual campus centers. District-wide coordination was viewed as necessary in order to develop consistency in philosophy, goals and objectives, service delivery expectations, and to provide necessary support structures for faculty, service sites, and students. However, we have also tried varied approaches to address differences in campus administration, faculty, surrounding community, student body composition, and service-learning office support.

### Campus Administration

A major consideration in meeting the needs of diverse campus constituencies is local administration support. Even with a sympathetic district administration, individual campus support varies considerably. Thus, we have had to address several key questions in order to map out appropriate strategies for the individual campuses. What are the key concerns of the individual campuses: retention, research, public relations, teaching, change, student enrollment numbers? What leadership style do local administrators favor: micro-management, laissez-faire, autocratic, shared? Do faculty follow the leader or run away from the leader?

Service-learning staff also need to learn the appropriate administrative protocol on each campus; i.e., the chain of command, what requests go to whom. Since each campus may have pressing needs or priorities that will be impacted by service-learning activities, meeting one-to-one with key local administrators is often essential. Related to such one-on-one meetings is the strategy of enabling local administrators to get recognition for their campus's service-learning achievements. We have learned that effective service-learning programs need and support both administration and faculty. Since district-wide support can mean financial resources to even the playing field on different campuses, knowing how to use faculty incentives and/or mini-grants in a skillful and timely way is essential.

### Faculty

Faculty length of service at the college and their teaching disciplines make for distinct differences in service-learning participation and support. One of our campuses has many faculty nearing retirement age and a majority who teach vocational or technical courses. The CSL uses mini-grants for service-learning course development and provides extensive incentives whenever possible (e.g., travel and supplemental contracts to recruit and keep faculty involved). The CSL office here, as on all the other campuses, does the routine placement and support of student service-learners, so faculty do not view service-learning as just additional work. Key faculty contacts are used to recruit other instructors to try the service-learning pedagogy.

On another campus, the instructors are in general younger and teach largely in the liberal arts. The CSL on this campus provides short, precise information pieces on how to incorporate service into the curriculum. More instructors have service experience and realize its benefits. Good placement and support are still needed; however, servicing effectively the large number of faculty involved is the biggest challenge on this campus.

On a small campus, which has a balance of liberal arts and technical/vocational faculty, a few respected faculty who use service-learning effectively have been the best recruiters. CSL support to students and the establishment of a CSL presence have been vital to our efforts.

## Community

The nature of surrounding communities and the availability of resources lead to different strategies in working with community organizations. Adjacent to one campus is a very impoverished community with real needs but not much in the way of service sites or diversity of agencies. The CSL attempts to help this area with grants targeted to develop services. Service-learning program collaborations are vital in sharing resources or creating programs with the community. Recently, the CSL has initiated an African-American history project here and has received a large grant to collaborate with the local high school, Police Athletic League, and Youth Services Center in developing an at-risk youth service program which targets community safety. A Habitat for Humanity project involves BCC students in building houses right on the doorstep of the campus. School mentoring/tutoring programs have also been successful.

Another campus is located near a large community with tremendous resources and placement opportunities. A clearinghouse approach with students placed in a plethora of organizations is the priority of this CSL office. Since the campus is fairly close to three high schools with a large number of early admission and dual enrollment students, K–14 collaborations receive special attention.

## Student Demographics

Student body composition has been another major factor in customizing services. On one campus, the majority of students are technical and vocational students, who usually are older, must work more, and are financially less secure. When recruiting here, the CSL staff must really emphasize concrete outcomes related to scholarship opportunity, job connections, résumé building, and career enhancement. Work-study service positions and academic credit incentives are also very important. Short-term exposure experiences and one-shot projects help get students involved, while service clubs and organizations are used as a conduit for longer-term projects and commitments.

On another campus, most of the students are associate of arts students who will be transferring to universities. These liberal arts students, though diverse, are younger and wealthier overall, and many have a service ethic from already having been involved in service activities in high school or because of their parents' community service activities. The most important tasks of the CSL in this case are to smooth the transition for students to meet community needs. Because these students have more time to serve, even the night classes prove to be fruitful recruitment grounds. Incentives such as academic credit are important, but students respond to a wide diversity of recruitment motivational methods. Much of the CSL effort here is focused on follow-through and commitment.

## Service-Learning Office Support

Campus service-learning centers have had to vary their approaches. For example, on the campus with many faculty approaching retirement age, we have prioritized recruiting younger, new instructors as soon as they are hired. The CSL office on this campus also provides the main administrative support for all CSL offices; therefore, time here is at a premium. Staff have to handle both general administrative and local student needs. Not surprisingly, it is this office that has the most experienced staff, capable of fulfilling its dual function. The director, coordinator, program secretary, and two student workers are located here. Since this office is the paperwork and communications hub, the students help almost entirely with general administrative matters.

On another campus, the large number of faculty and students involved in the program dictate much more direct constituent work. Staff emphasis is on quality of customer services to meet volume demand. Office hours need to be adjusted to this emphasis (some evenings), since providing constant coverage is a necessity. Located in the Student Center, this office supports a service-learning classroom in the same building. Most of the stand-alone service-learning courses are located here. Staff need to be student-oriented and able to handle several students simultaneously, especially during the CSL's prime recruitment time, weeks two through six of the semester. Staff at this office are cross trained to effectively do routine administrative tasks while handling community agency and student matters. Although student workers assist with some administrative support tasks, they are used primarily to provide first line support for students, community organizations, and faculty. They also do community on-site visitations, recruit students, and at times, are the main contact for the center.

On other campuses the center provides a presence with limited staff. Here, visibility as well as constituent support is a priority. Indeed, students on the smaller campuses are often supported by larger campus service-learning staff via telephone and written communication. Of course, such support has its limits. At a time when many students feel disconnected, the CSL offices need to be the very antithesis of isolation and depersonalization.

## Conclusion

Community colleges can be at the forefront of service-learning in the United States. Although they differ from their four-year counterparts, most service-learning programs are basically similar. Indeed, community colleges would seem to have many advantages with regard to service-learning: a very diverse student body, an emphasis on teaching, a more malleable curriculum, and students who live in the community they serve.

In less than ten years, BCC has developed a comprehensive service-learning program that impacts a significant number of students, faculty, and community organizations. Although 90% of what goes on in service-learning at four-year institutions would fit at Brevard as well, it is the remaining 10% that gives us our uniqueness and allows us, as a community college, to be exceptional in the field. Just like Sisyphus, we have to push hard and accept the challenge of building a successful and engaging program. Unlike Sisyphus, our burden is enjoyable, exciting, energizing, and life-changing.

*For actual Brevard Community College service-learning documents, see*
*Appendix A: Organization Chart*
*Appendix B: Student Opportunity Overview—Continuum of Service and*
*Learning Experience*
*Appendix F: Administrative Forms*
*Service-Learner's Checklist*
*Placement Confirmation Form*
*Service-Learning Contract*
*Service Hours on Academic Transcript (SHOAT) Guidelines*
*Student Volunteer Hour Report*
*Volunteer Insurance Enrollment Record*
*Student Volunteer Mid-Semester Progress Record*

## REFERENCES

*Blueprint 2000.* (1991). Tallahassee, FL: Florida Legislature.

*Brevard Community College catalog, 1996–97.* (1996). Cocoa, FL: Brevard Community College.

*Brevard Community College institutional self-study, 1991–93.* (1993). Cocoa, FL: Brevard Community College.

Kendall, J. C. (1990). Combining service and learning: An introduction. In J. C. Kendall & Associates. *Combining service and learning: A resource book for community and public service.* Vol. 1. Raleigh, NC: National Society for Internships and Experiential Education.

Porter, H. E., & Poulsen, S. L. (Eds.). (1989). *Principles of good practice for combining service and learning.* Racine, WI: Johnson Foundation.

Sigmon, R. L. (1979, Spring). Service-learning: Three principles. *Synergist, 8* (1).

# 6

# Rediscovering Our Heritage: Community Service and the Historically Black University

**Beverly W. Jones**
*North Carolina Central University*

## INTRODUCTION

Founded in 1910, North Carolina Central University (NCCU) is a four-year, historically black liberal arts institution with 19 departments, two programs, and five professional schools. It enrolls over 5,500 undergraduate and professional degree students. Of these, 89% are North Carolina residents.

Like most historically black institutions, North Carolina Central University was founded in order to "... seek the regeneration of the Negro," as outlined by W. E. B. DuBois in his seminal 1903 work *The Souls of Black Folks*. Seven years later, when James E. Shepard founded North Carolina Central University, he operationalized DuBois's vision in his mission statement for the university. For Shepard, the regeneration was possible only to the extent that the university was able to develop in young men and women the character and sound academic training requisite for real service to the nation. Service, in this context, could be considered a code word for community-based and community-focused regeneration.

The DuBois-Shepard service mission for higher education is even more relevant today, because many urban African-American institutions are surrounded by seamless poverty, epidemic crime, and physically deteriorating inner cities. Historically black institutions cannot be oblivious to these issues for, geographically, they are located in the heart of deteriorating African-American communities. Now, perhaps more than ever before, historically black institutions have come to realize that the plight of urban cities is inextricably tied to their future and must be addressed effectively and proactively.

## THE AFRICAN-AMERICAN TRADITION OF COMMUNITY THROUGH SERVICE

African-American notions of community service are rooted in a traditional African legacy of connectedness and intergenerational obligation. African metaphysics emphasized three basic aspects of humanity (Joseph, 1996). The first is the idea that individuals and communities have the capacity to celebrate life, even in despairing situations. The second idea is that individuals and communities are visionaries who have the creative power to manifest their visions. The third idea is that individual identity is communal. The individual operates in a network which provides economic, religious, and political functions. African mutual aid societies, for example, stressed moral instruction and provided financial aid for the burial expenses of their members.

Enslaved Africans brought this communal nature with them to the Americas as they were dispersed in the Diaspora. The tendency to form voluntary, benevolent organizations not only survived the slavery experience, but was significantly shaped by it. African-Americans in the slave community viewed themselves as a familial group with a common lifestyle and interests. Slave communities, in addition, protected and fed runaway slaves. Many slave narratives and interviews with former slaves exemplify this connection.

During slavery, most African-Americans viewed family as a combination of extended family and friends in the community. This might include community leaders, conjurers, preachers, and peer group members. These individuals felt a responsibility to nurture, protect, and educate the younger members in the family. Younger slaves exhibited a respect for their elders and often cared for those members too old to care for themselves.

A cooperative slave community allowed African-Americans to survive the harsh conditions of slavery. Recognizing that their fates were connected, many slaves pooled their meager resources to benefit the entire community. Slaves built houses, sewed, weaved baskets, and washed for one another. In some instances slaves shared food from their garden patch if they were fortunate enough to have one. In addition, slave communities protected individual members from harsh conditions and abuse at the hands of the master.

Outside the slave community, black benevolence expressed itself in the creation of mutual aid societies, fraternal organizations, and churches. These institutions often operated like the extended family network in the slave quarters. Black benevolence groups provided financial resources among free blacks and helped to ease the transition from slavery to freedom. The earliest, formed in 1787, aided the development of the black church.

Throughout the African-American experience, the church has been instrumental in the struggle for black liberation and citizenship. Early black churches served as stations for the Underground Railroad. These institutions provided food, clothing, and shelter for many of the runaways escaping the bonds of slavery. Churches were also centers for education and recreation. The first historically black colleges and schools were associated with black churches that often provided financial and human resources.

The African-American communal mentality reached an apex during the civil rights movement. During the 1950s and 1960s, thousands of local grassroots organizations raised money, collected and distributed food, and recruited volunteers to participate in demonstrations and boycotts. In addition, black churches often served as centers for mobilization. During this mass movement for social justice, the black community looked within for resources, as it had during slavery and the first years of freedom.

African-Americans still exhibit communal tendencies in their institutions and associations. Black churches feed the hungry, provide shelter for the homeless, and offer educational activities. Some churches provide economic and social development programs in the black community. Black fraternal organizations and mutual aid societies also remain a major factor in the African-American quest for a better life. Organizations such as the Alpha Kappa Alpha sorority, the Kappa Alpha Psi fraternity, and others often provide college scholarships and operate senior citizens' organizations.

African-Americans have a long history of helping themselves and others in the community. This legacy of self-help and volunteerism has survived throughout the African Diaspora. Despite the harsh conditions African-Americans experienced during slavery, they pooled their resources and came through the terrible ordeal. This sense of community aided the transition from slavery to freedom and continues to support the black struggle for liberation. The current black perception of community service remains an extension of traditional African notions of family and community responsibility.

## THE SERVICE MISSION REEMERGES AS MORAL IMPERATIVE

Not surprisingly, many African-American universities were originally commissioned to serve local community needs and to solve community problems. However, in the wake of desegregation, many of these universities neglected their service focus in order to emulate and compete with white institutions. Thus, over time, instead of working to improve the nation's poor urban communities, HBCUs (Historically Black Colleges and Universities) abandoned them altogether, opting instead for purely academic/theoretical goals. In doing this, HBCUs ceased to be active partners with the communities that had supported them when few others had dared. In the decades following the civil rights movement, these institutions seemed to forget the reciprocal benefits inherent in service-based relationships with their communities. Both parties have suffered from that amnesia. History has a way of repeating itself, however, and the current *zeitgeist* among institutions of higher learning in inner cities now favors university involvement in community regeneration. Reflecting this development, a number of HBCUs have begun to reassert themselves as community partners by tapping the rich source of helping hands and positive role models in their student bodies and faculties.

Among these universities, few have repositioned themselves more squarely in the service-learning camp than has North Carolina Central. This dramatic repositioning began as a top-down strategy in 1993. Under the leadership of Chancellor Julius Chambers, who based his strategy on both ethical and pedagogical considerations, the primary mission of the university became to promote the consciousness of social responsibility and dedication to the general welfare of the people of North Carolina, the United States, and the world. The university recognizes, however, the mutually reinforcing impact of scholarship and service on effective teaching and learning. North Carolina Central, therefore, encourages and expects faculty and students to engage in scholarly and creative as well as service activities that benefit the larger community. This lofty mission is akin to John Dewey's progressive idea that educational institutions should focus on developing the social intelligence of their students through service. Chambers, a former director of the Legal Defense Fund for the NAACP, transposed this Deweyan concept of pedagogical mission to the realm of moral responsibility. Thus, the ethical underpinnings of the mission have brought NCCU's educational focus full circle back to the DuBois-Shepard vision which served the university and its community so well in the early years of this century.

## FROM MISSION TO FRUITION

Once the service-based mission was adopted by the board of trustees in 1994, the chancellor turned his energies to two objectives which he believed were critical to making the mission a reality. These objectives were: 1) to revise general study requirements for freshmen and sophomores to include service components in core academic curricula, and 2) to require a minimum of 120 hours (15 clock hours per semester) of community service volunteer work as a condition for graduation.

In 1994, the university's General College Studies program was revised and renamed CFAS (Critical Foundations in the Arts and Sciences). Of the many course offerings involved, Personal and Social Development became the first to incorporate community service. To implement the above two objectives, Chambers established the Community Service Office (CSO)—which was later renamed the Community Service Program (CSP)—as an ombudsman between the university and the Durham community. I, who was a tenured full professor of history, was asked to develop a five-year service plan for the university. The NCCU planning team included Rosa Anderson, Director of the Community Service Office and a Department of Human Sciences faculty member; Dr. Ted Parrish, Health Education Chair; Dr. Kenneth Chambers, Faculty Senate Chair; Dr. George Wilson, Criminal Justice Chair; Mr. Tyrone Cox, SGA member; and Mr. Derick Brown, SGA President. The plan included: 1) direct service to established community agencies by students, faculty, staff, and alumni; 2) a variety of means to incorporate service-learning into all academic courses; 3) development of university-community partnerships to improve the local urban community; and 4) creation of awards and university-wide activities to encourage an ethic of service on campus.

As a core discipline faculty member with experience in building service components into her course design even before the new mission was adopted, I brought credibility to the CSP and was named its director in 1994. To maintain my credibility among faculty, I retain a part-time teaching load (two courses per year) while serving administratively as head of the CSP. In addition, to ensure that community service would develop from concept to core and that the university would, in fact, become a community revitalization partner, a full-time staff of four was hired to implement the program year-round. With mission and department in place, NCCU joined the Campus Compact in 1995 in order to solidify its commitment and to link its campus-wide involvement in service to a nationwide arena. During that same year, I was invited to join the Invisible College, a national organization whose aim is to increase faculty involvement in service-learning.

## PROGRAM STRUCTURE

The CSP currently has a year-round staff of five: Beverly W. Jones, Director; Rosa Anderson, Assistant Director; Carla Alston, Student Placement Coordinator; David Williams, Service-Learning Coordinator;

and Regina Barton, Administrative Assistant. I serve part-time and report to the provost and vice chancellor for academic affairs. Day-to-day operations are divided among the remaining four employees. In addition, a cadre of 20 student volunteers serves within and for the program in a variety of functions, from clerical work to program promotions.

The director's responsibilities include: 1) implementing service-learning policy; 2) securing funding; 3) serving as university spokesperson on matters related to service; 4) establishing collaborative institutional and interinstitutional activities; and 5) promoting opportunities for faculty and students to collaborate with noted service-learning practitioners such as Robert Coles, Edward Zlotkowski, and Ira Harkavy.

The assistant director reports directly to the director. Ms. Anderson coordinates departmental functions, maintains daily CSP operations, and supervises three full-time staff. She is responsible for program and staff development and evaluation, some fundraising initiatives and grant-writing, volunteer training, and program policy implementation. Other responsibilities include agency site monitoring, interinstitutional partnership development, coordinating nonprofit agency collaborations, and overseeing student reflection activities. Ms. Anderson is a member of the North Carolina Association of Volunteer Administrators and holds the Certification of Service-Learning Training from the North Carolina Department of Public Instruction.

The service-learning coordinator's responsibilities include the design and implementation of specific service-learning projects on and off campus. Mr. Williams identifies appropriate community service sites congruent with students' interests and career goals. He also assists community service sites in developing curricula and ensures continuity between the NCCU service-learning program and the community. The coordinator frequently visits departments on campus and assists in the development of workshops and conferences, but the position's primary purpose is to assist CFAS faculty in the incorporation of service into their courses. Mr. Williams taught social sciences at the secondary level, completed NTE certification, and maintains membership in Kappa Delta Pi.

The student placement coordinator has experience in customer service, salesmanship, and public relations—all of which help ensure smooth implementation of the Community Service-Learning Graduation Policy. Ms. Alston is responsible for student registration and placement, and maintains all records and statistics pertaining to student volunteerism. She conducts service site visits, monitors agency needs and concerns, and coordinates and analyzes all data gathered from the various service sites to gauge the impact of student efforts on each community site served. She is also responsible for officially documenting service hours, determining the impact of service on all stakeholders, and disseminating student and agency evaluations.

The administrative assistant is responsible for coordinating office operations, maintaining CSP budgets, and facilitating the grant writing process. She also takes care of all departmental written correspondence and CSP publications. Ms. Barton designs, composes, and serves as editor for the Community Service Program's monthly newsletter, *Truth and Service*. In addition, she plans and implements all conferences, town meetings, and workshops on community service and service-learning, and supervises the student volunteers who staff the CSP. Staying as current with inner-office technology as budgets allow and keeping a physical inventory are still other duties of the administrative assistant.

## STUDENT INVOLVEMENT

While the CSP provides guidance on community needs and requests, NCCU's policy is never to stifle student creativity. Freshman students are allowed to perform service both on and off campus. Many students like to perform service collectively rather then individually. This sense of communalism and group dynamics is integral to the African heritage of tribalism, which provides the context and the purpose of the African ethos.

Hence, many African-American students who perform community service are especially interested in activities and projects that relate to community development (e.g., assisting small businesses in marketing plans, designing community-based grassroots tutoring projects, conducting community needs assessments, and engaging in community capacity-building activities). Such linkages to service reinforce this sense of communalism and self-identity.

Since a key objective of the CSP is to promote an ethic of service, this heritage and the inclination of our students has led to a natural alliance among the Office of Student Affairs, the Student Government Association, and the CSP. The result has been projects such as the following:

- Project GRASP (Generating Resources to Address Social Problems) in which NCCU students work with targeted community agencies to attend to persons with health problems—physical, mental, and emotional—through the identification of coping strategies, resources, and referrals critical to ensuring quality of life.

- New Hope Project in which students from NCCU and Duke University organized a house course (a course taught by students and/or faculty in the dormitory) on homelessness and coordinated a city-wide effort to raise money and the awareness of citizens to the issues of homelessness.

- Project ASSIGN (After-School Session in Guided Nurture) in which NCCU students work with the child and family service unit of the social services department to provide at least minimal substance and social needs for families. Each student partners with a child to identify and address health, material, and educational needs as well as to provide mentorship.

- Project FACE (Friendly Association for Cultural Enrichment) in which students work with Holton Middle School students to address problems of youth literacy, negative behavior, and health and environmental concerns.

Cumulatively, these efforts have begun to address some of the most critical needs of our local community while also beginning to rebuild the community's trust in our resolve to be its long-term problem solving partner.

To cultivate student leadership, CSP has also established a Community Service Ambassadors Program. Ambassadors are upperclassmen who have been active in service from their freshman year on. The process of choosing an ambassador is highly selective. The candidates must have at least a 2.8 grade point average and must undergo an intensive screening process by the CSP staff. Ambassadors commit to activities such as placing and evaluating students, disseminating service information to NCCU departments and to the Durham community, assisting with student reflection activities, and conducting site visit evaluations. There are currently 24 ambassadors chosen per year.

## FACULTY INVOLVEMENT

Involving faculty has been more of a challenge. One promising start was to involve the English department in promoting the concept of service. Thus, in 1995, the CSP and the English department jointly developed and sponsored an annual community service essay competition, providing a forum for students to reflect upon and communicate the meaning of service to them personally. However, winners of the competition do not receive any monetary awards for their reflections. This would be antithetical to NCCU's philosophy of service-learning. Instead, they receive volunteer credit hours, have lunch with the chancellor and the board of trustees, and are celebrated in the campus media. The following excerpts from the first year's competition highlight the synergistic relationship between service and a student's intellectual and social development:

> Many of us have been taught the concept of being "our brother's keeper," but it takes more than thinking about it to make the idea work. It is one's own personal and committed action that really makes the difference. And the wonderful part of shouldering some of our neighbors' burdens by serving our community is that it all comes back to us. Giving service to others

not only touches the lives of those being helped, but also helps to build our character, to provide much-needed interaction with others, and to improve the world in which we all dwell together.

*—Nacelle Johnson, first place essay, 1995*

There are a lot of blind people in the world. Until recently, I was one of them. Going on that midnight run changed my way of thinking, the way I treat homeless people, and the way I want to live my life. If you doubt this radical transformation, just try to think of yourself as the one who helps save her, the one who makes a difference. It's an insight that could change your life and the lives of those frightened children out there in all of our communities.

*—Kesha Moore, second place essay, 1995*

You would never believe how giving a few hours of your time each week can make a difference in someone's life . . . I did not believe [this] until I became a volunteer for Communi-Care three years ago. A nonprofit, community-based organization originating in Statesville, North Carolina, Communi-Care focuses on positive intervention in the lives of children. And, while volunteers do their worthy work, they reap additional benefits—developing leadership and organizational skills, all while giving back to the community.

*—Cheryl Parker, third place essay, 1995*

While the essay competition has proven to be a success, there is much more to be done to involve faculty. We acknowledge that service-learning at NCCU is still in an embryonic stage and has not yet been universally accepted by all faculty. However, a recent survey of faculty involvement indicated that there are at least 50 faculty members who are actively engaged in service-learning teaching or curriculum restructuring efforts. The survey also reported a heightened interest in service-learning among both old and new faculty. This increased faculty interest can be traced to three factors.

First, external speakers have provided insight and strategies. Edward Zlotkowski, from Bentley College in Massachusetts, conducted two workshops on restructuring courses for over 30 faculty members. Tom Ehrlich, former president of Indiana University and member of the Campus Compact Executive Board, validated the important role of higher education in the service movement in a keynote address to faculty and students. Robert Coles, Harvard professor and renowned author, spoke to the freshman class and faculty about his book *The Call of Service.* Ira Harkavy discussed with the faculty the salience of university-community partnerships in revitalizing inner cities. A symposium featuring Nancy Rhodes, then Director of Campus Compact; Dr. Gloria Scott, President of Bennett College; State Representative William Martin; and moderator Valeria Lee, Program Officer of the Z. Smith Reynolds Foundation, even convinced some reluctant administrators that community service is a bonafide pedagogical tool. The CSP has also made it a priority to introduce faculty from neighboring institutions involved in service-learning to NCCU faculty in order to discuss service-learning strategies. Another, related effort has been the distribution of a series of journal articles on service-learning to the faculty. Finally, the CSP has coordinated service-learning circles of faculty and students to reflect upon existing courses and the meaning of service.

A second factor responsible for increased faculty interest is of a rather different nature. In concert with the School of Education, the CSP has developed an evaluation tool for assessing the impact of community service-learning on faculty teaching, as well as student leadership and intellectual development. Twice a year, service sites are also evaluated by students, faculty, and CSP staff. And yet, despite these steps, there is still much room for strengthening the evaluative aspect of the program.

Still another strategy calculated to increase faculty interest concerns the reward system. We are currently recommending a rewriting of our tenure, promotion, and merit increase policies to include curricular service activities. To that end, our provost and deans have reviewed copies of service policies from institutions such as Portland State University. It is our belief that, together, these activities have begun to create a critical mass of theory, insight, and practical information that is essential to convince faculty to adopt service-learning as an ongoing component of their courses.

## COMMUNITY REVITALIZATION: A PROJECT IN PROGRESS

Community revitalization is the goal of the Community Service Program's strategic plan. The reason we are working so hard on a variety of means to convince faculty of the efficacy of service-learning and the importance of university-community partnerships is that without committed faculty participation, the service mission and strategic plan of the university can only be empty promises. To nurture our fledgling program, therefore, we enthusiastically communicate and promote each genuine effort made by faculty members to contribute to the community revitalization effort. In this regard, one especially exemplary service-learning course is Health Education 4200, Aging and the Aged: Health Perspectives, in which students have produced taped interviews as part of prescribed home visits to elderly persons. In addition, they make a minimum of five visits to nursing homes where they do whatever they can to assist the staff and patients. Students in the class have also "adopted" two families and provided food items for their Thanksgiving and Christmas dinners. Many of the students have continued the relationships with the elderly beyond the end of the class.

With a $3,060 grant from the HBCU Campus Network, Environmental Biology 2600 was revised to incorporate a service-learning module designed to increase awareness of environmental hazards in the Durham community. Students focused on Legionnaires' Disease, a condition that stems from contaminated water in closed environments. During the spring semester 1995–96, students conducted a university-wide survey investigating student, staff, and faculty awareness of this disease and its reported incidence on campus; conducted a community-based survey to compare the university data with that of the Durham community; identified and formed liaisons with community organizations—health, environmental, and social—that deal with outbreaks of the disease; designed an information booklet on the disease, its history, prevention methods, and prescribed treatments; and selected the best techniques for demonstrating to the community the steps that should be taken to disinfect devices that may harbor Legionnaires' bacteria.

During the 1995 spring semester, public administration students met their service requirement by participating in an interdisciplinary health appraisal project with students in the geography department. The dual-discipline course was called Public Administration 2100. While public administration students administered a survey which tapped health perceptions and practices of students and faculty at NCCU, geography students input the data into a geographic information system (GIS) program. Public administration and geography students analyzed the data and assisted in summarizing the survey findings. The findings on health perceptions and practices at NCCU will become part of a larger collection of state survey information that will be forwarded to the Centers for Disease Control in Atlanta.

In addition to the service-based course offerings that have begun to remake our curriculum, a community project has been created which may prove to be the core of our long-term commitment to the community and its well-being. NCCU firmly believes that if the community is transformed, so will NCCU's students and the university itself. Thus, while many university-community partnerships use a bipolar approach to service delivery, the CSP favors a more holistic strategy. In 1993, in response to the city of Durham's Partnership Against Crime efforts (PAC), North Carolina Central University joined city and county government, businesses, post-secondary institutions, and community residents for the purpose of revitalizing the most drug-infested, deteriorating local community—Northeast Central Durham.

A community-based committee of representatives from the local community, from NCCU, and from city and county government developed five task forces focused on: 1) family and child support, 2) economic development, 3) religion, 4) youth, and 5) health. Members of each task force included the same mix of university, community, and government representatives. An assets and needs survey was conducted by the Institute for the Study of Minority Issues at NCCU. The assets of the community indicated strong economic interest on the part of operating businesses, economic investments potential among black churches, and three public schools with quality education programs that could be leveraged for further development. A needs survey indicated four concerns of the community: 1) reducing crime, 2) creating jobs, 3) developing health prevention programs, and 4) encouraging children to stay in school.

Though Northeast Central Durham is located eight miles from the university, North Carolina Central University responded to the expressed requests of the community through research projects, student tutors and mentors, technical grant writing, and curriculum restructuring support. Each activity and funding proposal was approved by the community-based committee. To date, the most promising result of this effort has come from the task force focused on family and child support. Though numerous meetings were necessary to solidify trust between partners, faculty from the School of Education and the Human Resources Department have now successfully fostered the concept of "community capacity-building" by assisting in the development of a Family Resource Center which serves as a one-stop delivery for children's needs. The center is operated by the community task force and volunteers. Smart Start and Family Preservation Grants totaling $350,000 now fund the necessary infrastructure to improve the quality of life for children and families in Northeast Central Durham. In addition, one elementary school in the community is receiving support from NCCU's School of Education and the human resources department to improve the curriculum and training techniques of teachers. Meanwhile, the health education department is providing lead testing and vision screening for the children.

The School of Business is also actively involved in this project, examining ways to work with the Economic Reinvestment Committee to spawn business incubators. Other discipline-based units, like the School of Nursing, have assessed their curricula and plan to incorporate quality of life issues and service support for this Durham community into their course activities. Since interinstitutional support is important in community revitalization efforts, Duke University has volunteered its medical staff and Durham Technical Community College has helped with adult and work-preparedness training. All along the way, the community has been directly involved in planning and implementation in partnership with CSP staff.

The Northeast Central Durham model has now become the collaborative structure for Durham's city revitalization efforts. As a result of the program's success to date, the city has created three other opportunity zones on which to focus service efforts: Southeast Central, Northwest, and Southwest Durham. Another community revitalization project that students have participated in is the Knolls Development bordering on Chapel Hill. This project began in 1991 when a health education class became aware of the toll that crack cocaine had taken on many of the people in the development. Crime was up; several drive-by shootings had occurred; young mothers were prostituting themselves for drugs; and a NCCU professor, who had committed to living in the community, had experienced the first break-in at his own home. An experienced organizer and field supervisor, the professor decided to place students in this troubled community for an eight-week period. Their assignment was to work directly with the community by 1) interviewing community leaders, 2) collecting and analyzing data, and 3) assisting neighborhood residents with planning and implementing programs designed to address community problems. In other words, while students learned to practice health education, they simultaneously served a low-income community.

In 1991–92, three students served the Knolls Development by helping neighbors plan and implement a summer enrichment program. Child safety had become a real concern to mothers in the area, following a drive-by shooting which accidentally injured a nine-year-old boy. The summer program had such a positive outcome on residents that one of the students, upon graduation, wrote a small grant proposal which the local school system funded. Other students were then assigned to help her, and a regular after-school program continued what the summer enrichment program had begun. This, too, was successful, and today the city of Chapel Hill funds this after-school program, which is operated by the local YMCA. Two students assigned to do their fieldwork in the Knolls Development formed the Knolls Development Association (KDA), through which students study the history of the community. Through the KDA, the community learned that the first black homeowner in the area was a former slave who had worked for Chancellor Caldwell of the University of North Carolina at Chapel Hill. It was also learned that the Knolls Development had had numerous strong leaders in the past, including an 80-year-old woman who still lives there today. It was she who had organized the community to petition both Carrboro and Chapel Hill for annexation many years ago. Both municipalities had refused to accept the development, but when Chapel Hill elected its first African-American mayor, the community was finally annexed.

Lessons like these infused the fledgling organization with the belief that it, too, could succeed with its initiatives, particularly in addressing the crack problem and the housing crisis. By 1993, the NCCU professor who had moved to the community assigned more students to organize work crews from NCCU to assist in the remodeling of a few old houses that had been given to KDA by the Durham school board. With the success of this remodeling, more houses, loans, and grants followed. Every step of the way, several semesters' worth of students found opportunities to perform service for and learn about the Knolls Development, as well as to develop graphic displays showing what they had accomplished.

Since 1995, when the Community Service Program was formally adopted by NCCU as part of its curriculum, the mentor professor has used the display to tell the story of the Knolls Development to students anticipating their own community service work. He points out how many NCCU, Duke, and University of North Carolina students have participated in service-learning in the community. He notes the thousands of hours that these students have invested in building houses, developing brochures, and providing technical assistance to KDA. As the professor looks out his window, he can see two houses. One is a ranch-style house built by KDA and valued at over $110,000, but sold to a moderate income family for $54,000. A second is a two-story house, which was appraised at $75,000 when it was given to KDA. When it is completed, its value will be over $100,000, even though KDA will sell it for only $60,000. Since 1993, KDA has renovated or purchased for renovation 25 residential units for low to moderate income families. KDA has become a positive force in the Knolls Development and concomitantly in Chapel Hill, where affluent residents no longer wish that African-Americans would leave the Knolls Development for good. With only a community center and a dream in 1991, and with the ongoing support that now comes through The Community Service Program, KDA expects to complete projects that will exceed $3,000,000 in value by the year 2000.

## THE FUTURE OF SERVICE AT NCCU

Many faculty and administrators believe we have, by this point, correctly identified the elements necessary to create a reliable and long-lasting Community Service Program. Our energy must now be focused on strengthening each existing component. Based on the results of projects such as those just outlined, the CSP will have to concentrate on increasing faculty support for service-learning, evaluating the efficacy of the Community Service Graduation Policy, strengthening community-university partnerships, and aggressively seeking external funding in the face of declining enrollment.

## LESSONS LEARNED: A SUMMARY FROM AN HBCU PERSPECTIVE

Overall, the success of the Community Service Program at North Carolina Central University can be attributed to the following:

- Visible top administrative support for the program, particularly during its start-up years

- Institutionalization of service as a driving force for university activities, through formal revision of the mission statement

- Formation of a core team of faculty, administrators, students, and community members to advocate for service-learning on campus and to serve on the Community Service Advisory Committee for the community at large

- Selection of a veteran faculty member to lead the program; also, providing a committee and professional staff to serve as a liaison among students, faculty, staff, and community agencies

- Application for faculty development funds to introduce faculty to the service-learning pedagogy from a variety of perspectives and through different voices

- Creation of numerous opportunities for faculty to discover how others in their discipline and across disciplines in similar types of institutions have implemented service-learning

- Existence of multiple approaches to build service into the university, including traditional direct service, service-learning, and university-community partnerships

- Service efforts that focus on a limited population, as in the case of Northeast Central Durham, so that real progress can be made and accurately assessed

The DuBois-Shepard service-based mission remains a challenge for NCCU, a reminder that regeneration is a broadly beneficial process and that regeneration through service requires continuous commitment. As our students, faculty, and staff have worked with our community in renewing itself—economically, socially, and environmentally—they have testified, almost as one, that the integrity of their learning and their self-image is, and must be, grounded in the renewable soil of the community in which their university makes its home.

*For actual North Carolina Central University service-learning documents, see Appendix A: Organization Chart*

## REFERENCES

Coles, R. (1993). *The call of service.* Boston, MA: Houghton Mifflin.

Joseph, J. A. (1995). *Remaking America: How the benevolent traditions of many cultures are transforming our national life.* San Francisco, CA: Jossey-Bass.

# 7

# Communal Participatory Action Research & Strategic Academically Based Community Service: The Work of Penn's Center for Community Partnerships

Lee Benson
Ira Harkavy
*University of Pennsylvania*

## INTRODUCTION

The Center for Community Partnerships at the University of Pennsylvania (Penn) is founded on the notion that the vast range of resources of the American university, appropriately and creatively employed, can help us solve a central problem of our time—the problem of the American city. Within the city, the need for communities that are based on face-to-face relationships and that exemplify universal humanistic values is most acute. Working toward solving the problem of the American city is most likely to advance the university's primary mission of developing and transmitting knowledge. This resonates with John Dewey's claim that real advances in knowledge occur through a focus on the central problems of society (Westbrook, 1991).

For Penn, as well as all other urban universities, the strategic real world problem is what should be done to overcome the deep, pervasive, interrelated problems affecting the people in its local environment. This concrete, immediate, practical, and theoretical problem requires creative, interdisciplinary, and interactive scholarship involving the broad range of human knowledge located within the American research university. The Center for Community Partnerships is Penn's primary vehicle for bringing that broad range of human knowledge to bear so that West Philadelphia (Penn's local geographic community), Philadelphia, the university itself, and society benefits.

## THE CENTER FOR COMMUNITY PARTNERSHIPS

The center is based on three core propositions:

1. Penn's future and the future of West Philadelphia and Philadelphia are intertwined.

2. Penn can make a significant contribution to improving the quality of life in West Philadelphia and Philadelphia.

3. Penn can enhance its overall mission of advancing and transmitting knowledge by helping to improve the quality of life in West Philadelphia and Philadelphia.

The first proposition is self-evident. Safety, cleanliness of the area, and attractiveness of the social, physical, and cultural environment contribute not only to a general campus ambiance, but also to the recruitment and retention of faculty, students, and staff. The deterioration of the city and our local area has a direct impact on Penn's ability to enhance its position as a leading international university. As studies by the center have indicated, West Philadelphia has declined precipitously since 1980.

## WEST PHILADELPHIA'S URBAN CRISIS

West Philadelphia's severe urban crisis is evident in population decline; increases in poverty, crime, violence, and physical deterioration; and the poor performance of the schools, among other quality of life indicators. The population of West Philadelphia has been decreasing since 1960 as the following numbers show: (1960) 301,742; (1970) 275,611; (1980) 232,979; (1990) 219,705. From 1989 to 1993, the number of West Philadelphia residents receiving some form of public assistance increased by approximately 25%. Crime increased 10% from 1983 to 1993 in the neighborhoods surrounding the university. A study of the Mantua/Parkside/ Mill Creek area of West Philadelphia (population 68,000) shows the prevalence of violence in the area. For example, between 1987 and 1990 there were 172 violence-related deaths, 60% of which involved guns, and 94% of area males in their twenties made at least one emergency room visit. Physical deterioration in the area surrounding the university is well-documented in neighborhood plans prepared by local community-based organizations in partnership with the Center for Community Partnerships. Finally, ranked by performance on national standardized tests for reading and mathematics, three public elementary public schools proximate to the university ranked 107th, 130th, and 160th out of 171 elementary schools in Philadelphia. For Penn to advance significantly, West Philadelphia must be transformed from an urban environment that has become increasingly dangerous and alienating into a reasonably safe, attractive (in all respects), cosmopolitan urban community.[1]

But this first proposition does not take us terribly far. It can be argued that conditions are indeed deteriorating but that nothing can be done to reverse them. This argument views deterioration as an irreversible phenomenon beyond our control, which at best can be delayed or dealt with on a purely cosmetic basis. A somewhat less pessimistic scenario is that the deterioration can be reversed, but that Penn can do little to improve conditions. In this interpretation we are, in effect, completely dependent upon the actions of others—government at all levels and corporations, for example—for any significant improvements to occur in the quality of life in West Philadelphia/Philadelphia.

The center is founded upon a very different notion—our second proposition—that Penn can lead the way toward revitalizing West Philadelphia/Philadelphia. Its leadership role derives from its status as an international research university with extraordinary intellectual resources, its position as the most prestigious institution in the city, as well as the city's largest private employer. Appropriately organized and directed, Penn's range of resources can serve as the catalytic agent for galvanizing other institutions, as well as government itself, in concerted efforts to improve the quality of life in West Philadelphia/Philadelphia. The center has already taken a lead in initiating a number of projects based on this assumption. These projects include:

- The development of a citywide higher education coalition, the Philadelphia Higher Education Network for Neighborhood Development (PHENND)

- An action seminar comprised of senior Penn administrators and faculty members, and community leaders on Urban Universities and the Reconstruction of American Cities, 1945–2000; How Universities are Affected By, and Actively Affect, Their Off-Campus Environments: Penn-West Philadelphia as a Strategic Case of Institutional Policy and Action

- A West Philadelphia coalition of institutions, governmental agencies, community groups, and businesses (organized with the West Philadelphia Partnership) that is developing plans for a business corridor bordering the university

An additional argument is based on the third proposition: Enormous intellectual benefits for the university can accrue from a proactive strategy to improve West Philadelphia/Philadelphia. In fact, the center's guiding assumption is that significant advances in teaching and research will occur by focusing on the strategic problems of the city. Faculty and students will be increasingly able to put their ideals and theories into practice and test those ideals and theories as they work to solve important intellectual and real world problems. Undergraduates will be able to learn and contribute to society simultaneously. Their academic work will engage them with the central dilemmas of our time, as they focus their intellectual energy, skill, and idealism on helping to make West Philadelphia and the city better places to live and work.

The center was founded in 1992 to achieve the following objectives:

- Improve the internal coordination and collaboration of all university-wide community service programs

- Create new and effective partnerships between the university and the community

- Encourage new and creative initiatives linking Penn and the community

- Strengthen a national network of institutions of higher education committed to engagement with their local communities

The center is an outgrowth of the Penn Program for Public Service which was created in 1989 to replace and expand the Office of Community-Oriented Policy Studies in the School of Arts and Sciences (Benson & Harkavy, 1991).

The center's director reports to both Penn's vice president for government, community, and public affairs, and the provost. For complete position descriptions, see Appendix A-3. Through the center, the university currently engages in three types of activities:

- Strategic academically based community service

- Direct traditional service

- Community and economic development

## Strategic Academically Based Community Service

Strategic academically based community service's primary goal is contributing to the well-being of people in the community, now and in the future. It is service-rooted and intrinsically tied to teaching and research, and it aims to bring about structural community improvement (i.e., effective public schools, neighborhood economic development, and strong community organizations). The primary site for Penn's strategic academically based community service is its community of West Philadelphia (Harkavy, 1996).

Much of the center's work has focused on the public school as the educational and neighborhood institution that can, if effectively transformed, serve as the concrete vehicle of community change and innovation. The center has helped to create university-assisted community schools that function as the focal points of education, services, engagement, and activity within specific geographic areas. With its community and school collaborators, the center has developed significant service-learning programs that engage young people in creative work designed to advance skills and abilities through service to their schools, families, and communities. Penn students and faculty are also engaged in service-learning that requires the development and application of knowledge to solve problems as well as the engagement in active and serious reflection. This Deweyan approach might be termed "learning by community problem solving and real world reflective doing."

The mediating structure for on-site delivery of academic resources is the West Philadelphia Improvement Corps (WEPIC), a university-supported school and community revitalization program founded in 1985. WEPIC's goal is to produce comprehensive, university-assisted community schools that serve, educate, and activate all members of the community, revitalizing the curriculum through a community-oriented, real world, problem solving approach. WEPIC seeks to help develop schools that are open year-round, functioning simultaneously as the core building for the community and as its educational and service delivery hub.

Specifically, the center's strategic academically based community service activities include the following:

- Development and support for undergraduate and graduate seminars, courses, and research projects. By the 1996–97 academic year, 45 courses were offered which supported Penn's work in West Philadelphia

- Coordination of internships for students to engage intensively in work in the community, especially in the public schools. Of particular note are the following:

  1. Pennsylvania Service Scholars, a statewide higher education AmeriCorps program funded by the Corporation for National Service. Twenty-two full-time undergraduates work part-time over a period of three years in local public schools.[2]

2. Public Service Summer Internship Program, a project that supports 12 undergraduates during the summer to take a research seminar with the center's director and conduct a six-week summer institute for incoming sixth graders at a local middle school.

3. Undergraduate Social Science Initiative, a program funded by the Ford Foundation, which aims to enhance undergraduate social science teaching (eight courses created to date), expand undergraduate academic internships linked to work in the public schools (39 to date), and support interdisciplinary action research seminars for faculty and graduate students.

4. Program to Link Intellectual Resources and Community Needs, a new program funded by the W. K. Kellogg Foundation, which focuses academically based community service on cultural and community studies, environmental studies, and nutrition. In 1996–97, the program supported 15 undergraduate students working as academic interns; it also supported course development and seminars integrating action research into the curriculum.

■ Coordination of the National WEPIC Replication Project, a three-year, $1,000,000 grant from the DeWitt Wallace-Reader's Digest Fund to replicate Penn's university-assisted community school model at three universities (Miami University, Ohio; University of Kentucky, Lexington; and the University of Alabama, Birmingham). The project is also developing a national network of colleagues interested in this work through a journal, *Universities and Community Schools*; a newsletter; an on-line database; and a series of national conferences.

## Direct Traditional Service

The center coordinates Penn staff, faculty, and alumni service projects, including a mentoring program for 21 middle school students, a postsecondary scholarship program for 12 high school students from West Philadelphia who have actively served their communities and achieved academically, and annual drives to fill community needs.

In addition, the center coordinates—together with the Program for Student-Community Involvement (PSCI), Penn's student volunteer center—an extensive service program initiated by undergraduates. We also work closely with the Community Service Living/Learning Project, a residential program for students committed to community service. In 1995–96, 24 residents worked with WEPIC, Penn's university-assisted community school partnership. Finally through the center, the facilities management department coordinates Operation Fresh Start in which student, faculty, staff, and community volunteers work on the physical improvement of local public schools and community centers.

## Community and Economic Development

The center coordinates work-based learning programs in which students from a local middle school are mentored at Penn's Medical Center, and high school students serve as interns in various Penn publication departments and as paid apprentices in the Medical Center. In coordination with local community associations and the West Philadelphia Partnership—a mediating, nonprofit organization composed of institutions (including Penn), businesses, and community organizations—the center works on community planning projects that have produced the following:

- City funding for capital improvements to a major business corridor along the university's western boundary. A business owners' association has been formed to oversee the project.

- Strategic plans for housing and commercial revitalization of two West Philadelphia communities, Walnut Hill and Spruce Hill.

Moreover, the center works with Penn's purchasing department to create opportunities for minority and female employment and business ownership in West Philadelphia through minority purchasing contracts. As a direct result of the Buy West Philadelphia Program, purchasing from West Philadelphia suppliers increased from $2.1 million in 1987 to $15 million in 1994. In 1995, Penn signed additional minority purchasing contracts worth $2.8 million. Furthermore, we are working with Penn's Office of Information Services and Computing and the West Philadelphia Partnership to develop a highly accessible West Philadelphia data and information system. A World Wide Web site on West Philadelphia and the center has already been established. The center also coordinates Internet training, involving software and technical support for approximately 100 West Philadelphia teachers. Finally, along with the human resources department, we provide training and technical assistance to the West Philadelphia Partnership's Job Network and Referral Center, helping to implement a Hire West Philadelphia strategy at Penn and other institutions in West Philadelphia.

## STUDENT AND FACULTY INVOLVEMENT

Undergraduates can become involved in the Center for Community Partnerships in several different ways. In general, they learn about academically based community service courses through discussions with other students. Faculty members and graduate students also inform students about opportunities to link academics and service. Students can be employed by the center through work-study positions, government or foundation grants, or paid internships. Approximately 500 students do traditional volunteer work in the community with WEPIC. All undergraduates who work with the center are encouraged to participate in training/orientation sessions and enroll in academically based community service courses, and research projects.

Graduate students are employed through the center on research grants or in work-study positions. Several graduate students are working on academically based community service dissertations with a focus on West Philadelphia. Masters and doctoral dissertations are being written by students in anthropology, education, history, history and sociology of science, psychology, nursing, and sociology. In addition, graduate students are engaged in academically based community service research projects in English, fine arts, geology, history, landscape architecture, city and regional planning, social work, and urban studies.

The Center for Community Partnerships works to support faculty involvement in academically based community service by funding course development grants. The center also provides funds to faculty members to support teaching and research assistantships. Seminars and conferences help to spur interest and expand the number of faculty members participating in the center's work.

## PROGRAM HISTORY

Penn's renewed focus on the problems of the city, its efforts to comprehensively engage academic resources to help improve the quality of life in its immediate geographic neighborhood, and its efforts to create genuine, mutually beneficial partnerships with the community have been developing since Sheldon Hackney's presidency began in 1981. In 1983 two organizations at the center of Penn's new relationship with its neighbors were created: the West Philadelphia Partnership and the Office of Community-Oriented Policy Studies, the predecessor to the Penn Program for Public Service which eventually developed into the center.

The West Philadelphia Partnership represents an organizational innovation of broad applicability and significance. It is a vehicle that has freed the university from an operational role in the community. If the history of university-community relationships has taught us anything, it is that the role of operationalizing and managing community initiatives is a role that universities are ill-equipped to perform. C. P. Snow's concept of two cultures could easily apply to the world of academics and managers. Different orientations, styles, approaches, and types dominate these different worlds. Effective linkages must be created, but attempts to alter the "dominant institutional-individual style" are to be avoided.

Indeed, universities are not only ill-equipped to perform operational roles in society, but it is inappropriate for them to do so: Universities should be concerned with the production and transmission of knowledge. How well a university does both those things is how it should be evaluated. A university's service activities, which should provide genuine neighborly assistance and improvement, are best tied to its academic functions. Community initiatives should be carried out by other institutions in society. Although these points apply to universities in general, they hold particularly for elite, private, research universities. In and through the West Philadelphia Partnership (WPP), Penn has developed an organizational vehicle that enables it to be linked to and to learn from the community without directly implementing specific programs. Since it is comprised of both institutions and community organizations, it not only has a legitimacy among diverse populations that a more narrowly based organization could not have, but it is also able to match community and institutional needs and resources more effectively than would otherwise be the case.

The School of Arts and Sciences' Office of Community-Oriented Policy Studies (OCOPS) worked very closely with the West Philadelphia Partnership for many years. Created in 1983, OCOPS was designed to bridge theoretical and applied knowledge and to orient the university toward the problems of the city. At the outset, OCOPS cast a wide experiential net for Penn undergraduates, featuring interdisciplinary seminars, summer internships, and research affiliations with social service organizations throughout the Philadelphia area. Students researched social problems targeted by the agencies and proposed alternative solutions; yet given the geographic dispersion of these projects and the particular needs of individual sponsors, the students' early efforts were disjunctive and lacked intellectual coherence. In the spring of 1985, however, when OCOPS turned its attention specifically to improving the quality of life in Penn's immediate geographic community of West Philadelphia, significant intellectual progress finally began to occur (Harkavy & Puckett, 1991).

We began working on university-community relationships as a result of the failure of our earlier efforts to link the Penn undergraduate curriculum to contemporary problems confronting American society. Since the early 1970s, we had been increasingly troubled—personally and intellectually—by the accelerating decline of student participation in the American political system. Since we both had long been firmly committed to the idea of learning by doing, we developed a joint seminar on American student political participation which required students to propose and implement organized innovations likely to increase student political participation. However, despite a great deal of time and effort on our part and university financial support, the project proved disappointing. By late 1984, we reconsidered our strategy and decided to reorganize a seminar to focus on university-community relationships rather than on student political participation. For a variety of reasons, President Sheldon Hackney, himself a former professor of history, agreed to join us in giving an honors seminar for undergraduates in the spring 1985 semester. The title of the seminar articulated its general concerns— Urban University-Community Relationships: Penn-West Philadelphia, Past, Present, and Future, as a Case Study.

West Philadelphia was, by this time, rapidly deteriorating. We asked undergraduates to consider what Penn should do to remedy its environmental situation. They proposed solutions and learned how to do socially relevant independent research. It also seemed to be a good action-oriented, engaging question to stimulate Penn undergraduates to think seriously about abstract, high-level questions such as "Why Study History?" "Knowledge for What?" and "What are Universities Good For?" How to stimulate students to address such concerns had long been a question that concerned and perplexed us both.

At this time, we were unaware of Dewey's community school idea. We knew literally nothing about the history of community school experiments and had not given much thought, if any, to Penn working with public schools in West Philadelphia. Instead, as the 1985 seminar was organized, each student focused his or her research on a problem that adversely affected specific groups in West Philadelphia. During the course of the semester, four students decided to work cooperatively to study the problem of youth unemployment in the context of improving the West Philadelphia physical environment. Having done library research, consulted experts in Philadelphia and elsewhere, interviewed leaders of local groups, and made a commitment to conservative political and social ideas, they developed a proposal to create a better and much less expensive youth corps than existed anywhere else, including the federal government's Job Corps. More specifically, they proposed a neighborhood-based, neighborhood-improving, summer job training program for at-risk youth. Built into their proposal, however, was the possibility of expanding the program to include adults and other volunteers concerned with neighborhood improvement. They called for creation of a West Philadelphia Improvement Corps (WEPIC). WEPIC, originally conceived as a neat acronym, has been retained and remains appropriate, although it now identifies a radically different project than the one originally envisioned.

For a variety of reasons (including some that were wholly accidental), it became possible to obtain funds to implement the proposed youth job training program during the summer of 1985. Much of the summer activity became focused around the Bryant School, a neighborhood elementary school. To remove graffiti and improve Bryant's physical appearance, murals were painted around the school building and a nearby daycare center. With the help of a Penn landscape architect and undergraduates serving as summer interns, a comprehensive landscaping plan for the weed- and rubbish-filled school grounds was drafted and partially implemented. Trees, shrubs, grass, and groundcover were planted, brick walks were laid, benches set in place, and a general cleanup and area improvement organized.

As work proceeded on the school building and grounds, an extremely significant development, wholly unforeseen, occurred: Neighbors reacted positively to the school improvements, provided some volunteer help, and undertook improvement projects on their own properties. From the positive reactions of the neighbors, faculty and students realized that public schools could function as centers for youth work experience and neighborhood revitalization. As a result, thanks to a grant from nonuniversity sources, during the fall of 1985, WEPIC became an extracurricular after-school program at Bryant. Teachers incorporated the after-school projects into their curriculum. WEPIC has spread to an increasing number of schools in West Philadelphia. We and our colleagues have come to see that the best strategy to help improve our off-campus environment is to use the enormous internal and external resources.

Like other American urban universities, by the late 1980s our institution was paying an increasingly heavy price for its myopic failure to make the quality of its off-campus environment a significant institutional priority. It was experiencing the great and varied costs and stresses of trying to perform its traditional academic functions in an ever more difficult, hostile, and unsafe physical and social environment—an environment which could neither be blocked from view by ivied walls and multi-storied dormitories nor effectively policed by an increasingly professional, armed, omnipresent, and expensive Department of Public Safety. After dark, most Penn buildings were either locked and essentially unused or carefully guarded, and personnel were instructed to take all the precautions appropriate for people living in an urban danger zone.

Since the deterioration of our off-campus environment was having adverse affects on our institutional well-being, the institution began to pay significant attention to the problem. It had become empirically clear that Penn had to radically change its orientation and relationships with West Philadelphia and Philadelphia. In principle, Penn could no longer simply be *in* West Philadelphia and Philadelphia, it had to be *of* West Philadelphia and Philadelphia—an integral part of the community in which it was physically located. The university at last formally recognized that fact of life in its official annual report for 1987–88.

## The Turning Point

That annual report was a major turning point in Penn's real relationship with West Philadelphia/Philadelphia, distinct from what might be called its rhetorical public relations relationship. Entitled *Penn and Philadelphia: Common Ground*, the report focused on the dynamic, mutually beneficial interaction that potentially existed between Penn and its local community. Since elite private American research universities like Penn have notoriously tended to consider themselves in but not of their local communities, that change in focus was itself highly significant. Even more significant was the report's explicit affirmation that Penn's future and the future of Philadelphia were inextricably tied together. After summarizing some of the university's recent efforts, President Hackney wrote, "The picture that emerges is one of a relationship in which the university and the city are important to one another. We stand on common ground, our futures very much intertwined" (University of Pennsylvania, 1989).

Implicit in Hackney's statement was a recognition that Penn could no longer try to remain an oasis of privileged affluence in a desert of urban pathology and despair. Such a recognition should lead to a radical change in institutional orientation and acceptance of the proposition that the problems of Penn's local community are also the problems of the university. Given such a radically changed orientation, efforts to solve community problems would no longer be viewed as a minor matter or as a matter of moral choice. Instead they should become an institutional imperative. Stated in more theoretical terms, the argument takes this form: As is generally true of open systems, Penn's environment significantly affects its functioning. If its environment deteriorates badly, it must seriously devote its resources to reversing that deterioration or suffer the consequences.

For Penn to focus seriously on the effective use of its resources to help solve Philadelphia's problems would simply represent its rededication to a tradition begun 250 years ago by its patron saint, Benjamin Franklin. But it is not the Franklin tradition that we are invoking here. Aside from that tradition, even in terms of narrow self-interest alone, the university's annual report for 1987–88 formally declared that, for its present and future well-being, Penn must seriously work to help solve its West Philadelphia/Philadelphia problem. In principle, at least, that problem now constituted a significant university priority. Translating that principle into practice, of course, would be anything but easy. Two issues had to be confronted: 1) Other than affirm that it stood on common ground with Philadelphia, what specifically should Penn do as an institution? 2) How should Penn organize itself to effectively mobilize its considerable resources to help improve its off-campus environment?

In retrospect, we can now say that the 1988 decision to organize the Penn Program for Public Service in the School of Arts and Sciences had far-reaching, positive consequences. An organizational innovation, the Penn Program in Public Service helped translate the general, nonspecific, rhetoric of the 1987–88 annual report into concrete practice. Harkavy was appointed the program's director, given a small staff and budget, and a generous hunting license to secure outside funds to support public service projects involving Penn and West Philadelphia. By 1988 some federal and state grants had already been secured which enabled the WEPIC job training project to expand from its original site at the Bryant School to several other West Philadelphia schools. The newly created Penn Program for Public Service concentrated its efforts on strengthening and expanding the work underway at WEPIC schools.

By this time we had abandoned our original notion of using a variety of neighborhood sites and organizations to develop job-training programs for at-risk youth and concentrated our efforts on a small number of West Philadelphia schools. As WEPIC became exclusively a school-based program, and as the teachers in the program more or less spontaneously expanded their roles to encompass community improvement and engagement, we unwittingly reinvented the community school idea. As the program evolved, the initial problem with which we had begun—youth unemployment and job training—was subsumed under a far more comprehensive problem: How could schools effectively function as genuine community centers for the organization, education, and transformation of entire neighborhoods?

We and our colleagues came to identify a far more comprehensive and significant problem as a result of our increasing engagement with West Philadelphia teachers and principals in a genuinely collaborative participatory action research project. To help carry out that project, we focused our attention (for the first time) on John Dewey's ideas on schooling and learning. Reading Dewey, in turn, led us to search actively through the primary and highly specialized secondary literature dealing with the wider use of schools as social centers and community centers. As a result, we increasingly saw that neighborhood public schools could function as the catalytic strategic agents for community revitalization.[3]

## The Community School Tradition

A genuine sense of intellectual excitement developed as academics and West Philadelphia school practitioners learned about historical antecedents to their improvised efforts. It located them in a larger tradition, helped them draw inspiration from previous attempts and learn from past successes and failures. Most critically, the discovery of community schools in American educational history helped everyone better understand what they all had been groping toward conceptually, theoretically, and practically. Our goal was far clearer than ever before. We wanted to transform the traditional West Philadelphia public school system into a revolutionary new system of community-centered, community problem solving schools.

Revolutions in schooling, of course, require lots of resources—particularly money. Fortunately, since 1985 WEPIC had developed a successful track record, thanks in large part to significant grants from federal and state agencies. Excellent professional and personal relationships existed between Penn faculty members involved in WEPIC and strategic Pennsylvania state government officials. As a result, in 1989 those officials responded favorably to a request for a relatively large grant to begin the process of trying to transform West Philadelphia's conventional public schools into innovative community schools.

Given the limited extent of Penn resources, our long institutional resistance to serious involvement with West Philadelphia's problems, and the intrinsic difficulty of transforming conventional schools into community schools, we decided that our best strategy was to try to achieve a visible, dramatic success in one school rather than marginal, incremental changes in a number of schools. While continuing the WEPIC program at other schools, we decided to concentrate on the John C. Turner Middle School, largely because of the interest and leadership of its principal.

We made several general decisions in order to set the evolutionary process in motion and loosely guide it:

- A teacher with several years of experience at WEPIC would be appointed to the newly created staff position of community school coordinator.

- The roles for community members would be allowed to develop and expand in the process of working on school and community issues.

- Penn faculty and staff would be charged with making suggestions, encouraging new directions, trying to provide requested resources, and helping to develop ideas with Turner staff and community leaders.

- The WEPIC staff would administratively coordinate the project.

- Final decision-making power would be held by those officially responsible for Turner's operation, namely its principal and teachers.

The importance of this last decision cannot be overemphasized: Turner would be a community school, but it would not be controlled by the community in which it was located. It would, instead, be a university-assisted, staff-controlled and managed community public school.

As specific plans developed to translate the general community school idea into real life practice at Turner, the community school coordinator requested and received appropriate resources from Penn. Seminars, studios, practicums, and research projects focused on the Turner School were launched in a number of Penn schools, not simply the School of Arts and Sciences and the School of Education.

Previous experiments in community schools and community education had depended primarily on a single unit of the university, the School of Education, which is one major reason for their failure or limited success. The WEPIC concept of university assistance was far more comprehensive. From the start of the Turner experiment, we understood the concept to mean both assistance from and mutually beneficial collaboration with a wide range of Penn's schools, departments, and administrative offices.

Given WEPIC's history when the Turner project began, we placed a good deal of emphasis on job training and school subjects related to landscaping and building construction. It soon became apparent, however, that the best way to develop and sustain the community school project would be to initiate a school-based community health program. In the summer of 1990, a six-week institute for at-risk students was conducted and organized around the theme of community health. With the aid of faculty and students from the Penn medical school, the teachers developed a community health-centered curriculum which had Turner students participating in a hypertension screening program for community residents. The program, organized and supervised by Penn medical faculty and students, served as a real world, action-oriented, project-focused learning vehicle for the Turner students. Similarly, the 1990 summer internship program for Penn undergraduates was revised so that undergraduate research focused on the problem of how community health and student learning could be interactively improved through development of a community health facility at Turner. From then on, the school-based community health program has formed the main focus of the Turner community school project, with a greatly expanded scope of subject matter and number of students and teachers involved.

Expansion came about for a number of reasons. Not surprisingly, the first reason was the same one Willie Sutton allegedly gave for robbing banks: "That's where the money was." For example, after the relative success of the 1990 summer institute at Turner, a proposal was made to and accepted by the federal Department of Labor for funds to conduct a Health Careers Work-Based Learning Project during the summer of 1991.

Given the development of the community health program at Turner, Professor Francis Johnston, Chair of the Anthropology Department, and a world leader in nutritional anthropology, decided to become involved with the Turner project. He did so by revising Anthropology 210 to make it a strategic academically based community service seminar for the fall 1990 semester. Anthropology 210 has a long history at Penn and focuses on the relationship between anthropology and biomedical science. An undergraduate course, it was developed to link pre-medical training at

Penn with the anthropology department's major program in medical anthropology. Pre-med students are highly important in Penn undergraduate education, and the anthropology department's program in medical anthropology is world renowned. Johnston's decision to convert Anthro 210 into a strategic academically based community service seminar, therefore, constituted a major milestone in the development of the Turner community school project—and in Penn's relation to the Turner School.

Since 1990, students in Anthro 210 have carried out a variety of activities at Turner focused on the interactive relationships among diet, nutrition, growth, and health. The seminar is explicitly and increasingly organized around strategic academically based community service. Students are encouraged to view their education at Penn as preparing them to contribute to the solution of societal problems through service to the local community and to do so by devoting a large part of their work in the course to a significant human problem, in this case, the nutrition of disadvantaged inner-city children. As the seminar expanded in scope and its relationships with Turner teachers and students strengthened and became more trusting, Turner students themselves have become increasingly engaged in community service related to their nutrition and other health-oriented courses. Penn students serve as mentors and supervisors of the disadvantaged children.

Professor Johnston has increasingly focused his own research and publications on his work with Turner students and community residents, serving as an example for a number of other anthropology professors and graduate students who are now integrating their teaching and research with the Turner school-based community health program. Even more significantly, Anthro 210 has not only affected the anthropology department; its success has radiated out to other departments and schools. There can be no doubt that it has played a major role in the increasingly successful campaign to expand the strategic academically based community service at Penn.[4]

As of the fall of 1996, over 45 service-learning courses were being given. More and more faculty members, from an ever wider range of Penn departments and schools, are now seriously thinking about how they might revise existing courses or develop new courses. Students will benefit from the opportunity to become active learners and creative, real world problem solvers.

## Creating the Center for Community Partnerships

In July 1992, President Hackney, encouraged by the success of the university's increasing engagement with West Philadelphia since the university-community honors seminar he co-taught in 1985, created the Center for Community Partnerships. To indicate the importance he attached to the center, he located it in the Office of the President and appointed Harkavy to be its director (Harkavy continued to serve as director of the Penn Program for Public Service).

Symbolically and practically, the creation of the center represented a major change in Penn's relationship to West Philadelphia/Philadelphia. The university as a corporate entity was committed to finding ways to use its resources to improve the quality of life in its local community, not only to public schools, but also to economic and community development.

The emphasis on partnerships in the center's name was deliberate; it recognized that Penn could not try to go it alone. Moreover, it explicitly signaled that Penn would work hard to overcome the heavy burdens of history and habit in order to help create truly collaborative coalitions of all the institutions, agencies, organizations, and interests that held a stake in West Philadelphia. Creating such truly collaborative coalitions was—and remains—something not easily accomplished; it is a work in progress and is likely to have that character for considerable time to come. However, creation of the center was also significant internally. The president of the university would strongly encourage all components of the university to give serious consideration to the roles they could appropriately play in Penn's efforts to improve the quality of its off-campus environment.

An interim president and provost led the university from July 1993 through June 1994. Although the center's work continued to progress, it did not accelerate to the degree that would have been possible with a more settled situation.[5]

The appointment in 1994 of Judith Rodin as Penn's new president represented still another important milestone, creating conditions for a great leap forward in the community school project. A graduate of Penn and a native Philadelphian, Rodin was appointed in part because of her commitment to improving Penn's local environment and transforming Penn into the leading urban university. Her choice of Stanley Chodorow as provost illustrated Rodin's commitment to service-learning. Chodorow, a medieval historian and former vice chancellor at the University of California, San Diego (UCSD), had taken a leadership role in helping to engage UCSD faculty with the San Diego public schools.

Rodin and Chodorow made radical reform of undergraduate education their first priority. They established the provost's Council on Undergraduate Education and charged it to design a model for Penn's undergraduate experience for the 21st century. The provost's council emphasized the union of theory and practice, and engagement with the material, ethical, and moral concerns of society and community defined broadly, globally, and also locally within Philadelphia. The provost's council defined the 21st century undergraduate experience as:

... provid[ing] opportunities for students to understand what it means to be active learners and active citizens. It will be an experience of learning, knowing, and doing that will lead to the active involvement of students in the process of their education (Provost's Council on Undergraduate Education, 1995).

To put this approach into practice, the provost's council described academically based community service as a core component of Penn undergraduate education during the next century.

President Rodin also highlighted the centrality of the Penn-West Philadelphia/Philadelphia relationship to her administration when she convened a President's Forum on the University and its Communities. This day-long retreat, which involved the provost, the deans of Penn's 12 schools, senior vice presidents, the vice provost for university life, and the director of the Center for Community Partnerships (Harkavy), evaluated the state of academically based community service, volunteer service, and corporate service (e.g., Penn's role as an economic entity). The president's forum concentrated on

- Establishing general guidelines and principles for each type of service activity

- Formulating strategies for integrating all three types of service and for engaging the range of Penn's intellectual resources in all university interactions with the community

- Evaluating the impacts of Penn's efforts both on and off campus

Building upon themes identified by the prost's council and the president's forum, Rodin entitled Penn's 1994–95 annual report *The Unity of Theory and Practice: Penn's Distinctive Character*. While describing a series of Penn efforts to connect theory and practice, Rodin wrote:

Finally, there are ways in which the complex interrelationships between theory and practice transcend any effort at neat conceptualization. One of those is the application of theory in service to our community and the use of community service as an academic research activity for students. Nowhere else is the interactive dimension of theory and practice so clearly captured.

For more than 250 years, Philadelphia has rooted Penn in a sense of the "practical," reminded us that service to humanity, to our community is, as [Benjamin] Franklin put it, "the great aim and end of all learning." Today, thousands of Penn faculty and students realize the unity of theory and practice by engaging West Philadelphia elementary and secondary school students as part of their own academic course work in disciplines as diverse as history, anthropology, classical studies, education, and mathematics.

For example, anthropology professor Frank Johnston and his under-graduate students educate students at West Philadelphia's Turner Middle School about nutrition. Classical studies professor Ralph Rosen uses modern Philadelphia and fifth century Athens to explore the interrelations between community, neighborhood, and family. And history professor Michael Zuckerman's students engage West Philadelphia elementary and secondary school students to help them understand together the nature—and discontinuities—of American national identity and national character (University of Pennsylvania, 1996).

This annual report illustrates and advances a cultural shift that had begun to take place across the university. By the end of their first year in office, the president and provost had increased the prominence of under-graduate education, defined the linkage of theory and practice (including theory and practice derived from and applied within the local commu-nity) as a hallmark of Penn, and identified academically based commu-nity service focused in West Philadelphia and its public schools as an integrative strategy for advancing research, teaching, and service. In short, Rodin and Chodorow created an institutional vision and climate that enable the promise of the Center for Community Partnerships to begin to be realized on a significant scale in actual practice.

## COMMUNAL PARTICIPATORY ACTION RESEARCH AS A STRATEGY FOR ADVANCING PENN'S WORK WITH WEST PHILADELPHIA: SOCIOLOGY 302 AS A CASE STUDY IN PROGRESS

Penn's 1994–95 annual report legitimized the center's research strategy and approach to community problem solving. We have called this form of research communal participatory action research which is different from traditional participatory action research (PAR). Both research processes are directed toward problems in the real world, concerned with applica-tion, and are, obviously, participatory. However, they differ in the degree to which they are continuous, comprehensive, beneficial, and necessary to the organization or community studied as well as to the university. For example, traditional PAR is exemplified in the efforts of William Foote Whyte and his associates at Cornell University to advance industrial democracy in the worker cooperatives of Mondragan, Spain (Whyte & White, 1988; Greenwood & Santos, 1992). Its considerable utility and the-oretical significance notwithstanding, the research at Mondragón is not an institutional necessity for Cornell. By contrast, the University of Pennsylvania's enlightened self-interest is directly tied to the success of its research efforts in West Philadelphia; hence its emphasis on communal participatory action research. Proximity and a focus on problems that are institutionally significant to the university encourage sustained, continuous research involvement. Problem-focused research, in turn, necessitates sustained, continuous partnerships between the university and its geographic community. A crucial issue, of course, is the degree to which these locally based research projects result in general knowledge. The center's position is that local does not mean parochial and that the solution to local problems requires an understanding of national and global issues as well as an effective use and development of theory.

In 1995, Penn's Zellerbach Family Professor of Sociology and Research, Frank F. Furstenberg, Jr., began a communal participatory action research project at University City High School. A distinguished scholar of the family, Furstenberg has published widely on teenage sexuality, pregnancy, and childbearing as well as divorce, remarriage, and stepparenting. In recent years, Furstenberg's work has focused on the family in disadvantaged urban neighborhoods, concentrating on adolescent sexual behavior, changes in the well-being of children, and urban education. Adjacent to Penn's campus, University City High School has consistently placed at or very near the bottom of Philadelphia's high schools. With 88.5% of its students from low income families, 50% of its students receiving a D or an F in at least one course each semester, an average combined SAT score of 643, and the eighth worst suspension rate and seventh worst absentee rate among Philadelphia's public high schools, University City High School is visible testimony to Penn's need to do more and better in its work with West Philadelphia (School District of Philadelphia, 1995). Furstenberg was the first of approximately 15 faculty to connect his or her academic work with University City High School. This wave of Penn involvement is the direct result of an extraordinarily able, progressive, Deweyan principal.

Harkavy had known Furstenberg since 1967, when Furstenberg was a new assistant professor and Harkavy a sophomore at Penn. From the early 1990s, Harkavy had made the case to Furstenberg that he turn his research and teaching toward West Philadelphia. A grant from the Ford Foundation to the center and the College of Arts and Sciences to develop academically based community service courses in sociology as well as three other departments provided an additional incentive for Furstenberg to pilot a West Philadelphia seminar. Since he cared deeply about the dreadful condition of public schooling in Philadelphia and wanted to do something to change that condition, and since he found University City High School to be in particular need of assistance and advantageously located for serious, sustained engagement, Furstenberg focused his attention on that school.

Designing his work to both study and help reduce teen pregnancy, Furstenberg's project was participatory action research in design from the outset. At the core of this work is a two-semester senior thesis seminar, Sociology 302: Community Research and Community Service. Seminar students work with teachers in four small learning communities (groups designed to break up large impersonal schools into smaller, learner friendly units), helping to incorporate a teen pregnancy prevention project into the curriculum.

Sociology 302 is also divided into task forces responsible for putting together a proposal for reducing teen pregnancy at University City High School. One task force focuses on designing a sexuality education program for teens; another, on the transition from high school to the workforce; and a third, on the transition from high school to college. Each task force produces a paper and presents it to a group of teachers that meet regularly with Furstenberg to discuss how to lower the high school's pregnancy rate, increase its attendance, and lower its dropout rate.

Each Sociology 302 undergraduate also writes an individual research paper based on his or her experiences at University City. Papers have focused on such topics as race relations, school culture, teenage fatherhood, and the impact of work. Finally, Furstenberg and his students have been conducting a baseline survey of the school, collecting data on teen parents and demographics of the school population in general. This information is being used by the principal and teachers as well as by Furstenberg and his students to develop a more comprehensive intervention designed to reduce teen pregnancy at University City.

Reports from the field and from seminar participants have been exceedingly positive. Furstenberg has described this work as the "most electric teaching I have done in nearly 30 years at Penn." Although at a very early stage, Furstenberg's work seems to illustrate the potential of communal participatory action research both for integrating research, teaching, and service and for contributing to scholarship, the university, and the community.

## CONCLUSION: WHERE DO WE GO FROM HERE?

The Center for Community Partnerships is part of a series of recent organizational innovations designed to improve higher education and create a better society. Three noteworthy examples include the University of Illinois at Chicago's Great Cities program, created in 1993 as an additional unit within the office of the chancellor; the State University of New York at Buffalo's vice president for public service and urban affairs position, created in 1992; and Campus Compact, created in 1985 as an organization of college presidents dedicated to advancing community service and citizenship, with a current membership of more than 550 presidents. These examples illustrate a movement that needs to be encouraged and supported. The crisis of the American city is testimony enough that the self-contained, isolated university will no longer do. Community problem solving, and socially responsible, civic colleges and universities are needed as never before if we are to achieve sustained intellectual and societal progress.

In 1982, Harvard's President Derek Bok called on universities to function as genuinely civic, socially, and morally engaged institutions in order to fulfill their educational mission:

> If we would teach our students to care about important social problems, and think about them rigorously, then clearly our institutions of learning must set a high example in the conduct of their own affairs. In addition to responding to its students, a university must examine its social responsibilities if it wishes to acquire an adequate understanding of its proper role and purpose in present-day society (Bok, 1982).

The Center for Community Partnerships is a vehicle for helping Penn to function as Bok describes. It has much more to learn and do if it is to make a significant difference. To continue this process of organizational learning and doing, we colleagues at the center, including a group of undergraduates, are proposing still another initiative to bring about the intellectually, socially, and morally engaged university (Whyte, 1991). We propose to use the past, present, and possible future of West Philadelphia as the real world site for a highly integrated, interdisciplinary, action-oriented, morally driven curriculum in problem solving (Gallagher, et al. 1992). The aim of the curriculum would be to significantly improve teaching and learning through communal participatory action research. It would test the possibility of developing the knowledge and trained personnel needed to significantly improve the quality of life in West Philadelphia by means of strategic academically based community service. Future reports on the center's successes and failures in implementing this as well as other innovations will, we hope, contribute to the growing and much needed discussion of what Bok has termed "[the university's] proper role and purpose in present-day society."

*For actual University of Pennsylvania service-learning documents, see Appendix A: Organization Chart*

## ENDNOTES

1.  Sources for the statistics cited can be found in Bureau of the Census, *Census of population and housing, 1960–1990*. Washington, DC: U.S. Department of Commerce; Philadelphia City Planning Commission. (1994). *The plan for West Philadelphia*. Philadelphia, PA: City Planning Commission; University of Pennsylvania Division of Public Safety. (1994). "Safety is everyone's right, everyone's responsibility; let's form a partnership."; Schwarz, D., Grisso, J. A., et al. (1994). "A longitudinal study of injury morbidity in an African-American popula-

tion." *Journal of the American Medical Association, 271*, 755–60; Center for Community Partnerships. (1994). *Walnut Hill strategic neighborhood plan*, Philadelphia, PA: unpublished manuscript; *Spruce Hill community renewal plan*. (1995). Philadelphia, PA: unpublished manuscript; and School District of Philadelphia, *School Profiles*. (1994). Philadelphia, PA: School District of Philadelphia.

2.  AmeriCorps is the central program in President Clinton's effort to develop and extend national service. The Corporation for National Service is the federal administrative entity responsible for Ameri-Corps and other national and community service programs.

3.  With John L. Puckett, Benson and Harkavy are writing a book tentatively titled *The Rise, decline, and revitalization of America's community schools, 1886–2006*. Works that they have found particularly useful include Dewey, J. (1902). The school as social centre. *Journal of the Proceedings of the National Education Association*, 373–83; Perry, C. A. (1911). *Wider use of the school plan*. New York, NY: Russell Sage Foundation; Dewey, J., & Dewey, E. (1915). *Schools of tomorrow*. New York, NY: E. P. Dutton; Glueck, E. (1927). *The community use of schools*. Baltimore, MD: Williams and Wilkins; Samuel Everett, S. (Ed.). (1938). *The community school*. New York, NY: Appleton-Century; Clapp, E. (1939). *Community schools in action*. New York, NY: Viking; Nelson B. Henry (Ed.). (1953). *The fifty-second yearbook of the National Society for the Study of Education, Part II: The community school*. Chicago, IL: University of Chicago; Cremin, L. (1962). *The transformation of the school: Progressivism in American education, 1876–1957*. New York, NY: Viking; Peebles, R. W. (1980). *Leonard Covello: A study of an immigrant's contribution to New York City*. New York, NY: Arno Press; and Reese, W. J. (1986). *The power and promise of school reform grassroots movements during the Progressive Era*. Boston, MA: Routledge and Kegan Paul.

4.  For a more complete account of Professor Johnston's work, see Benson, L., & Harkavy, I. (1994). Anthropology 210, academically-based community service, and the advancement of knowledge, teaching, and learning: An experiment in progress. *Universities and Community Schools, 2* (1/2), 66–69.

5.  One major development did occur in 1994 that contributed significantly to the continuity of undergraduate participation in the WEPIC community school project. In 1992, the university created a residential program for students committed to community service and housed it in an attractive former fraternity house, symbolically located at the very center of the Penn campus. In 1994–95, the 24 residents of the Community Service Living/Learning Project decided to devote their activities primarily to working in the community school

project and developed some organizational innovations that proved highly constructive. The honors seminar which Benson and Harkavy continue to give on university-community relationships is now held in the "Castle" (as the fraternity house has long been known).

## REFERENCES

Benson, L., & Harkavy, I. (1994). Anthropology 210, academically based community service and the advancement of knowledge, teaching, and learning: An experiment in progress. *Universities and Community Schools, 4* (1/2), 66–69.

Benson, L., & Harkavy, I. (1991). Progressing beyond the welfare state. *Universities and Community Schools, 2* (1/2), 1–25.

Bok, D. (1982). *Beyond the ivory tower: Social responsibility of the modern university.* Cambridge, MA: Harvard University Press.

Bureau of Census. (1960–1990) *Census of population and housing.* Washington, DC: U.S. Department of Commerce.

Center for Community Partnerships. (1995). *Spruce Hill community renewal plan.* Philadelphia, PA: University of Pennsylvania.

Center for Community Partnerships. (1994). *Walnut Hill strategic neighborhood plan.* Philadelphia, PA: University of Pennsylvania.

Clapp, E. (1939). *Community schools in action.* New York, NY: Viking.

Cremin, L. (1992). *The transformation of the school: Progressivism in American education, 1876–1957.* New York, NY: Viking.

Dewey, J. (1902). The school as social centre. *Journal of the Proceedings of the National Education Association,* 373–383.

Dewey, J., & Dewey, E. (1915). *Schools of tomorrow.* New York, NY: E. P. Dutton.

Everett, S. (Ed.). (1938). *The community school.* New York, NY: Appleton-Century.

Furstenberg, F. F., et al. (1992). *Caring and paying: What fathers and mothers say about child support.* New York, NY: Manpower Demonstration Research Corporation.

Furstenberg, F. F., & Cherlin, A. J. (1991). *Divided families: What happens when parents part.* Cambridge, MA: Harvard University Press.

Gallagher, S. A., Stephen, W., & Rosenthal, H. (1992). The effects of problem-based learning in problem solving. *Gifted Child Quarterly, 36,* 196–200.

Glueck, E. (1927). *The community use of schools.* Baltimore, MD: Williams and Wilkins.

Greenwood, D., & Gonzales, J. L. (1992). *Industrial democracy as process: Participatory action research in the Fagor cooperative group of Mondragón.* Assen Maastrich: Van Gorcum.

Harkavy, I. (1996). Back to the future: From service-learning to strategic academically-based community service as an approach for advancing knowledge and solving the problem of the American city. *Metropolitan Universities, 7* (1), 157–170.

Harkavy, I., & Puckett, J. (1991). Toward effective university-public school partnerships: An analysis of a contemporary model. *Teachers College Record, 91* (4), 556–581.

Henry, N. B. (Ed.). (1953). *The fifty-second yearbook of the National Society for the Study of Education, part II: The community school.* Chicago, IL: University of Chicago Press.

Peebles, R. W. (1980). *Leonard Covello: A study of an immigrant's contribution to New York City.* New York, NY: Arno Press.

Perry, C. A. (1911). *Wider use of the school plant.* New York, NY: Russell Sage Foundation.

Philadelphia City Planning Commission. (1994). *The plan for West Philadelphia.* Philadelphia, PA: City Planning Commission.

Provost's Council on Undergraduate Education. (1995, May). The 21st century Penn undergraduate experience: Phase one. University of Pennsylvania *Almanac.* s–1.

Reese, W. J. (1986). *The power and promise of school reform: Grassroots movements during the Progressive Era.* Boston, MA: Routledge and Kegan Paul.

School District of Philadelphia. (1995). *School profiles.* Philadelphia, PA: School District of Philadelphia.

Schwarz, D., & Grisso, J., et al. (1994). A longitudinal study of injury morbidity in an African-American population. *Journal of the American Medical Association, 271,* 755–760.

Snow, C. P. (1959). *The two cultures and the scientific revolution.* New York, NY: Cambridge University Press.

University of Pennsylvania. (1989). *Annual report 1987–1988*. Philadelphia, PA: University of Pennsylvania.

University of Pennsylvania. (1996). *Annual report 1994–1995*. Philadelphia, PA: University of Pennsylvania.

University of Pennsylvania, Division of Public Safety. (1994). Safety is everyone's right, everyone's responsibility. Philadelphia, PA: Unpublished manuscript.

Westbrook, R. (1991). *John Dewey and American democracy*. Ithaca, NY: Cornell University Press.

Whyte, W. F. (Ed.). (1991). *Participatory action research*. Newberry Park, CA: Sage.

Whyte, W., & Whyte, K. (1988). *Making Mondragón: The growth and dynamics of the worker cooperative complex*. Ithaca, NY: ILR.

# Comprehensive Design of Community Service: New Undertakings, Options, and Vitality in Student Learning at Portland State University

**Amy Driscoll**
*Portland State University*

## Introduction

Thomas Kuhn in his classic *The Structure of Scientific Revolutions* (1970) describes the emergence of a new idea as "a process of accretion"; that is, it builds upon what has gone before. He reminds us that it also requires a kind of leap of faith. The process is counter-intuitive in that those embracing the new idea must "have faith that the new paradigm will succeed with the many large problems that confront it, knowing only that the older paradigm has failed with a few." Defiance and faith emerge as traits that characterize those who create new ideas. Those creators build on the genius of others. They look to the future. They interpret what's ahead and what has gone before. They create new ideas, develop new paradigms, and often provide leadership for others.

The story of service-learning at Portland State University has been very much a process of accretion. It has built on previous tradition while moving forward with new thinking. It has built on the genius of others with a look to both the future and the past. Those involved—faculty, administrators, students, and community members—have needed to take that leap of faith, and their early moves are best described as defiant. The story began in 1992 and is full of insights and candid declarations of challenge and concern. It is not a finished story. There is potential for both successes and failures ahead. There are untried approaches and unforeseen problems in the process, and there are both certain and uncertain outcomes. What is certain at this time is that community service-learning at Portland State University (PSU) will be comprehensive, integrated throughout the curriculum, and a primary learning experience for students from the time they arrive on campus until they graduate.

## Mapping the Geography of PSU for Community Service

The layout of this map will establish a foundation for understanding the design of PSU's service-learning initiative by providing a description of institutional leadership, institutional fit, student characteristics, and faculty characteristics. Developing organizational literacy can be considered a first step in any action plan. It is also essential to any satisfactory analysis of what has happened at PSU. Organizational literacy means understanding what is going on, recognizing who's who, and knowing how to get things done. It helps one probe the normative values of all the players, the history and context relevant to work intended or action planned. The following section will help the reader develop such organizational literacy by mapping the geography of Portland State University.

### Leadership at Portland State University

In 1992 PSU was guided—and sometimes directed—by President Judith Ramaley and Provost Michael Reardon. Judith was already well-known on campus, in the community, and on the national higher education scene for her commitment to PSU's role as an urban research university with a defining interest in community involvement. At a time of ferocious budget cuts and public apathy, Judith urged faculty to nurture community partnerships, and she personally crafted her own role as one focused on community relationships. Michael Reardon, on the other hand, maintained the focus of his office of academic affairs on academic issues of community involvement. Michael began raising faculty and administrative awareness of issues of general education at the same time as Judith encouraged community involvement. With student learning as PSU's priority, Ramaley's and Reardon's commitments and concerns were well-aligned.

In 1992 university leaders faced increasing pressure from both inside and outside of the academy due to financial constraints, demands for accountability and enhanced productivity, and growing concerns about student learning and values. This was also a time when students and

their families raised intense concerns about employability and the availability of jobs after graduation. From many directions (Boyer, 1990, 1994;
Edgerton, 1995) came demands for higher education to consider a new
paradigm, one that "connects the work of the academy to the social, economic, and environmental challenges beyond the campus" (Hirsch &
Lynton, 1995). The leadership at Portland State University developed a
comprehensive response to those multiple pressures, concerns, and
demands while simultaneously creating a vision for the university.

In addition to these two dynamic individuals, there were others
among the faculty and in the community with similar commitments and
issues. Without support or even recognition, many faculty and administrators were already engaged in curricular innovation and in partnerships with community groups and organizations. These two engage-
ments had the potential for future integration and provided informal
direction to the changes that followed.

An example of curricular innovation was the development of a child
and family studies program. The program was developed by faculty from
16 departments and offices on campus and 60 representatives of agencies
and organizations serving children and families in the metropolitan area.
The program is directed by a faculty/staff consortium representing all 16
disciplines and projects and a community advisory board. Students
majoring in child and family studies (CFS) look at children and families
from diverse perspectives; e.g., sociology, psychology, public health,
black studies, anthropology, women's studies, education, and speech
communication. They also have a wide range of community experiences
to extend and enrich their perspectives on children and families. CFS students currently assist at the Children's Museum, Head Start centers, the
YWCA shelter for domestic violence, and the Multnomah County library;
in programs for teen parents; in hospitals; and in a range of social service
departments. These community agencies are seen as partners in the education of CFS students. At the same time, the community gains enthusiastic, energetic, and focused support from students and faculty.

An example of an existing community partnership was the Institute
of Portland Metropolitan Studies (IPMS), a well-developed and long term
partnership designed to link university resources with metropolitan
issues. The institute is governed by a board composed entirely of community members from a five-county metropolitan area. From its beginning, IPMS brokered connections between the university and the community. The institute's efforts facilitated the sharing of resources and
concerns—early partnerships between PSU and Portland's metropolitan
community. Today IPMS and the Center for Academic Excellence collaborate on the publication *Metroscape*, a publication designed to "bring
ideas about what kind of place Portland is and can be into the discussions
that shape our communities" (Godsey & Seltzer, 1996).

When early hints of reform were whispered, those involved in curricular innovations like the child and family studies program and in partnerships like the Institute for Portland Metropolitan Studies provided models and added strong voices to those of the PSU leadership. Thus, the university's approach to academic reform was characterized by broad participatory leadership both on the campus and in the Portland community and by clear direction from the top administration.

## Institutional Fit of Service-Learning

The second contextual element is institutional fit, and this could only be described as uneven in 1992. PSU's natural commitment to an urban mission contributed to the fit and provided the impetus for this story, but other factors suggested a mismatch. In support of its mission to "enhance the intellectual, social, cultural, and economic qualities of urban life," PSU had an inherent tradition of actively promoting education to serve the community. Its research agenda sustained a high quality academic environment as well as explored specific issues important to the metropolitan region. That tradition, however, lacked the clear support of a reward system attached to promotion and tenure guidelines. Like most institutions of higher education, PSU's notion of scholarship was not congruent with its mission, and, in fact, probably "blurred its mandate and sent confusing signals to faculty" (Rice, 1991). There was an unspoken, traditional understanding among faculty that community involvement was an add-on to the faculty role. Service was most often fulfilled by serving on a university committee. With such a blurring and gaps in institutional support and recognition, most faculty involvement with the larger community occurred with little coordination. But without campus-wide coordination, there was little awareness of the efforts of individuals or groups, little potential for duplication of their efforts, and scarce resources for such work.

The issue of institutional fit must also address the demographics and assets of the Portland community. PSU is situated physically in the downtown area, surrounded by myriad distinctive neighborhoods. The majority of the university's students come from those neighborhoods. Portland is unusual in the planned livableness of its downtown, its attention to transportation issues, and its involved citizenry. Involvement with the university is congruent with Portland's vision, its citizen dynamics, and its urban lifestyle. Unlike Harkavy's West Philadelphia (1992), Portland's areas of need are not centralized, but instead spread over a large metropolitan area. Numerous nonprofit agencies and groups operate on limited budgets and need assistance with traditional functions (research and evaluation, public relations, needs assessment, citizen education, and so on). Furthermore, Portland's location in the northwest part of the country places it in a region focused intensely on environmental issues and projects, so many community needs were attached to an environmental agenda. Since the Portland public schools and neighboring districts have had a rich tradition of enhanced programs and services using the resources of university students and faculty, they also had an important voice in the university's agenda setting. In short, the demographics, assets, and needs of the Portland metropolitan community could best be met by multiple forms of service-learning and the involvement of students and faculty from a range of disciplines.

## Student Characteristics

There are 15,000 full-time and part-time students enrolled in classes and programs at PSU. Approximately 4,000 of those are graduate students. In addition, 25,000 students are annually served through credit and non-credit courses through the School of Extended Studies. PSU is a university with multiple student bodies drawn from the metropolitan area: the traditional 18–22 year old cohort, the considerably older, and the in-betweens. Many of its students are nontraditional—older, married and with families, and working full or part-time (80%). Such demographics result in a commuter campus (90% commute).

Many PSU students have described the isolation of being a student there, and those reports of isolation have helped highlight a lack of interaction with both faculty and fellow students. Undoubtedly connected to this situation was a poor retention rate for first-year students. Approximately 75% of PSU students pursue and complete course work elsewhere—community colleges and other four-year institutions. Previously, most student community involvement took the form of internships, practica, and individual volunteerism.

Looking at PSU students in the context of the work of Astin (1992) quickly illustrates the challenges of working with them, since they have many of the factors found to have a significant negative effect on general education outcomes. Most prominent among these are living at home and commuting, lack of community among students, and full-time employment and off-campus employment (Astin, 1992). These factors were major considerations in the change process at PSU and its approach to community involvement.

## Faculty Characteristics

There are slightly fewer than 500 full-time faculty at PSU, with 154 part-time faculty. Although the average PSU faculty member is personally involved in the Portland metropolitan community in a variety of community activities involving the arts, environmental projects, criminal justice issues, human services connections, public schools, and city planning, teaching and research have been the faculty priorities. In 1992 many of Portland State's faculty were concerned about "how their careers would unfold in a changing academic environment, where external demands for productivity and attention to societal problems clashed with what they all [had] grown to value about their professional lives in the academic community" (Ramaley, 1995). As academic positions and entire programs were cut to adhere to mandated budget levels, PSU faculty often struggled to balance survival issues with reflective interpretation of the university mission.

## RECENT HISTORY OF THE INSTITUTION: CHALLENGES AND CHANGES

In 1990 PSU entered into a period of rapid and necessary change, generated in part by an impending budget crisis set in motion by a citizens' tax initiative. To guide budgetary and organizational decisions that would prepare PSU to do more with less, university leaders began comprehensive strategic planning which would operationalize the school's mission statement and create a set of institutional goals to guide administrative and academic reform.

### Planning and Action

From PSU's mission statement a set of the core characteristics of an urban land grant university was derived. Those characteristics focused on a commitment to the needs and opportunities of the metropolitan area and its students and a commitment to excellence in undergraduate education. As an urban land grant university, PSU conceptualized the metropolitan region as an extended campus and "text." At the same time as the core characteristics were identified, a comprehensive review and analysis of administrative structure and expenditures was conducted. Its purpose was to determine how to use administrative resources more effectively to support the academic components of the urban mission while at the same time preparing for painful budget cuts. A strategic plan was developed through a highly participatory process led by faculty and with community input. One outcome was the redesign of administrative services by clustering related units, redesigning campus operations, and introducing new technology. In addition, partnerships with other organizations were initiated for resource sharing and staff development. The ultimate goal was to turn campus operations into a genuine learning organization (Ramaley, 1995). From there the campus planning team turned attention to the effectiveness and productivity of the university's academic core.

Financially, the university had come to the end of a time when the quality of existing academic programs and enrollment goals could be protected from the impact of budget cuts and productivity demands. The higher education literature abundantly documented the lack of effectiveness of traditional undergraduate/general education requirements. PSU's own track record was characterized by a dismal retention rate and a wealth of anecdotal data that cast doubt on the success of the current program. As faculty began to study undergraduate requirements which they as well as students considered both costly and dissatisfying, Provost Reardon challenged them to, "Show me that the current general education requirements are meaningful." The unspoken agenda was to develop an alternative if those requirements weren't working. Once again, the forces from within the university and from outside of the university spurred both challenge and change.

## Portland State's Response

Given the scenario just described, one might expect that faculty morale would collapse, that thinking would focus desperately on maintenance of current programs and courses. Instead, what characterized this period can only be described as determined imagination. Maxine Greene (1996) describes the complete lack of imagination in traditional academic discourse. She notes, however, its essentialness when envisioning new pedagogical possibilities. She describes imagination's potential to counteract deadness and apathy, to combat meaninglessness. It would have been easy for PSU to shut down energy, creativity, and innovative thinking and maintain business as usual until a better economic and political time, but the situation was exactly the antithesis of shut down. As if touched by a stroke of imagination or creative genius, a number of events began to happen across the campus. Groups of faculty from varied disciplines were invited by the university to attend national conferences such as those of the American Association for Higher Education and gatherings of the national Campus Compact. For most faculty, this represented a unique experience. Faculty generally attend conferences only in their own discipline—to stay current with recent research, to network with colleagues, and to present their work. Instead, faculty now came in contact with the big picture of higher education, national trends, changes, and challenges on other campuses. Michael Reardon has described the "overwhelming tendency of university faculty and administrators to speak and act on issues related to their own culture and institutions based upon their experience as a faculty, and rarely on their knowledge of themselves as faculty" (1996). Faculty attendance at national forums and conferences initiated a new faculty understanding of themselves as faculty.

At the same time, articles and monographs began appearing in faculty mailboxes. The literature focused on reform in higher education and described concerns about the relevance of the traditional curriculum, the quality of teaching, lack of student involvement, and overall dissatisfaction with the state of higher education. Faculty read the work of Ernest Boyer, Peter Senge, Thomas Erlich, Ira Harkavy, and others. Terms such as "engaged campus," "curricular transformation," "scholarship of teaching," and "professional service" were heard in faculty conversations amidst the growing acknowledgment that educational reform was eminent at PSU. Faculty reading and discussion continued to develop their informal understanding of themselves as faculty.

Thus, even as faculty faced a growing lack of resources, they also faced a growing awareness of PSU as part of a national picture—an awareness of institutions poised for change, a picture of possibilities. Through readings, discussions, and conference attendance, faculty prepared themselves to lead the change effort and to design the possibilities. A number of faculty had previously conducted experiments in curricular redesign, such as the development of the child and family studies program. Those faculty were now joined by interested colleagues from all parts of the campus to examine the literature on student success and to study the experiences of faculty and students at other institutions. The conclusion presented by this General Education Working Group was that a fundamental rethinking of the general education curriculum was necessary. "We finally concluded that we could not state with conviction that the current distribution requirements are meaningful," was their response to Provost Reardon's charge.

In 1993 PSU was invited to join the Pew Higher Education Roundtable sponsored by the Institute for Research on Higher Education at the University of Pennsylvania. The new roundtable was charged with reexamining faculty roles and rewards, the curriculum, institution administration, and campus management. Since PSU was already immersed in a study of those areas, roundtable involvement recharged its continuing self-analysis by posing a series of difficult and challenging questions. Those questions revolved around several key issues:

- The alignment between areas of scholarship recognized and encouraged, and institutional purposes and expectations

- Responses to community that balanced public interest with concern for the nature and focus of scholarly work

- Effective modeling for students of a broad range of intellectual activities including teamwork, project management, collaboration

PSU study groups queried the most educationally and financially effective means of delivering education to a predominantly adult urban student population. Indeed, faculty approached these issues as a genuine research problem—with a literature review and application of the knowledge base to their recommendations. Their discussions emerged as the first step of a comprehensive change process.

## Reform of General Education
The group of faculty later referred to as the General Education Committee set their sights on the development of a curriculum that

would "build community, provide connected learning, and improve academic achievement" (White, 1994). The first draft of their proposal was completed in the spring of 1993. By May 1993, a second draft was presented to the complete faculty in three open meetings. Finally, the completed proposal was opened to debate and discussion at a campus-wide symposium. Throughout this process, the faculty task force's leadership was critical: They had been "turned loose on a problem that had to be solved, given the resources to do the work (released time, teaching assistants), and knew that their work was important" (White, 1995).

In November 1993, the faculty senate approved the new general education curriculum with all of its implications for scheduling, student support, community involvement, and changes in pedagogy. The work of reforming the general education curriculum was a first and critical step in responding to society. As Pelikan reminds institutions of higher education, "Of the university's duties to society, perhaps the most fundamental is the need and the possibility to initiate educational reform, including the work of self-reformation in the university itself "(1992). The magnitude of this general education reform significantly influenced the university's comprehensive approach to service-learning.

## THE CONTEXT OF PSU'S COMPREHENSIVE SERVICE-LEARNING DESIGN

Three major events facilitated PSU's movement to integrate service-learning with a comprehensive institutional design. The first was the implementation of the new general education curriculum, the alternative proposed by the General Education Committee after concluding that current requirements were "not based on any discernible underlying purpose or articulated goals" and that "no expected benefits for students or anticipated learning outcomes" could be identified. The second event was the funding of Students Serving the City—a PSU Learn and Serve grant. The third event was the opening of the Center for Academic Excellence in response to the recommendation of the General Education Committee that support was needed for implementation of the new curriculum. All three developments contributed to both the institutional design and the comprehensive quality of service-learning at Portland State University.

### Implementation of the New General Education Curriculum

The general education curriculum is best described as an integrated approach, one that blends content from the arts, sciences, and social sciences into a thematic study or clusters of inquiry. In the first year, students are grouped in cohorts to work with a faculty team (usually five faculty from five different disciplines) in a year-long thematic study called Freshmen Inquiry. Some of the initial themes have included: Getting To Know Home; Einstein–The Man and His Universe; and Our Pluralistic Society. Throughout their course sequence, students focus on models offered by different disciplines to describe phenomena and predict processes of change as a means for understanding current and future conditions and problems. Their studies are integrated with math, the fine arts, communication, geography, history, science, and technology. The goals of the general education curriculum have been developed to focus on inquiry and critical thinking, communication, human experience, and ethical issues and social responsibility.

Freshmen Inquiry courses (implemented fall 1995) are characterized by high levels of faculty/student interaction, group processes, and discovery approaches. Assignments typically require daily or almost daily communication. Classes are relatively small (30 students), and by design, the structure and organization of these courses is intended to create a learning community among students, faculty, and peer mentors (advanced students who assist freshmen with university logistics, study and tutoring needs, academic discussion groups, and group process concerns).

In their sophomore and junior years, students pursue clusters of related courses in addition to their major program of study. They begin with an introductory or entry course and proceed to various disciplines for different perspectives on a cluster theme. For example, a cluster called Families begins with an entry course, Current Perspectives on Families. From here students pursue courses such as American Family History, Sociology of the Family, Work and Family (PSY), and The African American Child and Family. As in the first-year experience, faculty work together to plan and connect content and course work. The themes are relevant to the Portland metropolitan area, to societal issues, and to the lives of PSU's students. As much as possible, courses in Sophomore and Junior Inquiry connect academic content with community service.

In their senior year, all students are required to complete a capstone experience. This new graduation requirement involves a community project conducted by a small team of students from several disciplines. Capstones are designed to meet significant community needs or to address significant problems and issues. Students engaged in capstone experiences should be able to demonstrate the achievement of general education goals as well as the expertise of their major. For example, a group of senior students are engaged in a capstone experience designed in partnership with Sponsors Organized to Assist Refugees (SOAR) and the International Refugee Center of Oregon (IRCO) to link recent immigrants with the resources of the community. The student team is working on the development of materials to support SOAR and IRCO staff who facilitate the process of settling refugee families. Students on the team represent the disciplines of public health education, psychology, sociology, child and family studies, women's studies, and foreign languages.

The entire general education curriculum is aimed at "bringing together . . . ideas from different disciplines and perspectives" (Hirsch & Lynton, 1995) in order to respond to what Greiner, President of the State University of New York at Buffalo, has called "a chaos of cries for help, understanding, new frameworks and ideas and solutions" (1995). Service-learning was an obvious extension of that integrated curricular response.

## Funding of Students Serving the City: PSU's Learn and Serve Grant

Concurrent with the implementation of the new general education curriculum, the Corporation for National Service issued a call for proposals from colleges and universities seeking to implement service-learning programs. The kind of work to be funded so complemented the general education plan, it was as if the call for proposals had been designed for PSU. Already described community service activities and early partnerships provided direction for a Students Serving the City proposal. The proposal represented a plan to assure that "existing and future . . . service-learning would be fully integrated [into the] curriculum in ways that ensured the quality of the students' experience and community satisfaction with the partnerships" (Holland, 1994). Those faculty who were already involved in service-learning were recruited, and their work was used as a foundation for the proposal. The Learn and Serve grant submitted by PSU was designed to "increase the quality, quantity, and impact of service-learning opportunities by developing greater connectedness among programs, common strategies for planning and evaluation, and systems for matching and monitoring community needs" (Holland, 1994). These goals supported curricular reform and would help create the infrastructure necessary to support a comprehensive university-wide service-learning effort that could involve every PSU student.

Students Serving the City was funded by the Corporation for National Service for two years. The major objective of the grant in year one was to provide incentives and training for faculty to experiment with service-learning—to revise curricula so that community service was integrated with academic content. Additional funds were earmarked for student support—transportation, materials, child care. Approximately 28 courses were funded involving 24 faculty and 610 students. The enthusiasm generated by those courses was contagious, and the faculty teaching Freshmen Inquiry for the first time sought community projects to integrate with their curriculum. During the third quarter of the Freshmen Inquiry sequence, most of the 700 first-year students were in the community working on projects that enhanced their understanding of their inquiry theme. For example, the students in Our Pluralistic Society were tutoring recent immigrants in refugee centers throughout the metropolitan area. Students in Getting to Know Home were engaged in projects with neighborhood associations. Finally, funding facilitated student recruitment and an increased effort toward community partnership development.

In year two, support for service-learning courses (faculty incentives and student expenses) continued, but the grant's major focus was on the development of pilot capstones and an assessment model for service-learning. Forty-two more community-based learning courses were implemented involving 33 faculty and 743 students with 30+ community groups. By spring quarter 1996, seven pilot capstones had been implemented with the participation of 12 faculty and 64 students. Capstones facilitated the development and delivery of health education programs to high school and university communities as well as to neighborhood clinics; surveyed the population receiving services through the Oregon Health Plan; and conducted a program evaluation of Healthy Start's services. It was estimated that approximately 400 individuals had had direct contact with PSU students during the students' capstone experiences. Several projects had the capacity to indirectly affect 1000 residents both statewide and in the metro area.

During year two, a comprehensive case study model (Driscoll, Gelman, Holland, & Kerrigan, 1996) was developed, and research was conducted to assess the impact of community-based teaching and learning in four classes. The model was comprehensive to the extent of measuring the impact of community-based teaching and learning on four constituencies—students, faculty, community, and institution. Each case study consisted of a combination of quantitative and qualitative approaches to describe and measure the impact of community-based teaching and learning. More importantly, the case studies had the potential to provide insights about the most effective and practical way to measure service-learning outcomes. PSU was part of a larger national community seeking to strengthen the literature base by addressing the "scarcity of replicable research on the effects of service-learning on student learning and development, the communities in which they serve, or on the educational institutions" (Giles, Honnet, & Migliore, 1991).

## Opening of the Center for Academic Excellence

The final report of the faculty committee that designed the general education curriculum included recommendations for a center for teaching and learning, a center for community service, and a center for assessment. In a time of continuing budget cuts, creating three centers was quite unrealistic. Faculty insights into the need for support in all three areas were, however, heeded and a single comprehensive center was developed. Although budgetary constraints provided the initial impetus, the integration of teaching and learning, community service, and assessment immediately proved a wise and logical way to provide needed faculty support.

In January 1995, the Center for Academic Excellence was organized with a director of teaching and learning excellence, a director of community/university partnerships, and a faculty assessment team. With respect to service-learning, the center provides leadership in creating community partnerships conducive to achieving PSU's student learning outcomes, while supporting appropriate accompanying changes in teaching and learning and in assessment. The director of community/university partnerships supports faculty efforts to connect their teaching and research to community issues, needs, problems, and resources. To provide that support, the director frequently serves as a broker who assists a community representative in connecting with a faculty member with an expertise that matches a specific community need, or who assists a faculty member in finding a community group or organization with activities that match his/her academic interests. The director of community/university partnerships also mentors faculty in course development activities, provides workshops and seminars on topics related to service-learning, and supports faculty documentation of the scholarship of service. In addition to workshops and seminars, the center provides technical assistance, resources (a library and a database), incentives, and some funding for expenses associated with curricular changes that involve service-learning.

A significant change in the university's guidelines for promotion and tenure has highlighted the need for faculty support in the documentation of community-related scholarship. At this time there is a paucity of samples of documentation or models of portfolios of such scholarship. The concept of professional service described by Lynton (1995) has affirmed the need to rethink criteria for reviewing faculty achievements related to the community. To begin meeting this need, the Center for Academic Excellence staff have developed cases of faculty professional service accomplishments (Johnson & Driscoll, 1996) and used them for faculty and administrative group discussions about how to evaluate such scholarship. Four faculty are participating in a national project funded by Kellogg to develop portfolios documenting community-based service scholarship (Driscoll & Lynton, 1996). One additional support provided by the Center for Academic Excellence is the ongoing development of a database of community partners and projects. Faculty, students, and community members can search for possible partners, projects, and curricular connections. There are examples of partnerships, community-based learning courses, capstone courses, and other forms of service activities available as an additional support for faculty efforts.

The Center for Academic Excellence represents a support for curricular change that extends campus-wide and into the community. Its structure, a blending or integration of three areas of support, complements the comprehensive design of the university's commitment to service-learning: "The center's goals are to link the three—teaching and learning excellence, community-university partnerships, and assessment—and by drawing them together, to improve student learning outcomes, support faculty scholarship, and contribute to the Portland metropolitan community" (from the center's brochure). In many ways, the center represents a permanent institutional commitment to faculty development in all three areas.

## COMMUNITY SERVICE-LEARNING AT PORTLAND STATE UNIVERSITY

Service-learning at PSU has been intricately woven into the curricular reform process and changes in administrative infrastructure, basically "changing the way we do business" (Hirsch & Lynton, 1995). The resulting program represents a linking of experiential learning and faculty/student outreach as "two essential, mutually reinforcing facets of an institutional commitment to link theory and practice, campus and community" (Hirsch & Lynton, 1995).

It is, however, important to remember that community service, service-learning, and community partnerships all existed at PSU well in advance of the reforms that have occurred in the last few years. From this perspective, the problem was not so much their absence from the university as their presence in fragmented forms with little visibility. Indeed, at the start of the curricular reform process, it was explicitly recognized that the "best coverage of community needs and assurance of the greatest impact on the community were inhibited by the disjointed and unconnected nature of service-learning activities" (Holland, 1994). Even less assurance could be given as to the impact of those activities on student learning outcomes at that time. One difference today is the existence of 1) coordination, 2) support, and 3) recognition for faculty and students engaged in those activities. Another difference is the context in which faculty and students embrace service-learning—a context in which PSU finds itself a national leader in curricular reform and community partnership development. And a final difference is the change in faculty roles and rewards that is being articulated and supported on campus and in national forums. From a faculty core group of about 12, service-learning participation has grown to at least 90 individuals who either teach community-based courses, coordinate a capstone experience, or formally collaborate with community partners.

Given such success, perhaps a word of caution is in order. While the curricular goal of PSU's comprehensive service-learning design is that students become engaged members of the community within the campus and beyond the campus from the moment they enroll at the university, that goal is anchored in a core educational conviction; namely, that learning itself can be enhanced by community involvement, that community members can serve as co-teachers with PSU faculty. Thus, the curricular goal is never sacrificed to community involvement. It remains the focus. PSU's philosophy of community partnerships is one that recognizes that the community has much to teach and many resources to contribute to students' learning. In the process of providing community service, students gain enhanced and often extended understanding of their academic course work. After much discussion and reflection, faculty at PSU have actually come to prefer the term "community-based learning" to "service-learning"—in part because of the former's emphasis on student outcomes and its implicit recognition of the contribution the community makes to those outcomes.

## Community-Based Learning Courses and Capstones

There are approximately 90 community-based learning courses offered at both the undergraduate and the graduate level. Faculty teaching those courses represent all seven schools and colleges as well as 23 departments. Students in Freshmen Inquiry continue to work in the community in the last quarter of their course sequence. In 1995–96 there were seven capstones offered; in 1996–97, 20 were scheduled. In 1997–98 there will be more than 1,000 seniors working in teams on community problems and issues.

Many of the faculty involved in community-based teaching have begun to see their teaching from a different perspective because they now involve the community as co-teacher. Their students bring new questions and complex understandings from their off-campus experiences into the classroom. They connect readings and videos with their own field observations. Faculty have had to learn how to use reflection to sustain and develop those connections between academic content and community experience, and student reflections have become a rich source of data about both teaching and learning (Williams & Driscoll, 1996; Arante & Driscoll, 1996).

As faculty examine their own teaching and experiment with alternative forms of assessment, their work has gradually assumed the character of research projects. The Center for Academic Excellence, with Learn and Serve funds, has supported those projects and nurtured faculty scholarship associated with speaking and writing about them. Currently 19 faculty have presented their work at national conferences—at both higher education and disciplinary meetings—and 12 faculty have published their work.

## Community Service Internships

A recent addition to the menu of service-learning experiences at PSU is an internship project funded by an anonymous donor. The Community Service Internship Project has two goals: to provide high quality interns in service projects that benefit community agencies, groups, and institutions; and to study the internship process for insights into how to make it an effective experience for students, the community, and the institution. Internships currently exist in many departments on the PSU campus, but with fairly loosely organized, if any, coordination. There is, moreover, a paucity of literature about these internships, aside from occasional anecdotes about both satisfying and disappointing experiences from either the student or the community perspective. Now, however, the coordinator of the Community Service Internship Project has weekly contact with both interns and community members. Interns meet weekly with the coordinator in a seminar format to discuss issues, share insights, and reflect on their experiences. An assessment tool is being developed to measure the impact of these internships on all stakeholders.

## Community/University Partnerships

Ultimately, the Center for Academic Excellence seeks to promote and develop authentic partnerships with community agencies, groups, and institutions. An ongoing and comprehensive example of a community/ university partnership is the PSU/City of Portland Bureau of Environmental Services Partnership—a partnership focused on watershed restoration and protection. Within the partnership, university involvement takes the form of community-based learning courses, senior capstones, graduate assistantships and internships, faculty research, and curriculum development. The Center for Academic Excellence facilitates the partnership by recruiting students and faculty, supporting the course work with logistical and other resources, coordinating educational activities, and coordinating faculty participation.

Achievements of the first year of the partnership include the development of a curriculum for certification of citizens to become watershed stewards, development of a hub site for watershed activities, an inventory and database of current watershed activities, and the involvement of more than 100 PSU students in eight watershed projects. The partnership also involves a third partner—Portland public schools' Environmental Middle School. Future plans include the development of demonstration environmental learning sites on the campus of the school and within the watershed area.

## CONCLUSION

In 1995, the Learn and Serve advisory board recommended that service efforts at PSU be directed to "enhance both the metropolitan community's potential as a livable environment and a just society, and the university's potential for excellence in teaching, service, and scholarship." The development of a wide array of community-based learning courses, significant progress in capstone implementation, the Community Service Internship Project, and the development of focused community/university partnerships all contribute to the achievement of that mission. These multiple forms of service-learning ensure that all students will have the opportunity to learn from the community and to experience participation in community work. These multiple forms of service-learning lie at the core of PSU's comprehensive design for curricular reform in the context of its urban mission.

This story is not complete—it unwinds even as it is written. As faculty study their work in community-based learning, as students learn from community involvement, as the university works in partnership with community groups, new chapters take shape. While PSU's movement toward a comprehensive service-learning program is clearly guided by a vision, its development remains fluid, sculpted by the insights of ongoing efforts. In an address to a class in Community Psychology during fall quarter 1996, President Judith Ramaley encouraged the students with the observation that:

> This new way of learning, involving faculty and students, linked in meaningful ways to the needs of our metropolitan community, has indeed opened up new understandings, new options, and a new sense of vitality for those who have experienced it. It is deeply satisfying and wonderfully rewarding to know that ideas do matter, that learning can be fresh, that faculty and students can learn together, and that students and faculty who are learning can serve the needs of the community at the same time.

A student who completed a community-based learning course echoed the president's words with her own description of what her community experience has meant:

> My number one complaint about the educational system is that I have felt like I've been sitting in a box, learning about the world but not being part of the world. That's disappointing. These are my college years and they're supposed to be exciting and engaging, but they've been pretty academic and grueling. A lot of faculty have their experience to contribute, but a lot of students also have experience and knowledge to contribute. I would tell others that this was a good experience—I would do this again—I will look for this kind of learning experience.

*For actual Portland State service-learning documents, see Appendix G: Policies and Procedures for the Evaluation of Faculty for Tenure, Promotion, and Merit Increases*

## REFERENCES

Arante, J., & Driscoll, A. (1996). *Reflective writing processes: Connecting curriculum with community.* Paper presented at the National Gathering of Campus Compact, Indianapolis, IN.

Astin, A. W. (1992). What really matters in general education: Provocative findings from a national study of student outcomes. *Perspectives, 22* (1), 23–46.

Boyer, E. (1990). *Scholarship reconsidered.* Princeton, NJ: The Carnegie Foundation for the Advancement of Teaching.

Boyer, E. (1994, March). Creating the new American college. *Chronicle of Higher Education,* 48.

*Campus Compact. (1994). Project on integrating service with academic study: Mapping the geography of service on a college campus.* Providence, RI: Campus Compact.

Checkoway, B. (1996). Combining service and learning on campus and in the community. *Phi Delta Kappan, 77* (9), 600–606.

Davidson, S. (In press). Divide and flourish: Nurturing the nucleus of faculty change. *Journal of Public Service & Outreach, 2* (1), 26-32.

Driscoll, A., & Lynton, E. (1996). The documentation of professional service: A progress report. *Metropolitan Universities, 8* (1), 19-38.

Driscoll, A., Gelmon, S., Holland, B., & Kerrigan, S. (1996). An assessment model for service-learning: Comprehensive case studies of the impact on students, faculty, community, and the institution. *Michigan Journal of Community Service-Learning, 3,* 66-71.

Edgerton, R. (1995). Crossing boundaries: Pathways to productive learning and community renewal. *AAHE Bulletin, 48* (1), 7–10.

Erlich, T. (1995). Taking service seriously. *AAHE Bulletin, 47* (7), 8–10.

Giles, D. E., Honnet, E., & Migliore, S. (1991). Setting the agenda for effective research in combining service and learning in the 1990s. Raleigh, NC: National Society for Experiential Education.

Godsey, J., & Seltzer, E. (1996). *Metroscape, 2, 3.*

Greene, M. (1996). *A conversation: Imagination, possibility, and curriculum.* Invited address to the annual meeting of the American Educational Research Association, New York, NY.

Greiner, W. R. (1994, Fall-Winter). In the total of all these acts: How can American universities address the urban agenda? *Universities and Community Schools.*

Harkavy, I. (1992). The mission of the Center for Community Partnerships. *Almanac,* 4–5.

Hirsch, D., & Lynton, E. (1995, Summer). Bridging two worlds. *NSEE Quarterly,* 10–28.

Hogan, T. J., Kerrigan, S., & Pittinger, D. (1996). *Organizing for community service: How to develop an approach.* Presented at the American College Personnel Association Annual Convention, Baltimore, MD.

Holland, B. (1994). *Students serving the city.* Proposal submitted to the Corporation for National Service.

Johnson, R., & Driscoll, A. (1996). *Supporting faculty community service through revision of promotion and tenure guidelines.* Paper presented at the conference of American Association of Higher Education, Atlanta, GA.

Kuhn, T. S. (1970). *The structure of scientific revolutions* (2nd ed.). Chicago, IL: University of Chicago.

Lynton, E. (1995). *Making the case for professional service.* Washington, DC: American Association for Higher Education.

Office of University Studies. (1994). *Portland State University, University Studies Program, Executive Summary.* Portland, OR: Portland State University.

Pelikan, J. (1992). *The idea of the university: A reexamination.* New Haven, CT: Yale University.

Ramaley, J. A. (1995). *Implementing the strategic plan: A progress report.* Portland, OR: Portland State University.

Reardon, M. (1996). *The esoteric and exoteric role of the academic administrator in aligning the faculty to the institutional mission.* Portland, OR: Commission on the Urban Agenda.

Rice, R. E. (1991, Spring). The new American scholar. *Metropolitan Universities,* 7–15.

White, C. (1994, Summer). Getting there from here—The process of change. *Connections,* 2 (2), 1.

Williams, D., & Driscoll, A. (1996). Connecting curriculum with community service: Guidelines for facilitating student reflection. *Journal of Public Service and Outreach,* 2 (1), 33–42.

# 9

# Making a Major Commitment: Public and Community Service at Providence College

**Richard M. Battistoni**
*Providence College*

## INTRODUCTION

Providence College, like many Catholic, liberal arts institutions of higher education, has a fairly long tradition of community service, understood primarily as voluntary and extracurricular. Prior to the creation of the Feinstein Institute for Public Service, however, the college had virtually no experience with service-learning and no formal institutional support for introducing community service into the curriculum. With the creation of the institute in 1994, service-learning has become a centerpiece of the college's liberal arts curriculum and has gained substantial institutional support. The institute's new flagship academic program, featuring a major and minor in public and community service, is being used to recruit prospective students and to distinguish our program among other institutions of higher education. A great demand among students exists for our service-learning classes, and our relationships with the larger community have grown much stronger. Since 1994, Providence College has moved from having no service-learning to speak of to having a model program, one worthy of inclusion in this volume. It is a remarkable story.

## PROGRAM HISTORY

In January of 1993, Alan Shawn Feinstein, a Rhode Island entrepreneur and philanthropist, invited all colleges and universities in Rhode Island to apply for a $5 million grant, to be awarded to the institution with the best plan for the establishment of a community service program at the undergraduate level. Providence College President Rev. John F. Cunningham, O.P., convened a committee of 18 faculty and administrators to advise him on applying for the grant. A subcommittee was appointed to draft the grant proposal. By the March deadline, five Rhode Island institutions of higher education had made formal proposals to the Feinstein Foundation. In June, Alan Feinstein announced the award of the grant to Providence College to establish the Feinstein Institute for Public Service and to create an academic major in public and community service. Of the $5 million, $3.5 million was designated as an endowment for the Feinstein Institute, and $1.5 million went toward the renovation of a classroom building, the Feinstein Academic Center, which would house the institute.

The announcement of the grant award marked the first of several milestones in the development of our service-learning program. Since the approved proposal only called for the establishment of an institute for public service and an academic major leading to a degree in public service, the hard work of developing a mission, goals, and objectives for the institute, and of designing the academic program in public service had just begun. Work on the new program would take two years, the first a research and planning year and the second a year to pilot many of the courses and concepts in the new curriculum. This in itself is somewhat unusual. Most grantmakers want to see immediate results, especially when community service is the goal (the Corporation for National Service, for example, touts "getting things done" as its main motto). But the Feinstein Foundation approved the college's request that it be allowed the time to plan and develop its new and unique academic program.

The fact that Providence College had virtually no prior experience with service-learning was both a blessing and a curse. The absence of existing practices or courses combining service with academic study meant that the new program would not be pieced together out of existing academic turf, but would be created from scratch, based on the desired outcomes for such a degree program and the students who would enroll in it. But it also meant that there was precious little experience on the Providence College campus to draw upon in designing this new curricular program. In July of 1993, Rev. Thomas D. McGonigle, O.P., Vice President for Academic Administration, invited applications from faculty for the position of acting director and for membership on the design team of the new institute. One month later, William Hudson was named Acting

Director and eight faculty, representing six different disciplines, were named to the Feinstein Research Team. They immediately added three students to the team.

During the 1993–94 academic year, the Feinstein Research Team met weekly, dividing into three subcommittees: one to study other service-learning programs around the country; one to assess campus-based community-related resources; and one to develop contacts with community partners. These subcommittees, in turn, drew upon dozens of other individuals—both on and outside the campus—to advise them. Besides drafting a mission statement and a curriculum proposal for a major and minor in public and community service studies, the research team devised strategies for incorporating service-learning throughout the college's curriculum, conducted a national search for a permanent institute director, and designed a pilot year program for 1994–95, beginning with a summer seminar for faculty and students in 1994. A corps of 18 students—from an applicant pool of nearly 60—was recruited during the spring of 1994 to serve as pilot students for the first year's experiment.

I began my work as director in June 1994, just as the summer seminar was to begin. Over the next year, I oversaw the piloting of ten new Feinstein Institute courses and four other auxiliary service-learning courses in discipline-based departments outside of the public service program—which together enrolled a total of 250 students. We were awarded major grants from the Corporation for National Service and from the Rhode Island Foundation to establish a program for Providence College's elementary education majors to use service-learning as a pedagogy in their teaching, working with two local urban elementary schools. Fifteen additional faculty were recruited to teach new or adapted service-learning courses through a faculty development program instituted that year. The major and minor were further developed and brought before the faculty senate and the college's curriculum committee—final approval came in May 1995. We also witnessed the dedication of the renovated Feinstein Academic Center, with the accompanying honoring of three public servants: Millard Fuller, Kathleen Kennedy Townsend, and Alan Shawn Feinstein. In March, a team of faculty, administrators, and students from Morehouse College in Atlanta made a two-day visit to Providence College to observe our service-learning program in action, and we would follow up a month later with a visit to Morehouse, all part of a Campus Compact Campus Team Forum grant. And in May of 1995, Providence College hosted the first national gathering of the Invisible College, a new association of service-learning educators. Over 200 participants attended.

The 1995–96 academic year brought even greater success. Working with a total of 42 community partners, 560 students were enrolled in 14 Feinstein Institute classes and an additional 12 service-learning courses offered through other departments. We began developing a curriculum-based alternate break program, which will be connected to core courses in the major and minor. The content and pedagogy of our curriculum were refined, and community partners entered the classroom as co-faculty in a number of our service-learning courses. The academic year ended with the graduation of the first nine students with minors in public and community service studies, and with our hosting a national high school conference for 150 participants representing 36 different states. In our second official year of existence as an academic program at the college (1996–97), we had over 40 declared public and community service majors and at least that many minors. Ultimately, we anticipate 25 majors per graduating class, with double or triple that number of students declaring a public service minor.

## PROGRAM VISION AND MISSION

The service-learning program conducted by the Feinstein Institute fits very nicely within the overall mission of Providence College, primarily a four-year college of the liberal arts and sciences with an undergraduate enrollment of 3,600 men and women. Providence is a Catholic college operated under the auspices of the Dominican Order, whose underlying values reflect the Judeo-Christian tradition. Providence College attempts to provide its students with a liberal education that will offer them "opportunities to advance their ability to formulate their thoughts and communicate them to others; to discover the facts about themselves and their environment; to evaluate their varied experiences, and to achieve insight into the past, present, and future of civilization," at the same time "equipping them to become intelligent, productive, and responsible citizens of a democratic society" (*Providence College Bulletin*, 1995–96).

The mission statement of the Feinstein Institute references many of the same concerns and values:

> The fundamental mission of the Feinstein Institute for Public Service is to provide the students of Providence College with an educational experience within our liberal arts curriculum which prepares them to become builders of human communities and responsible citizens of a democratic society. The mission of service flows from the understanding of the Judeo-Christian heritage that all human beings as sons and daughters of the living God are called to serve one another. The educational vision of the institute is built upon the unique Catholic tradition of the Dominican Order, which calls upon all persons to bear witness to the human and social dimensions of their religious faith as expressed in the mission statement of Providence College, and Alan Shawn Feinstein's dream of educating the young about the importance of compassionate service.

The central goal that flows out of the institute's mission is to offer to all students academically based experiences of service that encompass four broadly conceived principles: understanding human diversity, social justice, human solidarity, and engaged citizenship.

Before discussing the four principles and why they exist as the intellectual foundation of our program, a word about service is in order. From the earliest weeks of our introductory public service course, students are encouraged to explore the idea of service, both from their past and current experiences of community involvement and from different vantage points supplied by readings and other course materials. In classroom discussions, we have found that our students come to this new academic program with different understandings of service and a variety of motivations for doing it. Some come to our major or minor out of a sense of charity, usually grounded in religious faith. They see service as an act of giving of oneself, a basic responsibility to God and to one's brothers and sisters in need. Others see their service as part of a strategy to achieve systemic social change. Service, from this perspective, is not an end in itself, but instead is viewed as one strategy to be employed while seeking more fundamental changes in the social system. Still others see public service as a way to learn more about the workings of social institutions and to be more effective as individuals who will encounter such institutions upon graduation. Community service provides these latter students with experiences that will propel them in their careers after leaving Providence College.

We try to explore these and other meanings of service, rather than arguing that one approach is inherently better than another. In fact, confronting different philosophies of service is one aspect of understanding diversity, a principle to be discussed below. The biggest challenge for each of us is to practice whatever type of service we adhere to with the greatest degree of intentionality and integrity.

## Principle 1: Understanding Human Diversity

Diversity is one of the values at the heart of the college's service-learning program. One of the most important challenges in preparing students to be engaged in American public life into the next century is to push them to examine their role in a multicultural society. I have written elsewhere about the powerful insights concerning diversity that can come from a curriculum incorporating community service involvement (Battistoni, 1995). Here at Providence College, students like the following (quoted from their written reflections) reveal the possibilities of learning about diversity through service:

> I do not come from a diverse background. My contacts and friendships have always been with people very similar to myself. I do not think I chose not to be diverse, but rather I have never been exposed to diversity. . . . My service is helping me become a more diverse person . . . [by] coming into contact with people of cultures different than my own.

My images of race come from the media and movies mainly—unfortu-nately. Dealing with different races through community service provides alternative images of other races than what is fed to us on the news or in movies. At [my service site] I am able to interact with all different races who are positive people/role models for the community. Probably being involved in service could improve race relations in the general public. Those being helped and those who help get alternate images of different races. Not to say that all students [at my site] are minorities or all tutors, teachers, volunteers are white: it is just the opposite—all races occupy all roles and provide an alternative to classification and stereotyping.

The images of diversity and difference that emerge in a service-learning curriculum like ours are not simple or unproblematic. Moreover, at an institution like ours, which is relatively homogeneous with respect to race/ethnicity, religion, and economic class, interactions with a larger community that is diverse—at two elementary schools with which we work, students come from over 40 different countries of origin—raise dif-ficult and critical questions for students and faculty alike about equal access, power, and the capacity of service to make a difference in such a social environment. Still, we believe that it is these questions surrounding diversity and multiculturalism that go to the heart of a liberal education at this time in American life, and as such, we integrate them in several places into the institute's curriculum, including a specific core diversity requirement for both the major and minor in public and community ser-vice studies.

## Principle 2: Understanding Social Justice

As with our dedication to appreciating human diversity, our commitment to social justice requires that as people serve they pose critical questions concerning the ways in which social, political, and economic institutions affect individuals. Service entails more than just assisting others; it means collaborating with people in a community and developing the awareness and skills necessary for participating in positive social change. In this area, we take our inspiration from words attributed to an aboriginal Australian woman: "If you have come to help me, you are wasting your time. But if you have come because your liberation is bound up with mine, then let us work together." Through a balanced program of courses, practical experience, reflection, and community partnerships, the Feinstein Institute aims to model commitment to work for the libera-tion and equality of all.

## Principle 3: Advancing Human Solidarity

Our advancement of the principle of human solidarity flows from the col-lege's spiritual mission and its concomitant attachment to the idea of community. In his social encyclical *On Human Concern,* Pope John Paul II defined solidarity as "a firm and persevering determination to commit oneself to the common good, that is to say, to the good of all and of each individual, because we are all really responsible for all." From the onset of our introductory course, where readings and actions stress community and interdependence, to the senior capstone seminar, the Feinstein Institute seeks to increase the level of personal solidarity with the community of which we are a part, and to instill in our students a deep appreciation of community.

## Principle 4: Achieving Engaged Citizenship

Finally, engaged citizenship is one of the most powerful principles that guides our work. We believe that in a democracy, community service—whatever the particular connection to courses or the curriculum as a whole—must be seen as a crucial aspect of civic responsibility: a model of the relationship between rights-bearing citizens and the many communities to which they belong. To be a citizen is not merely to possess a knowledge of government and its workings or to have legal rights, but to take responsibility, to see ourselves and our interests as flourishing only as our communities flourish. The connection between liberal education and democratic citizenship is one that has a long tradition in American higher education.

But to claim an intimate connection between service-learning and civic education means to move beyond the confines of our individual courses or the interdisciplinary academic program we have developed here, to examine the place of our educational institutions in the larger public world. This requires that, in addition to the civic content of our courses, we pay greater attention to two essential matters: the pedagogy of higher learning and the nature of our campus-community partnerships.

Those involved in experiential education and service-learning have made the case for a more democratic pedagogy before, but it is worth reiterating here, given its centrality to the Providence College program. Democracy demands equal participation and voice by all citizens. However, even with all of the reforms of the past generation, the college classroom often suggests hierarchy: what Paolo Friere termed the "banking model of education," with the knowledgeable teacher "depositing" information into the minds of passive student-ATM machines. Moreover, in most classrooms, even those with experiential components, students do their work and are judged solely as individuals. A model for service-learning concerned with engaging citizens that does not challenge the traditional pedagogy is not modeling what it wants students to learn about democratic public life. Our experiences at the Feinstein Institute teach us that the creation of community-building, democratic classrooms is not an automatic consequence of service-learning; it involves much greater time and effort to coordinate and structure activities and class discussions, and much more attention to process, than does the traditional classroom. Additionally, we have found that even when successful, our efforts to create democratic service-learning classes often cause students pain and cognitive dissonance, when our more democratic pedagogy conflicts with the institutional and academic culture of more traditional offerings in the college's core curriculum.

In addition to being concerned about pedagogy, a commitment to engaged citizenship means that we must pay attention to the overall institution's relationships with the larger community. If students are to think about citizenship as being actively involved in a committed relationship with others in the public realm, then the campus as a whole—not just the service-learning program—needs to mirror the values of neighborly civic responsibility. We read and hear a lot about a growing disconnection between the academy and the public/society, between gown and town, but we firmly believe that much of this disjuncture comes not from students or from the community, but from the apathetic citizenship of colleges and universities, which are not engaged in the life of their surrounding neighborhoods. At Providence College, we have found that the more our students get involved in the community as part of their academic curriculum, the more the explicit message of our service-learning program—that of the connection of service to civic engagement—pushes an implicit message on the college itself to be a better institutional citizen (in return for the community's role in helping to educate our students).

For example, we have been asked increasingly to work together with and provide tangible resources—like campus space and faculty time—to our community partners. But we have also been asked, as we work with low-income youth in a variety of projects, whether Providence College will be an inviting place for them when they graduate from high school. Such a developed sense of relationship not only more fully models democratic citizenship; it also makes it easier for our students to connect their actions to those of citizens in the larger urban community, to join in a common cause, and to learn about their neighbors and the possible solutions to their concerns.

## THE ACADEMIC MAJOR IN PUBLIC AND COMMUNITY SERVICE STUDIES

While the existence of a substantial endowment to run the program puts Providence College on the map of leading college service-learning programs, it is the creation of an academic major and minor in public and community service studies that makes our program unique. Much credit goes to Alan Feinstein, who tied the resources he made available to the development of an undergraduate degree program focused on community service.

Analogously, while Feinstein's endowment has been essential to the creation of the program, what has given our program its distinctive character is the result of the conscious decisions of involved faculty, administrators, students, and community partners. One of the central features of the major and minor in public and community service studies is their interdisciplinary, liberal arts nature, with a primary focus on quality teaching and learning, and a secondary emphasis on faculty and student research.

Early on, the Feinstein research team had proposed that the major and minor in public service be an interdisciplinary, liberal arts degree program, rather than a professional degree in public service. Initially, some faculty and administrators assumed that the best route for Providence College to take would be to create a business-oriented not-for-profit management major, drawing upon the college's existing faculty and curriculum in the business, social work, and public administration departments. But given the existence of numerous other academic degree or concentration programs in this area, we believed a more challenging approach—and one more consistent with the spiritual and liberal arts culture of the college—was to design a major and minor within a liberal arts framework, one that would be attractive to students interested in pursuing a variety of career or post-graduate paths. Thus, what we have developed is a sequenced, four-year degree program that encompasses the four principles of human diversity, social justice, human solidarity, and engaged citizenship discussed above through the use of ideas and faculty drawn from a multiplicity of disciplines and perspectives.

## The Core of the Major

The conceptual core of the major consists of the following six courses (18 credit hours):

| | |
|---|---|
| PSP 101 | Introduction to Service in Democratic Communities |
| PSP 202 | Foundations of Organizational Service |
| PSP 301 | Community Service in American Culture |
| PSP 302 | Diversity, Community, and Service |
| PHL 201 | Ethics, Moral Leadership, and the Common Good |
| THL 322 | Catholic Social Thought |

Since the major and minor in public and community service studies makes the Providence College service-learning program unique, the core curriculum of the major/minor merits extended discussion. PSP 101, Introduction to Service in Democratic Communities, is considered the gateway for both the major and the minor in public and community service studies. It is also the course that students who are exploring the possibility of electing the major or minor take, as well as those who are interested in service-learning more generally. The introductory course is designed to expose students to the basic concepts and issues that provide the conceptual foundation of the Feinstein Institute and provide them with the opportunity for a range of service experiences integrated into the course content. The three central concepts of the course—service, community, and democracy—are examined from an interdisciplinary perspective; the course is always team-taught, either by two Providence College faculty representing different academic disciplines, or by a combination of faculty and community representatives. Because PSP 101 so aptly captures the approach and the values that underlie the Feinstein Institute's service-learning program, I have included a sample PSP 101 in the appendix.

Crucial to student learning has been the experiential component in the course. Students select from a range of four to six service placement options and engage in several hours of community service each week during the semester. Placed at community organizations in teams and led by teaching assistants as well as course faculty, students are able to reflect upon, analyze, and discuss their service experiences in class as a regular part of their course work, with the aim of connecting their service experiences with issues raised in class readings and discussions. From our own evaluations and those of our students, we have concluded that this course is not only an essential part of the major, both as a gateway to entering students and as a practicum for advanced student teaching assistants, but also has been a main mechanism for student recruitment.

PSP 202, Foundations of Organizational Service, offers students an introduction to the basic concepts of organizational behavior and organizational theory that provide the context within which public and community service takes place. In the course, students are exposed in some depth to theoretical and methodological perspectives on service in and through organizations and associations, which exposure permits them to understand organizational structures and processes essential to effective service. In addition to examining the historical development of approaches to organization, management, and bureaucracy, and critical dimensions of organizational service such as leadership, motivation, decision-making, and goal achievement, students have the opportunity to experience the organizational dimensions of service through a combination of observation and practice. PSP 202 is also cross-disciplinary, both in design and in instruction.

More than any other single course in the major or minor, Foundations of Organizational Service challenges and stretches our students. As has been observed nationally, young people drawn to service often tend to be anti-institutional, and thus either oblivious or hostile to the power and processes of established organizations. This course produces what Martin Luther King might have described as a creative tension, by forcing students to confront their initial hostility to institutional perspectives with the reality that to be effective an individual must understand and work with organizations.

PSP 301, Community Service in American Culture, provides students with historical perspectives on the social and cultural settings in which service takes place in the American context, as well as the history of attempted solutions to social problems. Students are introduced to the basic forms of community and public service that have developed historically in the United States, in order to understand the competing assumptions, values, and objectives that inform each type. In learning about each of the historic moments in which the meaning and practice of community service was profoundly transformed, students interpret the way each moment impacts the present by themselves being engaged in service that represents these different historical forms. This core course has been necessary for our majors and minors as they attempt to improve current social systems and invent new means of addressing unmet human needs, as it enables them to critically examine human service organizations as historic entities grounded in time and space.

PSP 302, Diversity, Community, and Service, is the core public service course that most attempts to model the institute's foundational commitment to understanding human diversity. The course explores diversity in contemporary American society—including ethnicity and race, language, religion, gender, social class, age, and sexual orientation—and its implications for people involved in community service. Through community-based projects that encourage them to analyze the socio-historical forces that contribute to the structures within which service organizations are situated, students are sensitized to the challenges and opportunities of working with diverse communities.

PHL 201, Ethics, Moral Leadership, and the Common Good, and THL 322, Catholic Social Thought, are core courses for our majors that also satisfy the general education requirements in philosophy and theology. PHL 201 provides students with the philosophical foundations for an ethic of public service by exploring the principles of moral life and decision-making, and by reflecting on the common good and the call to service. A service component is integrated into the public service ethics course. THL 322 introduces public service majors to the social documents of the Catholic church in the modern era, examining the principles used by the church in its moral reflection on the various social concerns of the day.

## Individualized Tracks

Understanding that students will enter the major from a variety of intellectual and career interests, concerns, and motivations, the major we developed allows for each student to select a three-course track from among the college's course listings outside the Feinstein Institute for Public Service (PSP). Students are responsible for creating their particular track in conjunction with a faculty adviser and for demonstrating both the relationship of the track to service and how the track will deepen their understanding of a particular subject area in relation to service. Students are not allowed to use more than one introductory or survey course to comprise a track, but within these fairly broad parameters, students are free to create their own individualized signature within the major (even going so far as naming their track). This was a feature strongly urged by students involved in the research and pilot phases of the program. While certain tracks are fairly obvious, like a three-course not-for-profit management sequence offered in the business departments and a series of courses in public/social policy and environmental studies/problems, a few of our majors have developed unique tracks, including a children's issues track and one in community psychology.

## Leadership Skills and Fieldwork Experience

Typically, beginning in their junior year, students take three courses that carry with them an intensive community experience tied to leadership and communication skills development. Students are asked to enroll in a two-course, full-year practicum in public and community service, where they are required to spend six to eight hours per week as teaching assistants, working with a community-based organization to orient, manage, and supervise Providence College students coming from the lower-level PSP courses or from other service-learning classrooms at the college. The experience of serving as a service-learning teaching assistant carries with it communication, management, small-group, and leadership skill building, and a strong reflective component, both in the classroom and in written work outside the classroom. Additionally, students are required to do an internship with an agency or organization of their choice, ideally one that connects the general themes concerning community service from earlier classes to their individualized tracks and career or post-graduate work interests. The internship is conducted as a seminar that meets semi-regularly throughout the semester, with student interns coming together to listen to each other's presentations of the work they are doing as well as brainstorming or problem solving around issues and concerns presented by that work in the community.

## The Capstone Experience

The culmination of the major comes with a two-semester capstone seminar in the senior year. In the capstone seminar, students majoring in public and community service have the opportunity to explore in-depth—and fully articulate for themselves—the central concepts and issues concerning community, citizenship, social change, and public ethics raised in a more elementary way in earlier coursework. The capstone experience allows each student to spend the year on a major action-research project in collaboration with a community partner and in consultation with his/her lead faculty member, culminating in a significant written (or other medium) product that will also constitute the final component of the student's portfolio. This product could take the form of—but is not limited to—an action-research monograph; a research/analysis thesis; a comprehensive community or neighborhood audit, history, or needs assessment; or a proposal for a program designed to meet community needs. The capstone project is designed to be a culmination of work done by students in prior courses, especially within their tracks, as well as their internships. Students present their final work at a public forum arranged by the institute and in the community in which they have studied.

## Requirements for the Minor in Public and Community Service Studies

The minor consists of six courses (18 credits), including the first five courses that comprise the core of the major, plus an independent study taken in the senior year. The independent study project, done in consultation with a faculty member, could include anything from intensive community involvement and analysis to community action research, or reading and writing in an advanced, specialized area within the field of public and community service. The idea behind the requirements for the minor was to mirror at a micro level the core conceptual content of the major combined with an individualized, intensive senior project that would bring the student's experiences together at the end of four years of study in the minor.

## Program Evaluation

The uniqueness of Providence College's service-learning program has caused us to consider unique methods of evaluation and assessment, both of our students' work and of the program as a whole. While we are still in the process of developing the complete package of evaluation instruments, our assessment already includes traditional student and faculty course evaluations, community partner evaluations of the program and of individual student service work, as well as course and student portfolios. The course portfolios include syllabi; samples of assignments and students' work; and community, student, and faculty evaluations. These course portfolios are designed to determine how well each course is meeting its objectives in terms of the overall academic program. In this way we can make adjustments to or add materials to individual courses to ensure that the major and minor cohere and are properly sequenced. The individual student portfolios, which include work from all of a student's courses and years in the program, are intended to be used both to evaluate our success in achieving our intended goals for the program and to demonstrate to the outside world the quality of the student's work and his/her potential for a future career and/or graduate study.

## PROGRAM STRUCTURE

As a curricular program, the Feinstein Institute operates under the academic affairs wing of the college. As previously mentioned, a number of organizations devoted to community service existed before this program and continue to exist, largely as extracurricular programs operating out of the student affairs division. In any given semester, approximately 1,000 students are involved in service, many through the Pastoral Service Organization (PSO), the student service corps that operates as an extracurricular arm of the college's Campus Ministry. In addition, over 100 first-year students participate in Urban Action, a community service program that begins during orientation and continues throughout the first year. Our relationship with these campus service organizations is collegial, and we attempt to share information and some resources, but because of the different histories of the extracurricular and curricular service programs and concerns over turf, we work to maintain the autonomy of each program or organization on campus.

We have a four-person staff at the institute, not counting part-time student workers or those working on special projects or grants: a director (myself), an associate director (Keith Morton, formerly director of the Campus Compact Project on Integrating Service with Academic Study), a full-time service-learning coordinator (Meg Stoltzfus), and a full-time office manager (Judith Clark). Keith and I have faculty as well as administrative appointments, and our teaching load constitutes two-thirds of our overall responsibilities. Meg has been service-learning coordinator since September 1994. In this position, she is responsible for orienting, training, and supervising the Feinstein teaching assistants and for working with community-based organizations and agencies to develop relationships and establish student service placements and internships. She maintains the institute's volunteer and post-graduate information clearinghouse, and has recently taken on the responsibility of initiating and maintaining our home page. Finally, Meg has taken lead responsibility for recruiting, placing, and training our community service federal work-study placements, which stand at between 30 to 40 per year.

As office manager, Judi coordinates the work of all the full-time and project staff and hires and supervises the six to ten part-time student workers at the institute. She is responsible for the operations of the Feinstein Institute Resource Center, an independent library and information center for students, faculty, and the wider community. She also coordinates the extensive budget and purchasing functions of the institute.

This four-person staff functions as a team, due both to our commitment to democratic principles and to our understanding that this is a more effective and desirable organizational structure, given the goals we are trying to accomplish. Between the Feinstein Foundation endowment and the commitment of Providence College's institutional resources and outside grants, the service-learning program operates with an annual budget of over $600,000.

As an interdisciplinary academic program, the Feinstein Institute does not have departmental status for the purpose of housing faculty or faculty lines. This has created an increasing challenge for us, as we have a growing number of courses that must be taught while we have to rely on discipline-based departments for our faculty. In the 1996–97 academic year, in addition to the six institute courses taught by the director and associate director, we have faculty from other departments involved in teaching 11 public and community service program courses.

We have adopted a number of strategies for recruiting faculty and interesting them in service-learning, either as a way to enhance courses they already teach or plan to teach, or as faculty in one of our Feinstein Institute courses. For two years, we have conducted a mini-grant process for faculty interested in teaching in the institute or adapting an existing departmental course to make it a service-learning course. We have also developed a faculty seminar series on experiential and service-learning, have hosted visiting faculty from a variety of colleges and universities to share their own experiences with and insights into service-learning, and for two years have invited all to participate in a Faculty Service Day, a combination of direct service with one of our community partners and serious reflection on the way someone teaches out of that service experience. Still, our largest challenge has been to recruit faculty to teach in our interdisciplinary program.

The Feinstein Institute reports directly to the vice president for academic administration, as do other units that offer degree programs. Our relationship with the administration is positive, for the most part. Ours is a new academic program that has received unprecedented financial resources compared with other Providence College programs. This brings us administrative support but also causes comparisons and charges of unfairness by other academic programs.

Students have played a pivotal role in planning the new program and in managing its activities. This has also been a conscious strategy, necessitated by both our commitment to democratic community and the fact that, as an academic program, the tendency for faculty to control the curriculum has had to be balanced by a strong student presence and voice. Unlike other service-learning programs, where student leadership emerges to direct particular projects or service opportunities, our students have the chance to voice ideas and concerns as well as manage the academic program and its connection to the larger community as part and parcel of the curriculum of the major. In our lower-level courses, we have tried to model student ownership and responsibility, by both the flexibility of the course structure and the self-consciously democratic pedagogy we attempt to implement. This is particularly true of our Foundations of Organizational Service course where students are presented in the first week with the task of developing the course syllabus, as part of their learning about organizations (the class being the first example of one). At the upper level, typically in the junior year, Feinstein majors spend a year working as teaching assistants assigned to a particular class to assist with student learning and reflection as well as to serve as liaisons to community-based organizations with whom students in that course are working. Students take the lead in developing our curriculum-based alternate break program, serving as break leaders and organizers, assisting faculty who are incorporating the alternate break trips into their classes. In addition to all this, a number of students serve on the presidentially appointed Feinstein Public Service Program Committee, and will serve on the advisory board of the institute.

The larger community has also played an important role in the development of the Feinstein program from its inception. Community representatives sat on several of the focus and advisory groups established during the research and planning year. During the 1994–95 academic year, a community advisory group was formed—with the help of a Campus Compact Campus Team Forum grant—that met throughout the year, visited classrooms and service sites, and issued a detailed report containing several recommendations for the program, most of which we have tried to implement. One of the most important recommendations, one that also assists with our development of teaching resources, was that we invite community representatives into the classroom as advisers and co-educators with our regular faculty. We now have community advisers involved in a number of our courses, particularly the introductory/gateway course (PSP 101). We have had great success with community representatives in the classroom who give faculty and students the opportunity to test their ideas and experiences against those of someone with extensive work in the community. It has also been beneficial to our community advisers, who report being able to reflect more meaningfully on their own practices by being confronted with different ideas and questions from the academy. We are in the process of setting up and appointing an overall advisory board, which will be made up of equal numbers of community and campus (faculty, administration/staff, and students) representatives. This will further institutionalize the important role of the larger community in the structure and direction of our service-learning program.

## COMMUNITY PARTNERSHIPS

Because the mission of the Feinstein Institute is essentially to provide a liberal undergraduate education where community service is both subject matter and method, the role of community partners is especially important. On the recommendation of the community advisory group, we have designated two types of community partners: placement partners and core partners.

### Placement Partners

We work with approximately three dozen placement partners on a semester-to-semester basis to develop service opportunities that meet our educational interests and community needs (as defined by the partners). Some examples of our placement partners and the work students do with them include the following organizations:

*Amos House.*  A comprehensive shelter for homeless or transitional men and women. Two of the several programs Amos House operates are meals for breakfast and lunch and an overnight shelter. Students serve as overnight supervisors of the shelter one night every other week. This opportunity includes an evening of training and a shift that runs from approximately 9 p.m. through 7 a.m. Volunteers also serve a meal at the soup kitchen once during the semester.

*Esek Hopkins Middle School.*  A public school grades six through eight, located in Providence's North End that serves 600 students from across the city and many different ethnic/racial groups. Providence College students tutor Hopkins students in math and work in the new after-school program, assisting teachers with a variety of after-school clubs.

*Project Hope/Proyecto Esperanza.*  A Latino advocacy agency and social service center in Central Falls, R.I. Students have the opportunity to assist adult immigrants who are trying to obtain U.S. citizenship. Providence College students work with small groups of learners one night per week to prepare them for the INS citizenship exam.

*Sunrise Community Housing.*  A comprehensive social service organization supporting people living with AIDS and their families. Sunrise provides housing for individuals, couples, and families in homes throughout Providence. Providence College students provide assistance by serving as companions to residents and by helping with basic living activities such as laundry, cleaning, transportation, and shopping.

## Core Partners

While our core partners also provide the institute with short-term service placements, we move with them toward a deeper type of interdependence. This involves doing strategic planning together, learning about each other's organization in detail, inviting their staff to join us in developing our curriculum and in teaching our students, especially in our core courses, and generally working toward intentional interdependence. We provide our core partners with faculty expertise, campus space, library and information resources, technical assistance, and access to other institutional resources as well as student workers. We become a stable resource and partner on whom they can depend, and they become an educational partner in our classes.

*Smith Hill Center.* The Smith Hill Center is a multipurpose agency in a neighborhood proximate to the college. In addition to providing dozens of students from a variety of Feinstein classes to their youth and senior programs, we have students and faculty working on fundraising and economic development plans for the center, and have provided classroom space for adult education and ESL classes conducted by the center. In spring 1995, we joined with the center to develop an innovative community gardens project as one part of the economic development plan. The program involves three types of gardens: the first, a series of family gardens scattered around a number of previously vacant lots in the neighborhood, where area residents can grow flowers and vegetables; a second type for elementary schoolchildren as part of the local public school's own service-learning initiative, located on the Providence College campus; and the third, called Generation One, a large entrepreneurial garden managed by teenagers and young adults (supervised by Smith Hill Center staff and Providence College faculty) to teach participants how to develop a small business by raising crops for sale to restaurants and farmers' markets. Additionally, Feinstein Institute interns and work-study students placed at the Smith Hill Community Development Corporation are in the process of establishing a long-range housing collaborative in conjunction with the Rhode Island School of Design that will design, build, and rehabilitate low-income homes and teach prospective neighborhood homeowners about the proper care and financing of their homes.

As one can see from the example of the Smith Hill Center, relationships with core partners are time and resource intensive. As a result, only four or five core partners have emerged from among the organizations and agencies we work with on a regular basis. But given our educational and social change missions, it is especially in collaboration with these core partners that we hope to make a measurable contribution both to our students' learning and to the communities in which we work.

## CONCLUSION

The development of this academic major/minor in public and community service makes Providence College unique among those institutions of higher education committed to service-learning. Other strategies are being tried across the country to sustain service-learning on college campuses, and many of those strategies are represented by the other essays in this volume. Although many of those on campus here were skeptical about promoting service through a major/minor that existed nowhere else in the country, we are convinced that designing a major or minor around service-learning is an excellent way of institutionalizing a campus community service initiative, excellent in terms of our three major constituencies: students, the faculty, and our community partners.

### Student Benefits

A sequenced major or minor in public and community service allows students to carry over past experiences and learning into further courses in the sequence, thereby building a body of skills and knowledge about community, service, citizenship, and social change over time. Students are also able to amass a wealth of community-based experience, working with a variety of community partners that may represent different ideas about service or different issue areas, or working with the same community-based organization over a four-year period. So often, service-learning programs offer students one- or two-time opportunities—in individual courses scattered across the curriculum—to become involved in curriculum-based community service. But the sequenced major and minor has created a series of experiences and courses that build upon and interact with each other throughout the student's undergraduate career. We have seen remarkable growth in our students, and most of this is attributable to the fact that students take a series of courses over a sustained period of time as part of an academic major or minor.

### Faculty Benefits

For faculty, the major places service-learning at the center of the curriculum, and as we all know, the curriculum is primarily a faculty concern. The faculty has taken seriously its role in creating and fine-tuning the program, and I have actually witnessed the creation of a learning community on the campus, where faculty from fields as diverse as education, sociology, management, English, American studies, philosophy, political science, chemistry, art history, theology, and social work come together to define the problem to be studied and the different perspectives that bear on that problem. It has been exhilarating to talk with one another about the meaning of community, the organization of social institutions, and the ethical dilemmas of service, all as we work with students and the larger community. Faculty have also taken the lead in developing innovative methods of evaluation for the service-learning program and the students who go through it. This community of learners on campus models what we would like to see in the world, with people from different backgrounds and perspectives working together on issues of common concern.

## Community Benefits

For the community, the presence of an academic major of the kind we have developed allows for real, long-term collaboration. We are able to make the organizations and agencies we work with more than mere community service placements for our students; we can make them partners in education and can provide more sustained resources to them in the work they are doing. Whereas other service-learning programs might provide an agency, school, or organization with a student who works 30 to 40 hours over the course of a semester, we are able to provide students who are engaged in intensive internships or capstone projects as well as the single semester participant. An organization can make an investment in students who might continue working with it over a four-year period. Additionally, our faculty have made commitments to our community partners that go beyond a supply of student workers or even their own service. Our faculty are involved with our core partners in numerous ways: doing research, sitting on agency boards, and giving their time to discrete projects where the organization sees a need for faculty involvement. The presence of an academic major and minor makes possible the kind of intentional interdependence with our community partners— especially that handful of core partners—we are trying to model.

*For actual Providence College service-learning documents, see Appendix H: PSP 101 Syllabus, Introduction to Service in Democratic Communities*

## REFERENCES

Battistoni, R. (1995, Winter). Service-learning, diversity, and the liberal arts curriculum. *Liberal Education, 81,* (1), 30–35.

# 10

# Santa Clara University's Eastside Project: A Pilgrimage Toward Our Own Humanity

**William J. Wood, S.J.**
*Santa Clara University*

*We, as an intellectual community, must analyze causes; use imagination and creativity together to discover remedies; communicate to our public a consciousness that inspires the freedom of self-determination; educate professionals with a conscience who will be the immediate instruments of transformation; and continually hone an educational institution that is academically excellent and ethically oriented.*

—Ignacio Ellacuria, S.J., Rector, University of Central America
Commencement Address, Santa Clara University, 1983

## INTRODUCTION

Since 1986, the Eastside Project has offered Santa Clara University faculty a program for integrating and supplementing theory with practice in their courses by having their students spend an hour or two a week during the academic quarter interacting with underprivileged people in an appropriate community setting. The Eastside Project also organizes, principally for faculty and administrators, immersion experiences among oppressed populations in so-called developing countries.

There have been five Santa Clara delegations to El Salvador since the Jesuits and their co-workers were slaughtered there in 1989. More recent itineraries have included Haiti, the state of Chiapas in Mexico, and Guatemala. Although most of these international delegations have included student representatives, and the Eastside Project has co-sponsored student projects in Central America and Haiti, student interests are reflected first and foremost in the goal of eventually creating study abroad opportunities in such countries, where community-based learning and participant-observer research can be more systematically developed. As of the present, however, the regular curricular program of the Eastside Project works principally in collaboration with approximately 30 local community placement sites. These include agencies that offer services for children or teenagers, homeless individuals and families, seniors, and students of all ages learning English as a second language.

The founders designed the program to create situations in which Santa Clara students could be brought into face-to-face contact with underprivileged people. When given the opportunity and guidance to struggle reflectively with this often discomforting experience, students tend to undergo a shift of paradigms in their thinking. To borrow Tony Sholander's geological metaphor, we are hoping to facilitate an intellectual earthquake, where cognitive and affective plates shift and realign to form a new conceptual terrain (Sholander, 1994). Our hope is that the result will be significantly altered world views and that, in the end, the students will recognize that their own lives are actually intertwined with the daily struggle for survival of the vast majority who cannot take life for granted.

With courses spread throughout three concentrated quarters in any given academic year, the Eastside Project has grown from fewer than 100 students, ten courses, and eight placement sites in its first year (1986–87) to 1,547 students, more than 100 classes, and 31 placement sites in 1995–96. Such growth in numbers, of course, makes quality control a major challenge.

Whether connected with a course or not, this kind of community-based learning requires three phases of activity: preparation for and orientation to the field experience; conscious attention to and personal involvement in the reality of the community setting; and critical reflection, dialogue, and synthesis through oral, written, and/or artistic presentation.

The office of the Eastside Project expedites the efforts of three key sets of players in this university-underserved community partnership of mutual learning: 1) Santa Clara University faculty who choose and qualify to participate in the program; 2) Santa Clara University students enrolled in classes that offer participation in the Eastside Project as a requirement or option; and 3) representatives of the community, principally managers and other staff of the placement sites.

In academic year 1996–97, the Eastside Project community-based learning program moved a step closer to institutionalization as part of the academic routine of the university. A proposal for an interdisciplinary community studies minor, which had been in the making for two years, received official approval and is closely linked with the Eastside Project, whose director is responsible for the introductory and capstone courses of the minor. The minor will provide a channel for the university to accomplish two important goals. First, it will enable us to move motivated students beyond community-based learning to the development of skills in cross-disciplinary social analysis and participant-observer investigation. Second, it will serve as a vehicle for effective reciprocity between the university, which has been mostly on the receiving end for the last ten years, and the community. The enactment of the community studies minor promises to embody solidarity between the university and the community by providing concrete ways in which the community of scholars, intellectual resources in hand, can take a stand on the side of those who are neglected and have no voice as together they reflectively engage in the rigorous inquiry and creative imagining required to fashion a more humane and just world.

## VISION AND MISSION OF THE EASTSIDE PROJECT

As its founder pointed out in a presentation at Georgetown University (Privett et al., 1989), the Eastside Project is not a center of activity nor is it any one specific program that someone can visit, observe, or even photograph for a university brochure. In terms of understanding the Eastside Project, one is not disadvantaged by never having been there. The Eastside Project is best understood by playing with metaphors rather than looking at photographs. We have chosen a bridge as the metaphor that is most expressive.

A bridge is the means by which one passes over into an area that is on the opposite side of an otherwise impassable chasm. Bridges allow persons on either side of a divide to interact with each other as well as to return home again. Bridges counter isolation with the possibility of interaction. The Eastside Project is predicated on the understanding that the university is generally cut off from and inaccessible to certain segments of the population. The result is that the experiences, questions, fears, hopes, doubts, frustrations, and concerns of these people make it difficult—if not impossible—for them to find their way into the academy across a chasm of separation that is broad and deep. Thus, the very institution that explicitly commits itself to exploring, distilling, articulating, and enhancing universal human experience is prevented from doing so because not all human experience can pass over into the consciousness of the university. This is a problem for any university, but doubly so for a university that claims to stand in the Catholic Jesuit tradition.

Those whom society pushes to the margins of its consciousness as unimportant are the very persons that the Gospel would have us attend to with special care. Contrary to the popular wisdom, it is the poor, the meek, and the persecuted who the Gospel declares are especially blessed by God. Close association with them can save us—faculty, staff, students and administrators—from being hopelessly confined to the narrow horizon and limited ethos of our particular milieu. The mission of the Eastside Project, therefore, is to create a partnership between Santa Clara University and the community of voiceless and powerless people who are excluded from society's benefits, a lasting partnership that fosters continuing conversation between both parties, so that the university is directly responsive to and shaped by the community. We envision Santa Clara graduates who will serve as a leaven in the evolution of a critical mass of those who, whatever their profession or status in society, will have the compassion, conscience, and competence to act in solidarity with the poor and most neglected members of society as critically thinking agents of change committed to the fashioning of a more humane and just world.

In the 1973 phrase coined by the then international head of the Jesuits, Pedro Arrupe, our prime educational objective is to form "men and women for others" (Arrupe, 1973). That will require, Father Arrupe added:

> First, a firm determination to live more simply . . . Second, a firm determination to draw no power whatever from clearly unjust sources . . . Third and most difficult, a firm resolve to be agents of change in society, not merely resisting unjust structures and arrangements, but actively undertaking to reform them.

In other words, it will take more than good will and volunteerism to shape a just, participatory, and sustainable, let alone regenerative, future for Earth's community. Knowledge is required, wisdom, too, and prudence, the ability to govern and discipline oneself by the use of reason. None of these are acquired without the very stuff of higher education: disciplined study, critical thinking, hours of contemplation, creative imagination, cross-disciplinary dialogue, and vigorous debate.

The Eastside Project did not begin with a set of goals and objectives for the university—either a specified percentage of minority students by a certain date or a predetermined slate of courses to be added to the core curriculum. Instead, the project is rooted in a theory that views interaction between the university and neglected or overlooked groups of people as an effective means for refocusing and redirecting the energies of the university. Basically, the project is built around a widely supported but badly neglected research finding that attitudes—personal and institutional—are more effectively changed by experience than by position papers or forceful rhetoric (Cook & Flay, 1978). Developmental theorists tell us that we are more likely to act ourselves into new ways of thinking than think ourselves into new ways of acting.

Educators are familiar with outreach programs that place the human resources of the university—generally the students—at the disposal of local human service agencies. In contrast to these traditional programs, the Eastside Project's main intent is to promote interaction between the university and the community on the premise that, in the words of psychologist Robert Kegan (1982):

> We not only increase the likelihood of our being moved; we also run the risks that being moved entails. For we are moved somewhere, and that somewhere is further into life, closer to those with whom we live.

The Eastside Project offers opportunities to move further into the lives of the underserved, to hear more sharply "the cries of the poor" [Psalm 9:13], confident that direct experiences of their pain and distress will broaden the university's base for reflection and redirect its activities and resources.

This theory and practice of personal and institutional transformation focuses our efforts to establish even more firmly the Eastside Project in the community and at Santa Clara University. From the very beginning our principal challenge has been—and still is—to remain true to our conviction that while the university has much to offer the community, it is the disenfranchised and underrepresented people themselves who are the motors that drive the mechanisms that will change the university. In short, the Eastside Project is about allowing the poor and the marginalized—those who suffer most from our social, political, and economic structures—to vitalize the university by educating it to the demands that must be met if justice is to be realized in our community.

Justice cannot be effectively promoted without a prior and continuous attempt to find some solidarity with the poor—that is, those who are the victims of injustice—in a more experiential way, by sharing their lives, sorrows, joys, hopes, and fears. We know that this is what has to be done, and the Eastside Project is an attempt to help Santa Clara University find solidarity with those who are at or near the bottom of society—those on the other side of the chasm. With their help, we hope to fix a concern for justice firmly within the university's very self-identity.

## HISTORY OF THE EASTSIDE PROJECT

### 1980–84: Call and Response

In 1980 I had the rare privilege of spending about ten days at a conference of new Jesuit provincial superiors with Father Pedro Arrupe, general superior of the Jesuits, and 20 other Jesuits—from Africa, the Mideast, Latin America, the Caribbean, Eastern and Western Europe, and North America.

To add even more to the depth of that international dialogue, during the course of the conference we each had a private meeting with Father Arrupe to let him get to know us personally, as well as to report on our province; i.e., the region of the Society of Jesus we represented. As the vice-provincial for education of the California province of the Society of Jesus, I gave Father Arrupe a brief synopsis of my personal life, and then reported on the work of the over 300 Jesuits serving in the three universities and five high schools of the California province.

Don Pedro listened patiently and attentively, and when I had finished he spoke to me in his animated fashion that flashed with affirmation, joy, genuine affection, the wisdom of the ancients, and the simplicity of a child. "You must understand," he pleaded with an earnest smile, "the effect the U.S. has on the rest of the world."

Arrupe had personally experienced the destructive power of that impact 35 years earlier. He was living in Hiroshima when we dropped the atom bomb there. With a gentle and loving passion, he grasped my hands and continued to speak: "Yours is the most powerful and wealthy nation in a world in which the vast majority live in misery and powerlessness. You have the scientific knowledge, technology, and political might to destroy the world or lead it into a new era of justice and peace."

He concluded by noting that "This poses an extraordinary challenge to American Jesuits and particularly to your educational institutions." That international assembly and especially Father Arrupe's remarks aroused in me a greater sense of the urgent obligation yet to be met at that time by the three Jesuit universities in California.

The call for all Jesuits and Jesuit institutions to put the highest priority on the service of faith through the promotion of justice had first been sounded in 1974 at the thirty-second General Congregation of the Society of Jesus. At one end of the spectrum of response, some heard this as a call for Jesuits to get out of education and into the trenches of social activism and political protest. At the other end of the spectrum stood some who thought the new battle cry was a betrayal of the five-century Jesuit tradition of education of youth as the highest Jesuit priority. The rest found themselves somewhere in between the extremes, most convinced that promotion of justice was important, but not at all sure how that was to be spelled out in practice, especially in an institutional context.

The struggle was particularly difficult for universities like Santa Clara. For one thing, they were no longer under the legal control of the Jesuit order. Besides, even apart from their own lack of consensus in interpreting the justice issue, Jesuits formed an increasingly smaller minority among the faculty and administration. But the hardest part for the universities was figuring out how to respond to the call for the promotion of justice without compromising the integrity of the university as an institution of higher education.

Gerdenio "Sonny" Manuel and Stephen A. Privett were among the bright young Jesuits who were convinced not only that a concern for justice was of the highest priority, but that it was the soul and animating force of authentic education in the Jesuit tradition. As the California vice-provincial for education, I was their chief adviser as they went off in the early 1980s to do their doctoral work—Sonny in psychology at Duke University, Steve in theology at the Catholic University of America. Many conversations ensued over the years.

Wherever they might go, Sonny and Steve were determined that their individual teaching and research would be aimed primarily at education for transformation. The many conversations we had during their years of study, however, centered not on how they would achieve this in their own classes, but on how a university itself could be transformed, integrating a preferential option for the poor into the curriculum as the animating force of the institution.

Since Sonny and Steve had had previous connections with Santa Clara, and the university was anxious to have them back as faculty members, it was mutually agreed that they would apply for positions there and that, presuming they were accepted, they would be assigned to Santa Clara on condition that they be given the latitude to take up residence in what is commonly referred to as the "eastside" of San Jose and work on a special project that would link Santa Clara University with the lower-income, underserved, and mostly immigrant population of that area.

This was, in fact, what happened, and the two wasted no time getting started on their project. At this point they still did not know what shape their program would take. But they had clear plans for how they would start. They had hoped to be joined by another young Jesuit who would not be a Santa Clara faculty member but would devote his time to working in the community. When that fell through, they invited Father Daniel V. Germann, long-time director of Campus Ministry to join them, and Dan willingly assented to launching a second career as the third person in their Jesuit *troika*.

## 1985–90: The Early Years

Thanks to the work of others, the time was ripe at Santa Clara. In the winter quarter of 1985, the very year Privett and Manuel came to Santa Clara, a young assistant dean and professor of modern languages named Francisco Jiménez had organized a major University Institute on Poverty and Conscience. Growing up as a migrant farm worker in the fields and orchards of central California, Francisco knew more about poverty from first-hand experience than the Jesuits associated with the Eastside Project will ever know. He tilled the soil in which the Eastside Project would flourish. And throughout the following years, always hidden behind the scenes, he would play a major role in the maturation of the Eastside Project.

It was clear to the founders that the effectiveness of the project depended on their being credible members of both the university and the eastside communities. Dan's 16 years in Campus Ministry added to Sonny's and Steve's tenure track appointments and previous service to Santa Clara to establish their status within the university. However, to establish their credentials in the community, they decided to live in Most Holy Trinity parish on the eastside after only four months of consultation with representative community persons. This willingness to consult combined with their eventual parish involvement to give them a visibility and plausibility on the eastside that would otherwise have eluded them.

Another major contribution to their standing in the community came from a decision to invite Peter Miron-Conk, Director of San Jose Urban Ministries, to join them on the project. Peter's years of service to San Jose's marginalized peoples earned him the respect, confidence, and affection of the people with whom they hoped to work. Of equal importance for the project were Peter's outsider perspective and his skills at facilitating goal-setting and decision-making processes.

The project's original administrative structure further reflected the concern to have a solid foundation for both sides of the bridge. Dan Germann and Peter Miron-Conk anchored the community side while Sonny Manuel and Steve Privett, the university side. Dan devoted the bulk of his time to community and diocesan committees and to direct participation in the project's cocurricular immigration program. Sonny and Steve both received a two-course reduction in their teaching loads which freed some time to work on the qualitative and quantitative development of the curricular placements. The three Jesuits and Peter met weekly to coordinate and evaluate the ongoing work of the project and to direct ad hoc efforts (e.g., panel presentations, symposia, guest lectures).

From the very beginning, the seminal idea of the project—mutual interaction—was clear to them, but they wisely left its specific shape and form quite vague and amorphous. The nebulous nature of the project's institutionalization saved it from becoming just another patronizing attempt to serve the interests of the community. Rather, the community itself had a major voice in the preliminary discussions to determine the direction that the project would take. They were not creating structures to help Santa Clara learn about the community; the community and the university were going to learn from each other from the very beginning of the project. This process of creation modeled the fundamental dynamic at the heart of the project—university and community listening to and learning from each other.

In October 1986, after then-President Father William Rewak announced and strongly endorsed the project in a letter sent to every member of the university community, the Eastside Project began in earnest with a series of meetings that facilitated direct discussion between representatives from the community and the university; two sessions were held on campus and two in a meeting room at the parish. The bridge was under construction, and people were already crossing over, if only for a meeting.

Each session elicited responses to the project's underlying concept of cooperative interaction between university and community and then asked for specific recommendations on how this ideal could be implemented to the satisfaction and benefit of all. Prior to these meetings, the discussants had tentatively singled out three emphases for the project: curriculum, research, and a cocurricular program. The community spoke, and the university listened. It was encouraging and exhilarating to listen to local residents denounce past research efforts that had reduced their lives and their families to grist for the academic research/tenure mill.

The community had had it with university types paddling through, and said so. Santa Clara was not their university; San Jose State enjoyed that status. University people left these meetings with heightened sensitivities, piqued curiosities, and a desire to begin this program that offered the vague hope of learning more from the community. Community representatives were impressed with the number, quality, and apparent sincerity of Santa Clara representatives.

The minutes of these meetings were reviewed by the four directors and by the project's advisory board, which was constituted on the basis of qualitative participation at those initial meetings. The board's membership was deliberately balanced with six university and six community representatives.

While there was an immediate and clear consensus among board members not to sponsor research efforts during the initial phase of development, the board did endorse the project's curricular and cocurricular concentration and drew up a set of criteria to direct the development of the project. They opted for programs that responded to real needs, were manageable, could be successfully implemented at minimal cost but with high visibility, used existing structures, and were capable of absorbing all interested participants.

In addition to the above criteria, they settled upon a set of more long-range goals against which all decisions would be measured. They would support, for example, programs or opportunities 1) that capitalized on existing university resources and fostered a partnership between the community and the university; 2) that were initiated by the community and had a multicultural context; 3) that addressed a justice issue or focused on the underserved; or 4) that promised to have an impact on a number of different areas within the community or the university. Above all, they looked for programs that would involve a significant segment of the university, that could ultimately be institutionalized within the curriculum, and that had the potential for redirecting the university's educational mission.

In response to community recommendations and in line with the criteria, they directed the project's cocurricular component towards undocumented immigrants who had become a critical local—and national—issue with the passage of the Immigration Reform and Control Act of 1986 (IRCA). After some testing of the local waters, the Eastside Project opted to link up with the Diocese of San Jose's program to help immigrants acquire legal status. Dan worked so effectively with diocesan and volunteer personnel that he was salaried by the diocese to direct the on-site conduct of this legalization effort.

An unanticipated but positive consequence of successful involvement with the immigration issue was some bridge-building between the university and the diocese. This initial contact—greatly expanded by Dan's subsequent involvement with a number of diocesan groups—led to increased collaboration between and the mutual enrichment of both Santa Clara and the local church. At Paul Locatelli's presidential inauguration in 1988, San Jose's Bishop R. Pierre DuMaine singled out the Eastside Project as a ". . . unique witness to the sense of community and service that this institution [Santa Clara University] has always carried along with its academic distinction."

The cocurricular legalization program drew student volunteers from upper division Spanish classes, from appropriate courses in ethnic studies, and from the law school. These student volunteers assisted undocumented persons through the complicated legalization process. The project's cocurricular effort cut across departmental lines and even began to bridge the gap between graduate and undergraduate students.

Within the cocurricular program it was difficult to set up the structures that require participants to reflect upon and learn from their experiences. Three such reflective exercises were offered during each of the first two quarters of operation: an orientation program, a panel presentation by documented and undocumented persons, and an opportunity for students to share with each other their experiences with the undocumented. But, with the exception of the orientation evening, attendance was sparse at these events, and the grafting of a critically reflective component onto the cocurricular branch of the project remained problematic.

The project's curricular effort began with Sonny and Steve's contacting faculty members whom they knew personally or who had expressed some interest and enthusiasm for what they were doing. The departments that were initially most responsive to their overtures were psychology, modern languages, ethnic studies, and communication. Steve and Sonny worked in a highly individualized manner at finding the right venue for each teacher.

For example, the goals of the child psychology course were best attainable at Family Place or Gardner's Children Center, both of which offered students direct experiences with poor children. A course in TV production required that each student create a brief video program that featured some social service agency or justice-related problem in the community. The pattern of the project's curricular components was quite flexible. Some courses required direct involvement with the community; others offered such experiences in lieu of a written assignment or even as an extra credit exercise.

In the spring of 1988—after two years in operation—it was obvious to the founders and the university administration that the project was mushrooming and that an additional staff person was needed to function as project coordinator and as liaison with the placement sites. Laura Jiménez was selected to fill this position, and she brought to the job the requisite industry and imagination to keep pace with ever increasing student involvement. Laura was to become the mainstay of the Eastside Project.

For the first six years, the project was funded by annually renewable grants from the Bannan Foundation, which is specifically devoted to enhancing the Jesuit character of Santa Clara. While support from the Bannan Foundation affirmed the Eastside Project as a distinctively Jesuit enterprise, the eventual incorporation of the project into the university's operational budget would later prove to be a major step in institutionalizing it.

The year 1989 was marked by two events that signaled the coming into maturity of the Eastside Project as well as a turning point. The first event was the first national conference ever of assembled Jesuit and lay representatives of the 28 Jesuit colleges and universities of the United States. Sonny, Steve, Dan, and Peter traveled to Georgetown University in Washington, DC, in June to make a presentation on the Eastside Project. Second, a few months after the national assembly of Jesuits at Georgetown, an incident occurred that gave the thrust of the Eastside Project a sense of added urgency and confirmed the decision to expand and extend the bridge from Santa Clara beyond the confines of Silicon Valley.

Shortly before dawn on November 16, 1989, six Jesuit educators at our sister institution, the University of Central America (UCA) in San Salvador, their housekeeper, and her daughter were snatched from their beds and brutally murdered by Salvadoran soldiers under orders from their high command. The eight white wooden crosses that today greet visitors at the entrance to the Santa Clara Mission church at the center of our campus are a daily reminder of the impact of that event on our sustained commitment to the mission and vision of Jesuit education at Santa Clara University.

In the wake of the murders, the Eastside Project, at the initiative of Steve Privett and Dan Germann, organized the first of its international immersion experiences in underdeveloped regions. University President Paul Locatelli, S.J. led a delegation of SCU faculty, regents, and friends on a week-long visit to El Salvador in late March of 1990 to attend ceremonies observing the tenth anniversary of the assassination of San Salvador Archbishop Oscar Romero and to tour refugee resettlement villages. Similar delegations to Third World trouble spots, most of them organized by the Eastside Project, became an annual Santa Clara tradition. Luis Calero, S.J. organized four other trips to El Salvador on behalf of the Eastside Project. Tony Sholander, S.J. and I travelled with Steve Privett to investigate possibilities in Haiti after the restoration of President Aristide in 1994 and led a contingent of 16 Santa Clara faculty, staff, and students to the state of Chiapas, Mexico during the 1995 spring break. In 1996, Santa Clara's Center for Applied Ethics sponsored an early summer faculty tour to Guatemala, with the initiative taken by philosophy professors Michael Meyer and Mark Ravizza, S.J. who wanted to immerse themselves in the reality of that country and examine it from a systematic ethical perspective.

## 1991–96: Years of Growth and Transition

The global perspective that came to be associated with the Eastside Project only served to intensify local efforts through the course-imbedded community placement program. Our own backyard is a microcosm of the globe, including the splendid diversity and the widening gap between rich and poor. If the early years of the 1990s were marked by expansion of the bridge into international territory, they also witnessed a conspicuous swelling of traffic on the stretch of the bridge that extends from Santa Clara to downtown and the eastside of San Jose.

Though exact records of numbers were not kept in the earliest years, a chronology drawn up by the founders for their 1989 presentation at Georgetown informs us that approximately six classes participated at four community placements in the pilot year of 1985–86, and approximately twelve classes participated at eight community placements in 1986–87, the official first year of the Eastside Project. By 1988–89, the number of classes had increased to 71 (taught by 33 faculty members), and the number of placement sites to 13. The numbers of students participating, however, did not exceed 350 or so, since most of the classes in the early years offered the community-based experience as an option, not a requirement.

By 1995–96, the numbers had grown to 1,547 students who were enrolled in 105 classes, taught by 53 instructors, with participation at 31 regular community placements, plus some individually arranged projects. The number of classes and instructors reached a peak by 1993–94, but the number of student participants continued to grow by as much as 47% between 1993–94 and 1995–96.

In the midst of this continuing growth in the early nineties, the project was undergoing a major transition. For one thing, the time had come for the university to assume full financial responsibility for the program. Not only were grant monies for start-up costs coming to an end, but success and growth meant more expenses, and the intent from the outset was for this program to become an integral part of the operations of Santa Clara University as an institution of higher learning. Deciding on an appropriate budget was not easy.

A tough choice had to be made eventually, for example, as to whether to continue maintaining a residence on the eastside or use the rent money to hire a part-time secretary. Even shortly before the university assumed full financial responsibility for the Eastside Project, an even bigger question began to emerge. What salary and benefit provisions needed to be made for the eventual replacement of the founding Jesuits? Of the three, only Dan, as titular director, was paid a salary from the project budget, and that only half-time. The other two salaries were paid by the respective academic departments. But Dan was working full-time as anchor and liaison in the community, while Steve and Sonny, both able administrators, were basically contributing their management and program development services. What if they should leave the Eastside Project?

That question soon became moot. In 1991 and 1992 Steve and Sonny, respectively, quietly retired from the program to take other posts. Their departure forced the budgetary issue and left an immense gap in organizational leadership, creative energy, and credibility within the academic community. A year later, a new mission for Dan would leave a similar gap in the community.

Several steps were taken in an attempt to fill the gaps. First, in September 1991, another Jesuit, Tony Sholander, who had an MSW and was completing requirements for a license in marriage and family counseling, was hired in a new half-time position to apply his organizational ability and expertise in educational and social psychology, social work, and computer technology to the work of the community-based learning program of the Eastside Project. He and Laura Jiménez worked closely on the planning and logistics of the course-embedded placement program. Having co-facilitated the first faculty training workshop with Sonny Manuel the previous summer, Tony stepped in to take full responsibility for the direction of the subsequent summer workshops, with Laura handling the material needs of the five-day sessions.

As placement coordinator, Laura focused on selecting, supporting, and fostering relations with the community placement sites. Tony, as experiential-learning coordinator, acted as mentor to the Santa Clara students, particularly facilitating their systematic reflection on their experience in the community and monitoring their progress. Tony also took it upon himself to develop a computerized database network that would serve the administrative requirements of the placement program as well as evaluation and research purposes. And he spearheaded the development of an Eastside Project newsletter, *The Bridge.*

A short-lived confederation of Eastside Project departmental liaisons gave way at this time to a new configuration. The most intensely involved of the 50 faculty members making use of the placement program formed an advisory group called the Eastside Project Faculty Associates. Colombian-born Jesuit anthropologist Luis Calero volunteered to serve as convener of the newly formed faculty associates and as mentor to other faculty who might be interested in integrating community-based learning into their courses. Luis also organized three of the annual faculty excursions to El Salvador.

Jesuit theologian Paul Crowley experimented with serving in a similar capacity. Neither Jesuit scholar was in a position to contribute the kind of time and energy that founders Steve Privett and Sonny Manuel had put into the creation of the Eastside Project. But with Tony Sholander and Laura Jiménez attending to some vital pedagogical components and handling the nuts-and-bolts of the operation, the idea of a modified administrative role for one or more faculty members loomed as a promising option.

Under the direction of Associate Academic Vice President Francisco Jiménez, the faculty position being piloted by Calero and Crowley was given a title, Faculty Development Coordinator, and an appointment policy and job description were developed over a two-year period. The position was to be compensated by way of a course release. It was a good idea, but for a variety of reasons has not worked out, although conceivably it could be reactivated in the future.

At the same time, the geography and patterns of the Eastside Project's involvement with the community were changing. For example, Most Holy Trinity parish ceased functioning as the principal base for Eastside Project operations. Instead, Laura Jiménez's development of the project's working relationship with an increasing number of community service agencies was broadening and deepening the base of our vital presence in the community.

That was the scenario I entered in January 1993 when President Paul Locatelli asked me to relieve Dan Germann and take the reins as the first full-time director of the Eastside Project. My main role was to pilot the project through its transition from a new and innovative approach founded by charismatic leaders to institutionalization as a solidly established program within the mainstream of the university. What struck me very soon was that the Eastside Project was at heart a powerful experiential-learning program, but that it lacked clear definition, a sense of direction, and the kind of structure needed for it to reach its goals and realize its potential.

Tony Sholander was already hard at work on the issue of definition, articulating for various audiences the pedagogical theory and praxis driving the Eastside Project's curricular program. At the same time, he and Laura streamlined and refined the day-to-day community-based learning program, in effect laying the cornerstone for the second decade of the Eastside Project.

What unfolded otherwise over the next three and a half years can be summarized under five headings:

1. Applying the vision of the Eastside Project to the development of updated university statements of mission and guiding principles and to the new core curriculum which took effect in the fall of 1996

2. Spreading the message and the vision through collaborative efforts (for example, participation in the University Institutes on Ecology and Justice and the Arts); spin-offs like the campus community garden; and service on the planning and steering committees of the three-year, $700,000 grant project, Leadership for a Just World, funded by the James Irvine Foundation

3. Planning for and establishing of the interdisciplinary community studies minor in the College of Arts and Sciences

4. Developing a new policy requiring that the director of the Eastside Project qualify for and hold a permanent faculty appointment

5. Creating an advisory board to make it possible for 100 Latino students from the local community each year for the next ten years to be admitted into and graduate from Santa Clara University

To strengthen the crucial faculty role in Santa Clara's program and to meet the new challenges of embodying the Eastside vision in the community studies minor, the university has now hired Pia Moriarty as the director. Dr. Moriarty has an extensive theoretical and experiential background in such areas as social and cultural anthropology, education and sociocultural change, social analysis, participatory research, and the pedagogy of Paolo Freire.

## STRUCTURES AND STRATEGIES

The Eastside Project is one of a number of special academic programs—for example, ethnic studies, women's studies, international programs, environmental studies, and the honors program—that Santa Clara University offers to complement the degree programs of the undergraduate College of Arts and Sciences, School of Engineering, Leavey School of Business Administration, and Division of Counseling Psychology and Education.

### Budget

For fiscal year 1997, the Eastside Project has a budget of $162,636. Paid staff include a full-time director, who holds a faculty appointment; three professional staff with ten-month contracts: the placement coordinator at 80% time, the learning coordinator and administrative assistant each at 50% time; student workers for roughly 30 hours per week during the heart of each academic quarter and 50 hours per week at the opening of each quarter. Is this adequate for the task, especially given the new planning and activities connected with the community studies minor? Up to now, even if it were evident that the budget was inadequate, there was no way of increasing it, except by generating new revenues of some kind. However, commencing with the budget preparation process for the fiscal year 1998, the university has in place a strategic planning document, approved by the Board of Trustees on May 10, 1996, that provides some clear criteria for departmental budgeting. Budget requests are to be weighed according to the extent to which they advance the following strategic initiatives to take Santa Clara to the year 2001:

- *Community of scholars*: Foster a vital intellectual community whose members collaborate as partners in learning and scholarship.

- *Integrated education*: Foster the education of the whole person in a learning environment that enables people to make connections among different forms of knowledge, understanding, and experience.

- *Continuous improvement*: Implement ongoing processes to improve the quality of academic programs and administrative services based on evidence of performance outcomes.

- *Resources for excellence*: Develop the human, physical, technological, and financial resources necessary for excellence in teaching, learning, and scholarship.

### Faculty Involvement

Though the program was initiated by faculty and depends on faculty initiative, ingenuity, and commitment for its effectiveness, faculty participation is completely voluntary and informally arranged. The Eastside Project has no formal relationship with departments other than the program council of the newly established community studies minor. Nor has participation in the community-based learning program been factored into the criteria for advancement in rank and tenure.

Nonetheless, some 96 faculty members have availed themselves of the program at one time or another during its first decade, while 58 continue to use it on a regular basis. Of the 58 regularly participating faculty, as of the academic year 1996–97, 21 are tenured, 14 tenure track, and 23 senior lecturers or adjunct faculty. Except for one in the accounting department and three in education, all participating faculty members are in the College of Arts and Sciences. Of the 16 departments represented in the program, psychology, communication, and anthropology/sociology boast the largest number of courses and faculty involved, followed in descending order by modern languages and literatures, religious studies, political science, English, ethnic studies, philosophy, theater and dance, biology, music, art, and history.

Meanwhile, faculty in the natural sciences and the schools of business and engineering either have not been interested for one reason or another or have come to the conclusion that, if the nature of their discipline does not preclude the appropriate use of community-based learning with the underserved, they at least have not found it feasible. It is anticipated that the development of the interdisciplinary community studies minor and systematic participatory research will encourage faculty and departments in other disciplines to reexamine the question of whether an element of community-based pedagogy could not enhance one or another course in their disciplines.

Possibilities are already being explored, for example, of broadening the scope of an innovative interdisciplinary course within the School of Engineering by including scholars in the social sciences, philosophy, and religious studies in the dialogue as well as by introducing an element of community-based participatory research. Called simply The City, this course puts civil, computer, electrical, and mechanical engineering majors together to design cross-disciplinary projects that would contribute to a well-designed city.

Eight to ten faculty members, chosen by their peers, make up the internal advisory committee known as the Eastside Project Faculty Associates. Associates meet once or twice each quarter and generally make themselves available for individual consultation with their colleagues on experiential learning and the integration of community-based learning into courses. The faculty associates also assist staff in conducting an annual five-day faculty training workshop and occasional shorter sessions calculated to enhance effectiveness in the integration of this kind of community-based learning into the curriculum. Professors are also encouraged to broaden and deepen their knowledge of experiential learning in dialogue with people in need by participation in conferences and other events sponsored by professional organizations such as the National Society for Experiential Education (NSEE).

## Staff: Who Does What?

Reporting to the associate vice president for academic affairs, the director of the Eastside Project attends principally to faculty development, design and direction of the community-based curriculum, and overall review of the department's effectiveness in meeting its responsibilities for educating the university community to the needs, issues, and perspective of marginalized groups. The director holds a joint faculty appointment with the teacher education and undergraduate liberal studies divisions, both within the College of Arts and Sciences. The director also serves as a member of the community studies minor program council and has primary responsibility for the introductory and capstone community studies courses.

Within the Eastside Project the director works closely with two staff assistants: the coordinator of placements and the coordinator of student learning. The coordinators, with the help of an administrative assistant and several student workers, administer the diverse components and countless details of day-to-day operations: inviting, receiving, and processing faculty and agency applications to participate in the program; developing partnerships with the representatives of the participating community agencies; advising faculty, students, and agencies on their respective roles in achieving the mission and goals of the program; quarterly registration, placement, and orientation of students in the community setting most appropriate for them and the course they are taking; practical arrangements for fingerprinting, tuberculosis testing, transportation, as well as maintenance and servicing of vehicles; on-site supervision of students, facilitation of the process of critical reflection on and integration of experience in the community; and the administration of quarterly surveys and evaluations.

In sum, the staff sets up the environment and support system through which the three sets of key players—faculty, community representatives, and students—are enabled to concentrate on the hard work of integrating theoretical investigation with direct personal encounters with people who are socially neglected and economically overlooked. At the risk of oversimplifying, one can say that while the staff work together holistically and as a team, the director's attention is directed to faculty, the placement coordinator concentrates on the community agencies in which the students are placed, the learning coordinator focuses on the supervision and guidance of students, and the administrative assistant manages the office and material resources, as well as the clerical and technical support system.

In addition to handling office work, database input, generation of reports, and care of automobiles, student workers have gradually assumed greater responsibilities such as periodic telephone surveys of their peers. During the summer of 1996, selected students were trained for service as small group discussion animators for the process of critical reflection on experience in the community. This training of student discussion facilitators is a joint venture with the Center for Student Leadership, a division of student development, and Santa Clara University's Markkula Center for Applied Ethics, which is interested in developing the ability of faculty and students to recognize and address the ethical dimension of personal experiences in the community through the various disciplines.

Finally, a word needs to be said about the relationship between the Eastside Project and Santa Clara University's new community studies minor instituted at the end of the spring 1996 quarter as an interdisciplinary program within the College of Arts and Sciences. The idea of the community studies minor emerged in a discussion of the Eastside Project faculty associates about what shape or direction the Eastside Project should take as a way of institutionalizing within the curriculum the university's preferential option for the poor. The Eastside Project Director and Faculty Associate Rose Marie Beebe took an active role in the work of the ad hoc faculty committee that formed to develop a proposal for a community studies minor.

Some foresee community studies developing beyond the minor into a more ambitious operation. If that should happen, it seems reasonable to expect the Eastside Project to find a structural home as part of a department of community studies. Initially, however, the Eastside Project and the community studies minor, while closely interlinked, maintain separate identities, budgets, and lines of accountability.

## Conclusion

From the beginning, our key strategy at Santa Clara University has been listening to and letting the community shape the Eastside Project agenda. We have stayed faithful to that policy as we have developed the proposal for the community studies minor, convening focus groups with our collaborators in the community-service agencies and on our advisory board. It should also be noted that our advisory board has challenged us to another important strategic initiative for the transformation of Santa Clara University, as well as for the achievement of our long-term goal of active solidarity with the community.

Call this, if you will, the "mutual carrying of one another in faith" (Sobrino, 1994) phase of bridge-building. The Eastside Project and, in some sense at least, the Santa Clara administration has accepted the advisory board's proposal to enable 100 new Latino students from the local community, each year for ten years, to qualify for and graduate from Santa Clara University.

Father Mateo Sheedy, the champion of the poor who serves as pastor of Sacred Heart Church near downtown San Jose, was the original author of this proposal and pushed it for three years. He has made it clear that the Latino students we are talking about are the real flesh-and-blood children of our neighborhoods, and the precious people who inspired the founding of the Eastside Project as a two-way bridge between their neighborhoods and the university.

These are the youth who live in Sacred Heart Parish and Most Holy Trinity Parish and other neighborhoods where they often find themselves up against insuperable odds. These are the hidden children who find themselves more and more neglected and rejected by the prevailing culture and economy, and whom the Eastside Project purports to embrace on behalf of the university as the youth of our neighborhood.

From this perspective, we are not talking about competing with Stanford, Harvard, or the University of California system for the cream of the crop of those whose skin is dark or who have ethnic minority surnames. We are competing with the county jail and the local fast-food joints. And the ones for whom we are competing are the ones no one else wants. These are the ones that our faith tells us are God's loved ones, the ones in whom God chooses to be most actively present. We need them at Santa Clara University. And that is why this proposal does not represent an act of faith only, but a wise and profoundly practical decision.

Nor does this radical proposal suggest for a minute that Santa Clara should lower its standards or compromise academic excellence in order to be able to welcome these young people. We are talking about taking the steps necessary, in solidarity with the community, to make sure they are motivated and prepared to get into and make it at Santa Clara, just as the farm worker boy, Francisco Jiménez, was motivated and prepared to go through Santa Clara, earn his doctorate at Columbia, and become a scholar, author, and sometimes high-level administrator at Santa Clara University.

And so, we choose to target these neighbors of ours, not only for their sakes, but for the major contribution their presence at Santa Clara University will make to the transformation of this institution. We will get and maintain these students only to the extent that we learn how to welcome them and make them feel at home. A thousand of them over a decade will form a critical mass that can transform Santa Clara and, after Santa Clara, the world. They are our future.

*For actual Santa Clara University service-learning documents, see Appendix I: Educational Philosophy of the Eastside Project*

## REFERENCES

Arrupe, P., S.J. (1973). *Men for others*. Jesuit Conference-United States Assistancy, Washington, DC.

Cook, T. D., & Flay, B. R. (1978). The persistence of experimentally induced attitude change. In L. Berkowitz (Ed.), *Advances in experimental social psychology*, *V*, II. New York, NY: Academic Press.

Ellacuria, I. (1990). The task of a Christian university (undergraduate commencement address at Santa Clara University, June 1982). In J. Sobrino, I. Ellacuria, et al. (Eds.), *Companions of Jesus: The Jesuit martyrs of El Salvador*. Maryknoll, NY: Orbis Books.

Jiménez, F. (Ed.). (1987). *Poverty and social Justice: Critical perspectives, a pilgrimage toward our own humanity*. Tempe, AZ: Bilingual Press/Editorial Bilinge.

Kegan, R. (1982). *The evolving self: Problems and process in human development*. Cambridge, MA: Harvard University Press.

Privett, S. A., S.J., Gerdenio, M. M., S.J., Germann, D. V., S.J., & Miron-Conk, P. (1996). SCU's Eastside Project: Bridging the Chasm. In the Eastside Project's *Handbook of information*, (rev. 1st ed.).

Sholander, T., S.J. (1994, Winter). Am I my brother's keeper? Eastside as educational support program. In *The Bridge*, Santa Clara University Eastside Project Newsletter.

# 11

# We Make the Road by Walking: Building Service-Learning In and Out of the Curriculum at the University of Utah

Irene S. Fisher

*University of Utah*

## INTRODUCTION

Jen Moffatt, pacing through the union building with her characteristic Sherpa-style fleece hat pressed down over her brown curls, is the antithesis of the Generation X portrait of American college students. When Moffatt isn't studying for her environmental policy major or working at the university's outdoor recreation program, she is engaged with her major passions: environmental action and community service. Moffatt might be reflecting on the lessons she learned through the Student Environmental Advocates Project which she directed last year— lessons that might help her advise the new director of the Wildlife Project whom she's helping this year. Or she might be planning the next step in her Service-Learning Scholars Program: working to integrate service-learning into the College of Engineering and to publish a small book on reflection strategies for engineers. She's an engaging, intense, productive young woman, involved in both cocurricular and curricular service programs open to students through the Lowell Bennion Community Service Center at the University of Utah.

The Bennion Center, a student-affairs-based community service center where Moffatt wears her many service hats, has breached the wall between student affairs and academic affairs to offer Moffatt and other students over 60 cocurricular community service opportunities and nearly 90 curriculum-based service-learning courses and programs. The Lowell Bennion Community Service Center mobilizes some 5,000 campus citizens who give 80,000 to 100,000 hours of service to the community annually. Cocurricular and curricular service programs flourish side-by-side and continually grow in quality and quantity. The center's service activities are widely respected both on and off the campus with energy and enthusiasm still growing. Certainly continuous stumbling blocks exist as in any learning organization, but we learn from these experiences, strengthening the program further.

How can one understand the Bennion Center's development in a way that offers clues to center participants themselves and to others who are looking for models? What can be learned that is worth replicating? What weaknesses exist in some of the center's approaches? The nonidentical twin emphases of the Bennion Center—cocurricular and curricular service programs—each offer unique answers. Additionally, the Bennion Center's example may be of interest to those in community service centers who have seen the strong learning opportunities available through service but struggle with the task of building curricular connections.

## THE BENNION CENTER'S INSTITUTIONAL CONTEXT

Over 27,000 students—the majority commuters—attend the University of Utah, a major research institution located in Salt Lake City, a metropolitan area of just under one million people. In the recent past, the University of Utah has focused attention on strengthening undergraduate education, but the clear historical institutional priority and the faculty reward system, as in most institutions of its type, favor research. Promotion, retention, and tenure processes cite research, teaching, and service, but research is inarguably writ in larger letters.

The percentage of state funds supporting Utah higher education has eroded recently, and the legislature has set tuition rates that encourage enrollment in rapidly growing community colleges rather than the large state institutions. The resulting decline in enrollment has caused budget cuts at the University of Utah over the last few years. A mandated change from the quarter to a semester system in 1998 absorbs enormous faculty and administrative attention. Observers of the campus scene frequently note the high level of faculty and staff frustration with inadequate salary increases and the seeming lack of public support. Many of these factors might predict failure for those attempting to gain institutional support for service-learning, especially for those housed in student affairs.

Other less visible and infrequently acknowledged factors are more encouraging for service-learning advocates. Utah's struggling pioneers founded their flagship institution in the earliest days of Utah's history out of their strong belief in education and a value for community service. This service ethic is still visible in the university's mission statement: "The university's faculty, staff, and students are encouraged to contribute time and expertise to community and professional service, to national and international affairs and governance, and to matters of civic dialogue." The service ethic is also very much alive within the citizens of the state and was the focus of significant attention during the state's 1996 centennial year. Students have been readily attracted to community service offerings. When introduced to service-learning concepts, many faculty seem to readily reconnect with the motives for societal improvement that initially attracted them to teaching and find renewed energy as they explore this methodology.

## THE BEGINNING AND GROWTH OF THE CENTER'S COCURRICULAR FOUNDATION

The Lowell Bennion Community Service Center was born into this campus environment in the mid-1980s during the national wave of interest in campus community service brought on by the founding of the Campus Outreach Opportunity League (COOL), Campus Compact, and Stanford's Public Service Center, all of which contributed to the Bennion Center's development.

In 1985, a University of Utah graduate turned Palo Alto developer came in contact with the Stanford Community Service Center. He was impressed with the center and its mission and made a note to himself in his personal journal that the University of Utah could do the same thing in the name of Lowell Bennion, one of his heroes. This man of action—who prefers to remain anonymous—contacted Tony Morgan, the University of Utah's Vice President for Planning and Budget, offering a significant amount of money to begin an endowment for such a center.

Morgan initiated an exploration of the concept on campus and in the Salt Lake community, which ultimately resulted in the approval of the center's creation by the university's board of trustees. Morgan and others organized a board of advisers for the new center, developed a set of board bylaws and a mission statement, secured President Chase Peterson's agreement to join Campus Compact, recommended the center be located in student affairs and services offices, and initiated the search for a founding director.

Morgan and others received permission from Bennion (who died in 1996) to use his name for the center. During his career, he served as the first head of the Latter Day Saints' Institute of Religion at the University of Utah, as an associate dean of students, and as a faculty member of the sociology department. Following his academic retirement, he served as the director of the community services council, a multi-program human-service organization serving the Salt Lake community. He founded the Bennion Boys' Ranch in the Tetons. In Bennion's characteristically humble way, he resisted the suggestion of using his name, but ultimately agreed if it would help others.

In October 1987, I was hired as the founding director of the center to follow my passionate commitment to narrowing the gap between our society's professed values and the realities of poverty, injustice, violence, abuse, and environmental deterioration. At the time when I was selected as the center's director, I was directing Utah Issues, a nonprofit, low-income advocacy organization representing 13% of Utah's population who live below the poverty line. I had become convinced that more of the state's citizens needed to see these problems on a personal level if significant social change were to occur.

November 17, 1987, marked the birth of the Lowell Bennion Community Service Center when students, faculty, staff, and alumni of the University of Utah set out to save an old boarding house—home to 48 chronically mentally ill residents—that was slated to be closed by the Salt Lake City-County Board of Health. This service project, pictured on the front page of that Monday's campus newspaper, symbolizes the bias for action which has continuously characterized the center's participants and activities.

While state and higher education leaders fought a tax cap initiative that threatened all of higher education and particularly new programs, I stepped into a ten-by-seven foot-office with empty file folders, two desks turned on their sides, a phone with the wrong number printed on it so that people couldn't return calls, and a goal shared with a supportive group of people which soon won out over the physical limitations.

Within a month, eight student project directors—who barely knew what their job titles meant—became engaged in creating the center's first ongoing service projects, including partnerships with a local elementary school, an alcohol and drug recovery house, a literacy program, and a campus group for students with disabilities, as well as the Saturday Volunteers Corps. These student leaders and the center director traveled to their first Campus Outreach Opportunity League (COOL) conference at Stanford that spring and returned determined to live the theme of the conference—"ain't nothin' to it, but to do it."

## COCURRICULAR SERVICE LEARNING

### Cocurricular Student Leadership Development

From the beginning, the Bennion Center championed a student leadership model which empowers a student to take lead responsibility for each of the student-directed community service projects that the center offers. Each student project director agrees to lead a particular project for the academic year, receives training and ongoing support, and is reminded that "you are in charge of this project." As this model developed and the number of projects increased, a student coordinator—someone who previously directed a successful community service project—became needed to serve as the first line of support for a coordinating group of six to eight new project directors. Each coordinator also has a staff partner who serves as his/her first line of support.

Grouped by interest area as much as possible, these small coordinating groups provide a smaller home within the broader Bennion Center community. The groups support those students who take on significant leadership responsibility having little previous experience—but large amounts of enthusiasm and willingness to learn. Eight to ten coordinators meet weekly serving as the Bennion Center's cabinet or student planning and decision-making body. A student president provides the overall leadership for the student, or cocurricular, component of the Bennion Center.

The center experienced rapid initial growth: from eight ongoing student-directed service projects involving 546 volunteers in 1987–88 to 19 projects and 1,409 volunteers in 1988–89, and 27 projects and 2,762 volunteers in 1989–90. By 1992–93, the center was involving 5,000 volunteers per year in 45 projects and knew it had to curb its growth and focus on strengthening training, agency partnerships, and funding diversity. The center currently sponsors over 60 ongoing projects and continues to involve approximately 5,000 students annually in all its offerings.

In many ways, the Bennion Center looks like other comprehensive, student affairs-based community service programs across the country. The students who direct the 62 ongoing service projects provide the energy and foundation for all the cocurricular service activities at the center. Student volunteers serve children from at-risk environments, elderly people, those with mental and physical disabilities, refugees, recovering alcohol and drug abusers, the homeless, and many more. Students who direct projects receive ongoing training and are provided a high level of autonomy within the center's value system, liability constraints, and budget limitations. Academic credit for this normally cocurricular involvement exists, but students rarely seek it.

## Student Training and Summer Service Programs

Training is a key element for success in this student-led model. The center selects new project directors each spring, with the understanding they will assume leadership for their projects during the next academic year. Each new project director must attend a day of basic training, offered on multiple dates during the summer, which helps them learn the basics of volunteer recruitment, orientation, training, recognition, and reflection. All student leaders also participate in a two-day fall orientation just prior to the beginning of the school year which includes group service projects, community building experiences, and other skill building activities. Each Tuesday morning throughout the academic year, student leaders alternately attend community meetings with all directors and coordinating group meetings with the small supportive family of related project leaders. Both meetings offer community leadership skills, personal development opportunities, personal support, and a broader understanding of community issues.

All students applying to serve as coordinators engage in a summer of service with the Bennion Center through one of two programs. Three or four students each summer receive Bennion Center-Alumni Association fellowships which provide a $1,300 stipend, plus room and board, and the chance to serve full-time for ten weeks in a nonprofit organization in the community of their choice in the United States. Those selected must have directed a successful project in the previous year, plan to serve as a coordinator the following year, and be willing to share their learning with others in the center upon their return. Jonathan Jensen, for example, directed a project for the homeless during the 1995–96 academic year, worked with the Calvary Women's Shelter in Washington, DC the following summer, and currently supports a coordinating group of six new project directors leading the Bennion Center's partnerships at the Salt Lake Homeless Shelter and Resource Center, the (Homeless) Fourth Street Clinic, the School With No Name, and other sites.

Up to ten other students are selected to participate in the Bennion Center's summer Intensive Community Leadership Program, an eight-week, 200-hour, stipended program which includes 48 hours of group discussion, service, and learning, combined with an individualized service-learning plan for each student. Students plan and direct summer service projects, serve in community agencies that will broaden their learning, and prepare for their coordinator roles in the coming academic year. This preparation includes getting to know the new directors they will support and visiting the agency partners for the projects in their coordinating group.

## Unique Cocurricular Emphases

Several activities of the cocurricular component of the Bennion Center are unusual. A student-produced annual magazine, *Reflection*, periodic group reflection sessions for volunteers, winter retreats for student leaders, and several other offerings transform traditional service activities into rich community service-learning opportunities for the student directors and volunteers.

Students have developed and periodically revise a written document describing the values that center participants strive to embody in their shared work. Center participants intentionally and consciously strive to create an open, inclusive, caring, learning community across religion, race, gender, and political viewpoint. A stuffed koala bear called the Good-on'ya Guy circulates biweekly among student leaders who have exemplified the center's values through their actions. In defining these values, center participants have clearly articulated a desire to strive to live the elements of community described by Scott Peck in *The Different Drum: Community Building and Peace,* including the use of a consensus decision-making process which respects the views of all participants.

Most Bennion Center cocurricular projects provide opportunities for direct or indirect service. A few offer community organizing experiences. One public interest advocacy project organizes students to address legislative issues of their choice, advocating the issues in their own names, not in the name of the Bennion Center or the University of Utah. Increasingly, project directors want to move to public policy advocacy when they realize the limits of direct service and a need to change societal direction.

Bennion Center participants have developed a method for seeking consensus on advocacy initiatives or other types of center action initiatives which could be viewed as controversial among center participants. This consensus process has been used only twice, both times to seek group agreement on what actions the center should take to lower the incidence of AIDS/HIV among university students. Both times the consensus-building process has been painful because of the variety of viewpoints existing among Bennion Center participants. Both times the process has opened doors to rich and difficult learning opportunities as students attempted to listen—really listen—to people with widely divergent views and to assess their own capacity for respecting and working through differences.

## Cocurricular Organizational Structures

The organizational structure of the cocurricular arm of the Bennion Center reflects the desire to empower student leaders and to help them practice the skills of community service leadership by taking active responsibility for their projects. The message to new project directors is that "you are in charge." There are, however, some obvious limitations in regard to budget constraints, liability concerns, and the need to live within the center's values. Within those limits, students directing projects are encouraged to understand their issue or project, clarify their goals, and formulate and carry out the plans as they see as best.

The center's organizational structure reflects this emphasis on empowering individual leaders both to make decisions and move forward with their own plans, and to practice the skills and commitments of active community problem solving. Those new to the Bennion Center search in vain for the traditional organizational structure with its series of tiered boxes delineating a top-to-bottom hierarchy. Instead, the center's organizational chart, reflecting its empowerment orientation, looks more like concentric circles leading outward from a central staff and representative board of advisers to the community at large. Thus decision-making and action planning are highly decentralized.

Although students have been told that they are responsible for directing their projects, they still look for approval from above. Slowly they realize that the initial conversations were real: They can make their own decisions. The organizational and operating structure begins to make sense, as they find their place within the Bennion Center community and receive the support necessary to carry out their own community service leadership plans.

## Bennion Center Programs for Other Constituencies

The Bennion Center's mission calls for the involvement of university students, faculty, staff, and alumni. Thus, the center's organizational and program structure includes a university staff service committee which provides the leadership necessary to offer community service options to nearly 7,000 University of Utah staff members and their families. This 15–20 person group meets monthly and selects, organizes, and advertises periodic one-time service activities. Just over 70 identified staff liaisons encourage involvement from within their units. Over several summers, the group has invited interested offices to join in the summer service challenge and to organize their own co-workers to carry out a one-time service project in partnership with a community agency. Each year the committee has planned a summer service challenge kick-off event, a range of service options with identified community partners, and a final celebration. Approximately ten offices, such as career services, KUER radio, and the community relations office, have participated per year.

Since 1991, the center has organized Bennion Center alumni—past student leaders—in an informal network to encourage them to continue their service involvement after graduation. Each year all alumni are invited to a fall social evening and organizing meeting. Ten to 15 alums serve on a steering committee to identify and implement goals for the year which could include an alumni newsletter, periodic service events, and a fundraising phonathon. An alumni committee also selects the center's annual service award winners each spring. Other groups of alumni plan the final community meeting for current student leaders who reflect on their year's effort along with those who have gone through similar experiences.

The center maintains leadership programs for students, staff, and alumni—joined in a myriad of informal contacts—through Bennion Center staff connections and through a formal board of advisers. Representatives of the student, staff, and alumni components of the center serve along with faculty and community representatives on this board of advisers which thus unites all the center's constituencies for consideration of overall program direction. The 20-member board meets quarterly and has been charged with planning for the center's tenth anniversary and developing goals for its second decade.

An eight-person staff provides the other connecting tissue for all program elements. A director, administrative assistant, two full-time cocurricular service coordinators, two curriculum-based service-learning staff members, a half-time public relations director, a full-time VISTA volunteer, and a clerical support person comprise the paid staff of the Bennion Center.

## Funding the Center's Programs

The initial plan for funding the center envisioned raising a $1.2 million endowment, with earnings to constitute the annual operating budget. Today, the center's annual budget is just under $400,000, with two salaries and space deriving from university funds and the remainder from endowment earnings and community fundraising. As director of the center, I lead development efforts, with the support of the university's development office and the center's own development committee. The university is currently mobilizing for a major capital campaign, and the center is an active part of that effort. This funding arrangement is both good news and bad: The center is not limited by available university resources, but the effort to raise funds takes considerable staff time and energy. A major part of the tenth anniversary goal setting will focus on long-range plans for financial support of the center.

## CURRICULUM-BASED SERVICE-LEARNING: THE GROWTH AREA

In 1988, one year into the Bennion Center's existence as a community service program, I began to consider what the role of faculty should be in a center whose mission statement identifies its constituency as "students, faculty, staff, and alumni." In a fortunate coincidence, I received a document from Campus Compact written by Tim Stanton of the Stanford Public Service Center at Stanford University who raised questions about the nature of the faculty role in the growing campus community service movement and asked members to discuss these questions with their faculty.

## Public Service Professorship Award

In response to Stanton's challenge, the Bennion Center hosted a focus group discussion and gathered opinions from over 40 faculty members on their ideas about faculty involvement. One concrete result of the meeting was the idea for what became the Public Service Professorship Award. The Bennion Center organized a faculty advisory committee that was to implement the new award program and provide ongoing counsel and direction for building faculty roles into the center's activities and programs. The administration provided $20,000 to fund the first awards.

Both the award and the faculty advisory committee proved to be good beginnings in building the center's faculty connections, although the phrase "service-learning" was still not part of our vocabulary. The faculty advisory committee, initially composed of 15 highly respected faculty members with personal interests in the center's activities, was and still is a key element in maintaining academic credibility for the center's curriculum-based programs and activities.

The committee's first tasks were to create the Public Service Professor Award purpose statement, identify criteria for winners, issue an invitation to apply or nominate faculty, and select the recipients. The award essentially created a funded opportunity for one or two faculty members annually to develop a service-learning course or academically based community project. Faculty members who are selected receive release time to develop the ideas described in their proposals. Their departments receive $4,000 to cover the release time. The one or two faculty members selected each year became the pioneers in course-based service-learning at the University of Utah and received recognition at commencement and in the community. This award still exists in a modified form, and a growing gallery of Public Service Professors' pictures are visible in the foyer outside the Olpin Union Panorama Room, the campus dining room used frequently by faculty and guests.

The first two Public Service Professors selected were Carol Werner, Professor of Psychology, and Doug Rollins, Professor of Pharmacy, both tenured with strong teaching and research records. Werner, a social psychologist with a personal interest in environmental issues, modified a course to include an action research component in which students studied behavior and attitude change and then applied their learning to recycling problems in Salt Lake City. Students developed interventions which they applied with residents in a selected neighborhood. They followed the recycling truck on its weekly rounds to determine the effectiveness of their various interventions and made recommendations to the mayor's recycling committee on the most effective ways to increase recycling participation.

Rollins developed and taught a new elective pharmacy course in which students surveyed the Salt Lake community for needs which required pharmacy expertise and incorporated knowledge gained from this program into subsequent College of Pharmacy service-learning courses.

## Designation of Service-Learning Courses

As the Bennion Center ventured further into the academic arena and considered more service-learning initiatives, center staff began to see a need to develop criteria by which to judge whether or not a course should be considered service-learning. The faculty advisory committee accepted the challenge of creating such criteria and identified eight factors which seemed to summarize the elements necessary to distinguish a service-learning course. The process of developing these criteria provided an important learning opportunity for committee members who in turn helped to educate others within their own circles of influence.

The eight criteria identified by the faculty advisory committee draw heavily upon concepts articulated in *Principles of Good Practice for Service and Learning* developed by service-learning practitioners at the Wingspread Conference Center. These eight criteria have served well in the ongoing process of designating service-learning classes. The Bennion Center is developing a ninth criterion, the first change since the other eight were adopted. This addition will assure that faculty members offer a wide enough selection of service opportunities within a given course, so that no student will be forced to contribute a personal effort that has real world consequences to a community initiative with which he or she has serious disagreement.

## Service-Learning Scholars Program

Another significant step in creating the foundation for curriculum-based service-learning was the birth of the Service-Learning Scholars Program in 1991. This program, created through strong and effective student leadership, provides a structured opportunity for interested students to complete 400 hours of journal-documented community service, 15 hours of service-learning courses, and a final integrative service project which meets a recognized community need. The service-learning scholar selects a faculty-student-community committee that will oversee his or her work. Six to eight service-learning scholars have completed the program requirements and been recognized at commencement each year since its inception. Nearly 100 students are now actively engaged in the program although, due to staff limitations, the center has not publicized the program beyond word-of-mouth. The process of securing institutional approval for the program was remarkable: It was initiated and instituted within one academic year with a high level of support and ownership among student government leaders, faculty decision-makers, and the administration.

Since the approval of the Service-Learning Scholars Program, the Bennion Center has been assigned to determine which courses can bear the label of service-learning. Because the Service-Learning Scholars Program requires 15 hours of service-learning course work, there is a need to designate the courses which satisfy this requirement.

The center's faculty advisory committee made the process for designating courses service-learning as simple and nonbureaucratic as possible. After a period of consultation with Bennion Center staff, a faculty member wishing to have a course recognized as service-learning submits a summary to the faculty advisory committee. The summary describes briefly how the course addresses each of the eight criteria. Once approved, a small "sl" precedes the course number for these courses in the course catalog, and all service-learning courses are listed together in a special section of the catalog.

The University of Utah offers 85 officially recognized service-learning courses, embedded within 45 academic departments and eight colleges. Most of these courses are faculty dependent; i.e., only when a certain faculty member teaches the course will it be taught as a service-learning course.

## Service-Learning Course Development

The prospect of having service-learning scholars, generally viewed as highly motivated students, incites faculty to seek the service-learning designation for their classes. The Bennion Center offers additional incentives to encourage service-learning course development. The public service professorship was the first of these. A teaching assistant program provides first-time faculty members who are experimenting with service-learning an experienced service-learning student—which is probably the best incentive developed to date. A teaching assistant can help with community contacts, lead reflection sessions, and generally support the service component of the course. To be included in the teaching assistant selection pool, students must have prior experience in organizing service opportunities and participate in additional training. Almost all teaching assistants are undergraduates who have directed one of the Bennion Center's cocurricular projects.

## Borchard-Bennion Service-Learning Teaching and Research Project

An offer of financial support from a California foundation was the impetus for yet another of the Bennion Center's early service-learning initiatives: the three-year Borchard-Bennion Service-Learning Teaching and Research Project. This project offered an opportunity for four faculty members, each in in different disciplines, to teach a traditional course in the first year of the grant with release time to develop a service component for that course. In the second year of the grant, faculty taught courses with the service component included, and in the third year they revised and taught the courses again based on their own, as well as their students' learning outcomes. Another faculty member, who subsequently became the university's graduate school dean, organized a qualitative research design to assess outcomes in each of the three years. The faculty members involved were from communication, engineering, pharmacy practice, and special education. The four met quarterly with Bennion Center staff and the researcher to discuss their experiences, share ideas, problem solve, and discuss community contacts. The energy created among the faculty and others who observed the three-year project escalated campus support for service-learning.

Through a follow-up grant which will continue for eight years, the Borchard Foundation provides annual support to a Borchard-Bennion Service-Learning Faculty Fellow. The award offers recognition plus a $4,500 cash grant. The fellow promotes service-learning course development among faculty. In the initial year, Nancy Nickman, Professor of Pharmacy Practice, offered three faculty roundtables to discuss various aspects of service-learning. The second year, Doug Perkins, Professor of Family and Consumer Studies, continued the roundtables and created a local service-learning listserv. In 1996, Marshall Welch, Professor of Special Education, led a book discussion group for faculty and students, conducted several faculty discussion groups, and organized a service-learning conference in partnership with the newly formed Utah Campus Compact. All three have furthered service-learning course offerings within their own colleges and have assisted as needed in other tasks. Nickman was awarded the national Campus Compact's Thomas J. Ehrlich Faculty Award for service-learning in 1995–96 for her service with the center.

In 1993, the Bennion Center was awarded a service-learning grant from the then Commission on National and Community Service. This grant enabled the center to hire one staff person to focus exclusively on the development of academically based service-learning programs. A 1995 grant from a private foundation added a second staff person to support these activities. These two people, along with a full-time VISTA volunteer and intermittent student clerical staff, struggle to support the service-learning scholars, faculty, the faculty advisory committee and its three subcommittees, and a departmental initiative. These grants have provided critically needed funds to initiate curriculum-based service-learning programs. The University of Utah is now seeking ways to continue this and additional funding. A legislative funding initiative was considered in the January 1997 legislative session.

## Institutionalizing Service-Learning within Academic Departments

The Bennion Center's most recent curriculum-based service-learning initiative is perhaps its most ambitious and potentially important. Designed to institutionalize service-learning within academic departments, this initiative grows out of all the prior learning of the Bennion Center and out of a year's work by a faculty advisory subcommittee. This subcommittee, lovingly dubbed the "WOW" Committee, looked at "whether or why" to institutionalize service-learning within academic departments at the university. The committee's work produced an important document, the WOW Document, which presents a rationale for the integration of service-learning at this institution. It concludes that higher education has a responsibility to develop in students the broad background of a liberal education, the skills of a professional, and the skills and commitments of an active citizen. The document suggests that socially responsive knowledge is the reasonable outcome of service-learning and needs to be a valued part of a university education.

The process of creating the document educated key faculty members as to the importance of this ingredient of higher education and created articulate and vocal proponents for service-learning. Professor Irwin "Irv" Altmann, a highly respected psychology scholar and former University of Utah Academic Vice President, chaired the subcommittee and became particularly convinced of the value of this pedagogy for educational reform. He has become an effective spokesperson through presentations to the council of academic deans, the academic senate, and individual faculty.

Subsequent to the completion of the WOW Document, the Bennion Center's faculty advisory committee charged the subcommittee to work with Bennion Center staff to begin to institutionalize service-learning within departments. In the first year of this effort, the vice president of academic affairs, the vice president for student affairs, and the president all provided funds to enable the Bennion Center to invite academic departments into a partnership agreement to build service-learning into their course offerings. Eight departments accepted the offer and are one year into their initiatives, which include a variety of actions. The department of communication, for example, has modified its basic research methods course to be taught as a service-learning course when any of eight faculty members teach it. Family and consumer studies has added eight new service-learning courses; the department of psychology has added five and created a departmental service-learning committee to explore future initiatives. The English department created a course called Literature of Social Reflection: Homelessness, which will be taught regularly by other faculty who will create their own subtitles. The department of modern dance surveyed the community for its needs and interest in dance as a step toward creating a dance outreach program. The College of Medicine has researched what other institutions are doing with service-learning, as part of a long-term curriculum reform initiative.

In the second year of this initiative, the same funding sources, plus the vice president for health sciences, pledged funds to continue to expand the institutionalization initiative. Bennion Center staff believe that ten to thirteen departments will respond with interest in developing partnerships.

This summary of curriculum-based service-learning progress greatly understates the amount of effort necessary on the part of a small but constantly growing base of Bennion Center staff, faculty, and student advocates. The process used to build enthusiasm has been one of persuasion: sharing specific examples of successful service-learning courses, telling stories about the community impact of university action, students talking to students and faculty about the impact of service-learning on their education and personal development, and meetings, meetings, meetings. Advocates for service-learning courses have woven the vibrant threads—their own personal belief in the power of such learning to change lives and to change society—into the fabric of the institution.

As part of the center's tenth anniversary planning process, the faculty advisory committee will help the Bennion Center establish goals for curriculum-based service-learning for the next decade. This assignment requires those involved in the institutionalization initiative to look further into the future and to develop a shared vision of the next steps necessary to reach their service-learning goals.

## BENEFITS AND TENSIONS OF JOINT COCURRICULAR/CURRICULAR SERVICE-LEARNING INITIATIVES

Both cocurricular and curricular service programs thrive and grow within a common campus home at the Bennion Center. Is this a positive, effective organizational arrangement to maximize service-learning on the campus? There is little doubt that this co-housing arrangement provides more benefits than problems in the particular circumstances which exist on this campus. Several ingredients have been essential to making this arrangement work, however, and without them another arrangement might be preferable.

The arrangement requires flexibility and collaboration between two major divisions of an institution: academic and student affairs. More specifically, the vice presidents for academic and student affairs must be willing to share reporting lines, financial support, and responsibility for outcomes. The director of the service-learning program must have ready access to both vice presidents without worry about conflicting interests. During the center's development, and within the administrations of two consecutive presidents and two different vice presidents for student affairs, this healthy collaboration has been possible at the University of Utah.

Those responsible for service-learning program development must simultaneously be inclined to respect traditional organizational patterns and be willing to move beyond them in the interest of furthering the objectives of the service-learning program. A willingness to take risks on behalf of the program's objectives is critical to the success of this model.

Student energies and community goodwill generated from the cocurricular service programs provide two major sources of energy for the growth of both types of service initiatives. The ability of students to gain approval of the Service-Learning Scholars Program provides a clear example of this situation. Faculty members who have been introduced to service-learning through student persuasion provide another indicator of this student power.

Many student leaders of Bennion Center cocurricular projects serve as teaching assistants for new service-learning courses. These undergraduate students essentially share with their faculty colleagues what they have learned through directing their own cocurricular projects. Faculty members are almost universally impressed with the knowledge and commitment of these outstanding students.

Service-learning faculty members frequently refer their students to specific types of service placements within the Bennion Center's cocurricular projects. This arrangement benefits the projects as they obtain committed, informed participants; it also benefits faculty members who lack the confidence, knowledge, or time to make their own community placements.

In addition to these positive aspects of housing cocurricular and curricular service programs together, there are tensions. The working relationships between student project directors and faculty members using those projects for service-learning course placements must be carefully monitored and problems quickly addressed. To minimize confusion and additional work within agencies, the community contact people relating to both types of programs must understand the origin and responsibilities of the students who come into their agencies. Program staff involved with each type of program must be able to see the larger vision of civic education for all students, regardless of the type of program in which they are involved.

Bennion Center staff are currently engaged in a conversation about a perceived value imbalance between the cocurricular and curricular service programs within the center and within the university community. The level of concern about this issue within the center is not yet clear. But most institutions of higher education have a bias toward learning which bears academic credit and a tendency to undervalue cocurricular programs and learning. This real or perceived value imbalance will need to be addressed within the Bennion Center and possibly within any similar model which combines curricular and cocurricular service programs. The use of the term service-learning bears careful scrutiny in relationship to this issue. General definitions of service-learning embrace both classroom and nonclassroom-imbedded programs. Yet in the shorthand of the field, the term service-learning is frequently used—as in this volume—to mean only that service and learning which occur within a course or other credit bearing program. The Bennion Center is searching for less cumbersome language which articulates our belief that service and learning can be powerful transformative tools within structured credit or noncredit bearing settings.

## KEY FACTORS IN THE DEVELOPMENT OF A SERVICE CENTER

Almost any person who knows the Salt Lake area well would agree that a center named for Lowell Bennion could be predicted to have a positive and highly regarded program, matching the reputation Bennion developed during his years of active service to others. Regarded as a saint by some and as a friend by all who knew him, Bennion embodied service, respect for all people, intellectual acuity, strong social justice advocacy, and so much more. His name itself has been a key factor in gaining respect for the center. Bennion did not give the money for the center as some expect. As has been noted, an anonymous benefactor and admirer of Bennion gave an initial gift to the center's endowment conditional upon the use of Bennion's name. One phone call illustrates what this name has meant to the Bennion Center. A woman, extremely frustrated at being referred from one human service agency to another, called the Bennion Center, because, she said, any center with Bennion's name on it would certainly be able to help her.

### Initial Planning

The careful planning and preparation done by Tony Morgan, Vice President for Budget and Planning, was key to the center's success. Morgan consulted with all the players within the university and in the community who would have an interest in the center's existence, gaining the support and buy-in crucial to the center's ability to rapidly move forward. Student body leaders, faculty, the board of trustees, and potential community partners were all consulted and represented on the initial board of advisers created to hire the first director and to consult on program operations.

### Encouraging Leadership Among Students

As the first and only director, I have also played an important role in shaping the center's culture, structure, and bias toward action. Those responsible for hiring selected a community activist from off-campus, rather than an academician and scholar. My strengths included a passionate knowledge of the social problems facing the Salt Lake community, an awareness of the potential partner agencies addressing these problems, and personal friendships within the community developed through 20 years of activism. A corresponding weakness included my limited knowledge of the campus culture and organizational patterns, a deficiency that needed to be corrected quickly by students and faculty who became my teachers. I also believe in the power of people, choosing to guide rather than control emerging leaders who strengthen the center's programs.

This desire to encourage rather than control leadership is evident in the basic structure of the cocurricular student component of the center. The center acts on the belief that people of reasonable intelligence and personal strength who have a strong desire to make a difference can lead. From the outset, students selected projects, developed projects, implemented projects, faced the consequences of their choices with the support and positive responses from other participants, and learned in the process. The message "you're in charge" continues to frighten and excite students who assume leadership responsibilities. The energies created by those assuming these leadership responsibilities have fueled the center's growth. This factor, as much as any other single element, is the source of the Bennion Center's successes. One constant conversation within the Bennion Center is how to enable student leaders to learn by doing, how to maintain quality programs while allowing students to learn by seeing the consequence of their actions, and how to support rather than control. Finding this balance and trust is essential to preparing students for current and future community leadership roles. During the center's initial years, it was a common occurrence for a student to come into my office, describe a community need and possible action response, and to leave with the leadership charge to propose and work with the center to develop a project based upon that idea. Many of the center's current projects began in just this manner; however, the rapid growth of participation has limited the center's capacity to say "go for it" as regularly as it did in the past.

## Taking Action and Making Up the Rules Along the Way

The center's bias toward action has been a source of surprise and strength in a reflective scholarly campus environment. Service was the first activity of the center. Its organizational structure has developed secondarily, to support the active service already underway. Thus, especially during the first five years of the center's life, the players "made the road by walking." The first student president of the cocurricular component of the center once remarked that he thought we should probably close the doors of the center after about five years and start over, because the excitement of making up the rules as we went along created such positive energy. After eight years, this spirit has lessened, but is still visible.

Another indicator of this bias toward action was visible at nearly every center-sponsored group service project during the initial years. I always served alongside the students. The message: Service is for everyone. This message continues to be visible as staff and board members participate as frequently as possible in the center's service activities. The deans of the colleges of business and law have each modeled this behavior for their students at college-wide service projects. Painting a house or laying sod with a law school dean, a vice president for student affairs, or a respected faculty member provides an important egalitarian message to student service participants.

## Fulfilling the Pledge to Integrate Service-Learning into the Curriculum

Active student leaders were not only key developers of cocurricular service projects; they also led the creation of the Service-Learning Scholars Program, the linchpin of the center's curricular offerings. A Bennion Center volunteer running for student body president in 1990 promised to integrate service into the curriculum if elected. After a successful campaign, Andy Cooley created a three-person committee to carry out his campaign pledge. The president of the Bennion Center's cocurricular component, an Associated Students of the University of Utah (ASUU) representative, and the senior class president set out to fulfill Cooley's pledge within one year. They developed the basic idea for what became the Service-Learning Scholars Program and began a highly systematic plan to consult and revise and consult and revise with every key person and group on campus that needed to accept the idea. Their efforts culminated in academic senate approval and board of trustees sign-off within their one-year timeframe. This accomplishment would have been impossible for anyone other than students. When asked at any point, "What's your rush?" they simply reported that they would graduate that year, and they had to finish their task. To many people's amazement, usually recalcitrant faculty and administrative committees respected their goals and their advocacy approach, and said yes.

Students have been equally successful in convincing faculty members to teach service-learning courses and in helping faculty members learn how to make community contacts and how to lead reflection sessions. The strengths and capacities of undergraduate students are resources that have been incredibly valuable to the center, and their involvement in the development of service-learning has strengthened their own education. Indeed, Andrea Pinnock, one of the three students leading the charge for the Service-Learning Scholars Program, realized that her involvement in that effort was itself a service-learning experience in higher education policy development.

Academic credibility is a high need for a service center housed in student affairs and working in the academic arena. Highly respected faculty members who have been willing to serve as informal advisers and as members of the center's faculty advisory committee have assured that credibility. A much respected dean of liberal education sat on the initial center organizing committee and offered informal consultation to the center's director throughout the early years. The first chair of the faculty advisory committee was a highly regarded vice president for health sciences. A nationally known psychology scholar who formerly served as department chair and vice president for academic affairs has been a lead advocate for service-learning, articulating the center's message forcefully but with good humor. These individuals, plus many others from each college who have created service-learning courses, approved service-learning classes, selected public service professors, and created the basic philosophical document which guides the center's service-learning programs.

## Creating the Faculty Advisory Committee: A Working Committee

The creation of the faculty advisory committee in the early years of the center was in itself a key developmental factor. This group, with a representative of each college, gave visibility to faculty involvement and opportunity for regular consultation on program direction. Although the faculty representatives are technically named by the university president, Bennion Center staff consult with other faculty to identify candidates who have professional credibility and personal interest in the center's programs. The faculty advisory committee name is definitely misleading. This is a working committee. Members have always been actively involved in the work of creating the center's service-learning programs and have been willing to give time to this purpose. With leadership from Bennion Center staff, each faculty meeting is geared to consider alternatives, decide direction, and get important work done. Faculty members have often expressed their pleasure at working on a university committee that actually makes decisions and gets things done.

## Establishing Purpose: Socially Responsive Learning

A key element in shaping any new initiative is a broadly shared vision of the purposes of that initiative. Acting on that premise, in 1994 the faculty advisory committee undertook a critical piece of work. An outside evaluator observed in the prior year that although there was a great deal of energy and progress within the service-learning initiatives, there did not seem to be a shared vision of why the university should engage in service-learning. Responding to this challenge, the faculty advisory committee created the WOW Committee that charged itself with the task of creating a document articulating the shared vision. The process of creating that document was an important milestone in solidifying group purpose and direction. The document itself provided credibility to the effort and exposed more people on campus to the "why" of service-learning—socially responsive learning.

The availability of undergraduate teaching assistants to faculty teaching a service-learning course for the first time has been the single most important factor in encouraging course development. The support of the teaching assistant program's has encouraged faculty to move forward by easing initial community contacts and modeling reflection methodologies for both faculty and students in classroom.

## "WE MAKE THE ROAD BY WALKING"

Several years ago, I visited the Highlander Center outside Knoxville, Tennessee, and encountered the community organizing work of the center's founder, Myles Horton. Part of that powerful discovery included the book *We Make the Road By Walking*, a conversation between Myles Horton and the South American educator Paulo Freire. The title of that book offers a fitting concluding thought for this essay. Early leaders of the Lowell Bennion Community Service Center have practiced the belief that students, faculty, staff, and alumni who care about the problems they see in their communities, who want to connect their lives to others in those communities through service, who want to learn from that service, and who are willing to work to organize those opportunities for others, can find the path as they walk in service.

Jen Moffatt, the busy undergraduate student who works with both the Bennion Center's cocurricular and curricular service programs, has put herself in charge of her undergraduate education through her service-learning scholars project and her cocurricular environmental work. She will leave her mark on the Bennion Center, on her environmental community, and on the College of Engineering. And service-learning will leave its mark on her. She is still walking. We in the Bennion Center are still walking.

*For actual University of Utah service-learning documents, see*
    *Appendix A: Organization Chart*
    *Appendix B: Student Service-Learning Opportunities*
    *Appendix J: Educating the Good Citizen*

## REFERENCES

Horton, M., et al. (1991). *We make the road by walking*. Philadelphia, PA: Temple University Press.

Kendall, J. C., & Associates. (1990). *Combining service and learning: A resource book for community and public service.* Vol. 1. Raleigh, NC: National Society for Internships and Experiential Education.

Peck, M. Scott. (1988). *The different drum: Community making and peace.* New York, NY: Touchstone.

Stanton, T. K. (1990). *Integrating public service with academic study: The faculty role.* Providence, RI: Campus Compact.

# APPENDIX A
## Selected Service-Learning Organization Charts

### Appendix A-1
#### Brevard Community College

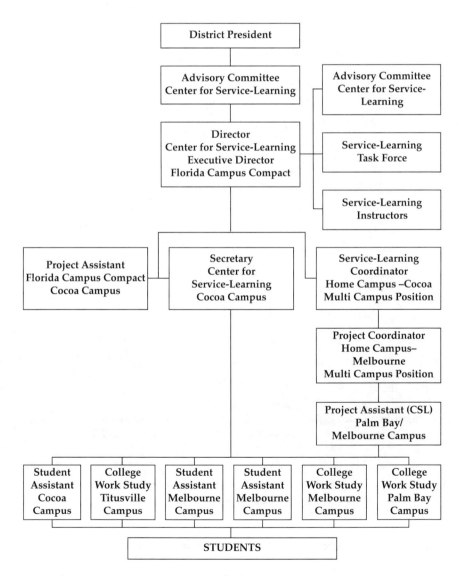

District President

Advisory Committee
Center for Service-Learning

Advisory Committee
Center for Service-
Learning

Director
Center for Service-Learning
Executive Director
Florida Campus Compact

Service-Learning
Task Force

Service-Learning
Instructors

Project Assistant
Florida Campus Compact
Cocoa Campus

Secretary
Center for
Service-Learning
Cocoa Campus

Service-Learning
Coordinator
Home Campus –Cocoa
Multi Campus Position

Project Coordinator
Home Campus–
Melbourne
Multi Campus Position

Project Assistant (CSL)
Palm Bay/
Melbourne Campus

Student
Assistant
Cocoa
Campus

College
Work Study
Titusville
Campus

Student
Assistant
Melbourne
Campus

Student
Assistant
Melbourne
Campus

College
Work Study
Melbourne
Campus

College
Work Study
Palm Bay
Campus

STUDENTS

# Appendix A-2
## North Carolina Central University

Chancellor Julius Chambers headed the administrative arm of the Community Service Program (CSP) at its inception. This provided the fledgling program with salient financial and institutional support. As of July 1, 1996, the CSP reported directly to the provost and vice chancellor for academic affairs. This transition was made to ensure that the efforts of the program continue to be regarded as integral to the university's academic objectives.

### Community Service-Learning Venture

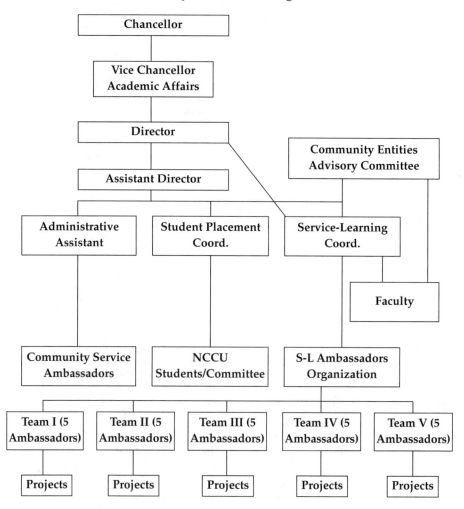

# Appendix A-3
## University of Pennsylvania

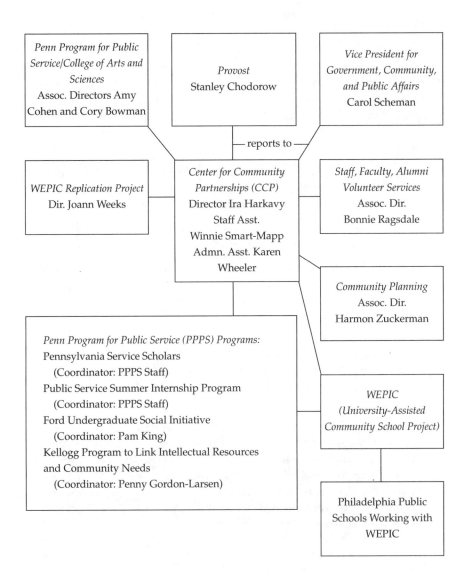

Penn Program for Public Service/College of Arts and Sciences
Assoc. Directors Amy Cohen and Cory Bowman

Provost
Stanley Chodorow

Vice President for Government, Community, and Public Affairs
Carol Scheman

— reports to —

WEPIC Replication Project
Dir. Joann Weeks

Center for Community Partnerships (CCP)
Director Ira Harkavy
Staff Asst.
Winnie Smart-Mapp
Admn. Asst. Karen Wheeler

Staff, Faculty, Alumni Volunteer Services
Assoc. Dir.
Bonnie Ragsdale

Community Planning
Assoc. Dir.
Harmon Zuckerman

Penn Program for Public Service (PPPS) Programs:
Pennsylvania Service Scholars
(Coordinator: PPPS Staff)
Public Service Summer Internship Program
(Coordinator: PPPS Staff)
Ford Undergraduate Social Initiative
(Coordinator: Pam King)
Kellogg Program to Link Intellectual Resources and Community Needs
(Coordinator: Penny Gordon-Larsen)

WEPIC
(University-Assisted Community School Project)

Philadelphia Public Schools Working with WEPIC

## University of Pennsylvania Position Descriptions

- Center Director Ira Harkavy supervises Center staff and directs Center programs. He also serves as associate vice president and reports to the vice president for government, community, and public affairs and to the provost.

- Center Staff Assistant Winnie Smart-Mapp, responsible for the Center's internal administrative, financial , and operational activities. Ms. Smart-Mapp also manages daily operation of the Center office. This includes supervising support staff and approximately 55 work-study students.

- Center Administrative Assistant Karen Wheeler provides administrative secretarial support to the associate vice president and director of the Center and to the Center in general.

- Senior Fellow Daniel Romer develops public health and education campaigns that link campus resources with the urban community.

- Associate Director of Staff, Faculty, and Alumni Volunteer Services Bonnie Ragsdale initiates, develops, and coordinates university staff, faculty, and alumni volunteer services in Philadelphia, particularly in West Philadelphia.

- Associate Director for the Program in Community Planning Harmon Zuckerman works with the West Philadelphia community to develop effective neighborhood plans, provide technical assistance to community organizations, and manage a geographic information systems (GIS) for West Philadelphia.

- Associate Director of the Penn Program for Public Service (PPPS) Cory Bowman reports to the director of the Center for Community Partnerships and the associate dean for undergraduate education in the School of Arts and Sciences. PPPS, the School of Arts and Sciences' office for the support and development of academically based community service, works to encourage and engage faculty, undergraduate, and graduate student academic activities with the Philadelphia community. The program encourages the development of university-public school partnerships. Bowman is the primary liaison with the University City and West Philadelphia High School clusters.

- Associate Director of Penn Program for Public Service (PPPS) Amy Cohen reports to the director of the Center for Community Partnerships and the associate dean for undergraduate education in the School of Arts and Sciences. Ms. Cohen is the primary liaison with Turner Middle School, a central site for the work of the Center and the West Philadelphia Improvement Corps (WEPIC), a university-assisted community school coalition.

- Director of the WEPIC Replication Project Joann Weeks reports to the director of the Center for Community Partnerships and the associate dean for undergraduate education in the School of Arts and Sciences. In November 1994, the DeWitt Wallace-Reader's Digest Fund made a three-year, $1 million grant to the University of Pennsylvania's School of Arts and Sciences to replicate nationally the West Philadelphia Improvement Corps (WEPIC) model of university-assisted community schools.

- Administrative Assistant of the WEPIC Replication Project Kimberlynn Taylor provides administrative and secretarial support to the director of the project and manages the replication office.

- Academic and Administrative Coordinator for the Kellogg Foundation–supported Program to Link Intellectual Resources and Community Needs at the University of Pennsylvania, Penny Gordon-Larsen coordinates relations among the undergraduates, graduate students, faculty, and community involved in the Kellogg Program. The academic and administrative coordinator is a full-time position designed for an advanced graduate student interested in academically based community service as a career.

- Grant Coordinator for the Undergraduate Social Science Initiative, Pamela L. King administers 19 undergraduate student internships and five graduate student teaching assistantships. She is also responsible for both administrative and programmatic oversight of the grant budget, coordination of a visiting fellows program, and grant-related seminars and meetings.

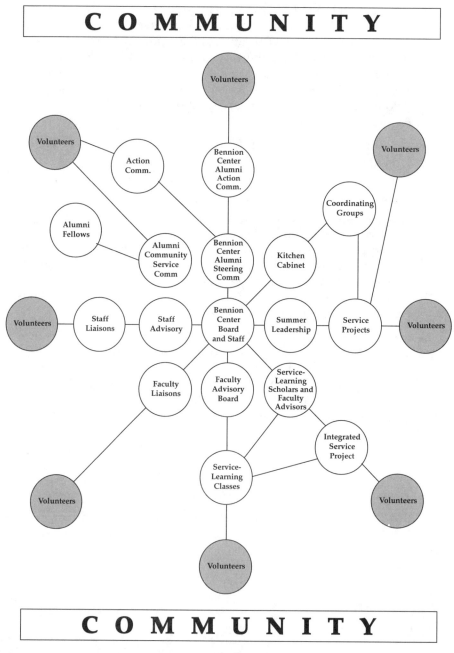

# APPENDIX B

## Selected Student Service-Learning Opportunity Overviews

### Appendix B-1

#### Categories of Student Positions  /  Bentley College

| | Community Scholarship Students | Community Work Program Students | Students in Internships | Students Doing Course Projects | Student Volunteers |
|---|---|---|---|---|---|
| *Number of hours per week* | 6–9 | 12–15 | 15–20 | varied | varied |
| *Duration of project* | Academic year | 1 semester | 1 semester | varied | varied |
| *Supervised by* | Coordinator of Student Programs | Coordinator of student Programs | Director of BSLP Internships | Faculty member | Volunteer center |
| *Students receive for service* | $2500 per semester | $7.00 hour | varied | none | none |
| *Academic or volunteer* | Volunteer/ Academic | Volunteer | Academic | Academic | Volunteer |
| *Purpose* | Work on a variety of academic or non-academic-based projects and serve as a community/ college liaison | Work on a variety of projects | Serve as professional business consultant | Work on discipline-specific project | Volunteer for various projects |
| *Phone number of supervisor or contact person* | (617) 891-2408 Jeannette MacInnes, BSLP Coordinator of Academic Programs | (617) 891-2408 | (617) 891-2534 | (617) 891-2977 Terry Robinson, BSLP Coordinator of Academic Programs | (617) 891-2433 |

# Appendix B-2

## *Continuum of Service and Learning Experience*

## Brevard Community College

| Service Opportunity | Co-curricular Community Service | Class related, Observational Assignments | Community/ Volunteer Service |
|---|---|---|---|
| Description | Episodic, short duration or special projects, usually 1–10 hours for specific service event. | Part of regular course assignment, 1–6 hours for points or percentage of grade. Students are oriented to service settings, societal concerns. | Student seek a voluntary/ service experience in a local service organization/project. Students usually volunteer 1–5 hours weekly. Student critically reflect on experience. |
| Example(s) | ▪ A Taste of Service Day ▪ Beach cleanup. ▪ Fundraising for runaway youth shelter. | ▪ Interview homeless service providers and prepare information speech. ▪ Visit (3) mental health agencies and prepare reflective report. | ▪ Serve meals to the homeless once per week for (3) months. ▪ Volunteer in hospital for (1) year, 12 hours monthly. ▪ Tutor a child for (2) hours weekly for 1 semester. |
| Service Opportunity | Service Pay | Service Learning Options Field Experiences | Community Service Credit/ 4th Credit Option |
| Description | Student serves in public service setting while receiving small stipend, scholarship, or pay. 2-12 hours weekly for semester | Service-learning options in regular classes usually 15–30 hours of service plus reflective writing tool for 5–40% of course grade. Often in lieu of term paper, essays, or exam. Students perform service as a way to gather, test, and apply content and skills of existing courses. | Student contracts with instructor or service-learning office. 20 hours of service, reflective journal, one required seminar. |
| Example(s) | ▪ Community service/learning for work study eligible students. ▪ Mini-grant school mentoring project which pays students minimum wage to tutor youth. ▪ $800 scholarship for outstanding student humanitarian. | ▪ Algebra: 15-20 hours of service to replace lowest test grade. ▪ Biology: 30 hours of service and essay for 10% of grade. ▪ Speech: At least 20 hours service, related analytical journal, and oral presentation for 60 additional class points toward grade. | ▪ Instructors offer an additional credit of Human Service Experience, SOW 1051 or 1052 or 1053. |

| Service Opportunity | Introductory Community Service Courses | Service-Learning Courses |
|---|---|---|
| *Description* | Community/public service is combined with classroom work to provide information, skill building, reflection, generalizing principles, assessment methods to help students serve and learn more effectively. Adaptable for various service-learning applications. | In-depth theoretical and practical courses which allow for maximum integration of service and classroom work. Satisifies social science general education requirement option. Reflection, action skill building, examination of theory/practice of citizenship. The 3,000 Gordon Rule requirement is fulfilled with journals, essays, or other reflective writing methods. |
| *Examples* | ■ Human Service Experience, SOW 1051, 1052, 1053, (1) credit hour elective, 20 hours of service, 4 seminars, and critical reflection (oral and written), can L(earn) total (3) credits.<br>* also used as fourth credit option. | ■ Community Involvement, SOW 2054, (3) credit hour elective, 32 hours of field experience combined with 16 hours of seminars. |

| Service Opportunity | Professional Development Offerings | Internships |
|---|---|---|
| *Description* | Seminars/Workshops/Courses offered to key constituents of service-learning: Instructors, student leaders, agency/service site personnel. Provide knowledge, skills for volunteer, and service-learning personal and community enhancement. | In-depth experiences usually toward the end of coursework. 6–20 hours weekly, but can be full-time (usually course prerequisites to enter). Individually arranged and tailored to student need. |
| *Examples* | ■ Volunteer/Leadership, LLX0064: A lifelong learning course for supervisors of volunteers, agency personnel, and student volunteer program leaders (30 hours of classroom work).<br>■ Teaching for Service Seminars: Inservice for instructors who use service-learning pedagogies. 15 hours of action and reflection learning strategies (graduate credit available).<br>■ Supervisor as Educator Workshops: Periodic seminars for agency supervisors of volunteers and students (usually 2–8 hours of training).<br>■ Community Involvement, SOW 2054: A course for recertification designed for elementary, middle, and high school teachers. | ■ Media Internships<br>■ International Service-Learning<br>■ Washington Intern Program<br>■ Other national, global immersion experiences<br>■ Medical field related internships |

# Appendix B-3

*Service-Learning Opportunities* / University of Utah

| Position | Time Commitment Responsibility | Service Achievement | Major Learning Available | Prerequisites |
|---|---|---|---|---|
| *CO-CURRICULAR* | | | | |
| *Casual Volunteer* | ■ irregular as schedule allows<br>■ short-term commitment<br>■ complete upon finishing task | ■ one-time, short-term help<br>■ frequently physical labor | ■ meet new population groups<br>■ glimpse of real community problems<br>■ skills and interest testing<br>■ basic understanding of community service | ■ personal interest<br>■ willingness and dependability |
| *Regular Committed Volunteer* | ■ regular or long-term commitment, usually one quarter or one year<br>■ 1–4 (or more) hours per week | ■ longer-term service tasks (tutor, mentor, befriend)<br>■ trusted, regular volunteer<br>■ higher skill level service possible | ■ deeper understanding of population/people<br>■ learning about agency, school, dominant problem<br>■ skills related to community need | ■ some criminal record checks<br>■ some experience with one-time volunteer services helpful<br>■ initiative<br>■ dependability<br>■ special skills for tasks tasks |
| *Committee Chair* | ■ short-term or ongoing generally 2–5 hours per week for period of commitment | ■ basic service<br>■ task of committee leadership to help group achieve tasks | all above plus:<br>■ basic understanding of group dynamics<br>■ interpersonal skills | ■ experience working with groups<br>■ some past related experience |
| *Community Service Project Director* | ■ 10+ hours per week for the academic year | ■ oversee and ensure service success of 5 to 500 other volunteers | all of the above plus:<br>■ leadership skills<br>■ group process experience<br>■ organization of tasks and people<br>■ knowledge of community problem<br>■ knowledge of nonprofit organization<br>■ philosophy of service related to a community issue | ■ volunteer experience<br>■ time availability<br>■ initiative/persistence<br>■ interpersonal/ organizational skills |

*Continued on next page*

| Position | Time Commitment Responsibility | Service Achievement | Major Learning Available | Prerequisites |
|---|---|---|---|---|
| *Coordinator* | ■ 10+ hours per week for academic year | ■ oversee and ensure service success of volunteers in 4–9 projects in a variety of settings<br>■ act as a resource and community link<br>■ encourage, help, and support directors | ■ all of the above plus:<br>■ learn how to empower / support others to succeed<br>■ advanced group process<br>■ organizational decision-making | ■ successful project director experience |
| *President* | ■ 10+ hours per week for academic year | ■ oversee and ensure success of volunteers in 60+ projects | ■ all of the above plus:<br>■ broad span of responsibility<br>■ leadership of a large group<br>■ represent group to the public | ■ same as Project Director and Coordinator experience |
| *Summer Leadership*<br><br>*academic credit available with extra initiative of volunteer* | ■ 200 hours (service and class time) | ■ ongoing and one-time service<br>■ short-term service projects | ■ understanding of how to direct project<br>■ development of philosophy of service<br>■ community leadership development | ■ commitment to direct a Bennion Center project the following year |
| *Alumni and Bennion Center Summer Fellow* | ■ 10 full-time weeks in summer in another city | ■ major involvement with an issue and a population | ■ in-depth understanding of a major issue<br>■ learn about an agency<br>■ experience with different populations in different settings; generally diverse people<br>■ learn about community issues in another area | ■ past experience volunteering—helpful if in issue applying for<br>■ application to committee<br>■ one-year commitment to Bennion Center before and after fellowship<br><br>*Continued on next page* |

| Position | Time Commitment Responsibility | Service Achievement | Major Learning Available | Prerequisites |
|---|---|---|---|---|
| *CURRICULAR* | | | | |
| *Service-Learning Classes* | ■ based on class requirements | ■ high skill level of service possible depending on level of course<br>■ exposure to different types of service | ■ experiential learning tied with course<br>■ deeper understanding of community issues<br>■ structured learning opportunities | ■ course prerequisites, if any |
| *Service-Learning Teaching Assistant* | ■ 10-15 hours per week for one quarter | ■ oversee and ensure success of volunteers in the course<br>■ facilitate service of others<br>■ facilitate meaningful discussion of service and related issues | ■ coordination of group<br>■ organizational skills<br>■ interpersonal skills, public speaking<br>■ work with faculty on a different level | ■ prior service-learning experience<br>■ ability to work with agencies<br>■ experience coordinating volunteers<br>■ ability to work with faculty<br>■ ability to lead groups in reflection |
| *Service-Learning Scholar* | ■ 400 hours of service<br>■ 15 credits of service-learning<br>■ integrative service project | ■ both short-term and extensive<br>■ final project which is left with the community | ■ experiential learning tied with courses and major<br>■ creation of a service project that meets a need in which individual is personally interested | ■ prior volunteer experience helpful but not required |

# APPENDIX C

## *Infusing Service-Learning Into a Course: A Timeline*
### Augsburg College

The following summary, written by Vicky Littlefield for Augsburg's faculty manual, describes a step-by-step developmental process and timeline for incorporating service-learning into an existing course.

## BEFORE THE COURSE BEGINS

### 1. Meet with Associate Director

At least one month prior to the beginning of the course meeting with the associate director, meet with the associate director to let her know that you are interested in developing a service-learning component for a course.

The associate director can help brainstorm ways that service-learning might fit into a course, suggest service-learning sites that are appropriate for different courses, provide resource materials (e.g., syllabi from other courses, readings on service-learning), and put faculty in touch with others who have used service-learning in their courses.

### 2. Develop the Syllabus

The most successful service-learning courses provide students with a clear picture of the place of service-learning in the course. The syllabus can show students how service-learning is an integral part of the course.

*Incorporate service-learning into the course's educational goals and objectives.* Examine the educational goals and objectives of the class. Identify specifically what students are required to learn from the service-learning experience: the knowledge, skills, understandings, or attitudes and list them as course goals.

*Describe in detail the service-learning requirement and related classroom activities and assignments.* These will include classroom-based activities and assignments, and activities at the service-learning site. Most instructors have students keep a journal which serves as the basis for many classroom activities. Consult with the associate director in developing site-based activities.

Instructors commonly require students to spend between 12 and 20 hours at the community service site. Several shorter visits, rather than one long one, provide a greater variety of experiences at the service site.

C-1

Instructors may require that all students participate in community service or may use service as one of several options. An advantage of requiring service is that it provides a common topic for classroom assignments or discussion. Instructors who provide other options should consider ways to integrate them with the service option.

*Describe how the service-learning component will be evaluated.* A general rule is not to evaluate the service-learning experience itself, but to evaluate what students make of the experience. Possibilities include written or oral exams, papers, interviews, questionnaires, observations, skill assessments, or other indicators of learning.

*Specify the contribution of service-learning activities to the course grade.* In order to be seen by students as an integral part of the course, rather than as an add-on, service-learning should contribute significantly to the overall course grade. Instructors have often specified a

---

## CHARACTERISTICS OF GOOD SERVICE-LEARNING SITES

- The site must be doing work that is connected to the course in ways that will be obvious to students.

- Activities at the site must give students opportunities to reflect on how course concepts relate to the activities.

- Whenever possible, students should have direct contact with client populations or constituency groups with which the organization regularly interacts.

- Ideally, students should be able to work in pairs or teams and not be isolated from other students, staff, or client populations.

- The work students do should have some clear connection to the main purposes of the organization. While some of the work may be generally clerical, etc., it should not be consistently repetitious or boring for long periods.

- The site supervisor should be present when students are there to directly oversee their work.

- The site supervisor should have done advanced planning so that students have assigned activities throughout their time at the site.

- The site supervisor should provide students with some background on the organization and orientation to the specific work they will be doing. (If there are mandatory and formal orientation sessions, they should be scheduled frequently so that students do not experience long delays before they can begin to work.)

- The site should be in the community near the campus (2–3 miles away at most) and/or is accessible by public transportation.

*Adapted from a handout by Norm Ferguson, Augsburg Department of Psychology, entitled "Criteria for an Environmental Psychology Experiential Learning Site."*

20% or 25% contribution of service-learning to the overall course grade, with some instructors going as high as 40%.

*Include a calendar of service-learning events.* A semester-long calendar that shows service-learning activities and due dates is a useful tool for students.

### 3. Finalize Service-Learning Sites with the Associate Director

Before the course begins, check back with the associate director to obtain the final list of service-learning sites and to find out how many students each site can accept, get a description of the activities that students perform at each site, as well as the names, addresses, and phone numbers of contact persons at the service-learning sites.

### 4. Send a Letter to the Site Supervisor

It is appropriate to contact the site supervisor prior to the students' initial visit. A courtesy letter introduces the instructor to the supervisor, provides a way to describe the integration of service-learning into the particular course, and allows the instructor to mention expectations about the students' service-learning activities. It is also useful to have had an initial positive communication with the site supervisor in the event that problems arise later on.

A generic letter, which can be adapted by individual instructors, appears below.

## AUGSBURG LETTERHEAD

Date

Service Site Supervisor
Address
City, State zip

Dear XXX:

Mary True, our Community Service-Learning Coordinator, has let me know that your organization has agreed to provide opportunities for a few students from my (course name goes here) class to work with you during our (fall/interim/spring) semester. I want to express my appreciation to you for your willingness to cooperate with us in this activity.

Mary has identified several organizations, including yours, willing to serve as service-learning sites. I will ask students to work in pairs and to select an organization at which to work. They will be expected to work for you for at least XX total hours and to (name other service-learning related activities here, e.g., write a paper in which they relate their work experiences to classroom material, etc.). Mary and I will attempt to balance the students across the organizations when they select their work sites in class on (give date, typically in the second week of the semester). I will ask students to contact you very soon after that date so that they can make their first visit and complete some hours of work before (give date, typically one month after the semester has begun), when the class is scheduled to have its first discussion of these activities.

As your organization's contact person, it would be very helpful to us if you would be willing to spend a brief amount of time describing your organization's mission and history to the students. This information will be very helpful to them in putting their work activities into a larger social and organizational context.

I am excited about this opportunity because I believe it will give my students a chance to do some direct "hands-on" experiential learning and at the same time will help your organization with its work.

Again, I want to thank you for your willingness to serve as a service-learning site. If you have any questions, please contact Mary at 330-1155 or me at 330-xxxx.

Sincerely,

Professor's name
Department

## DURING THE COURSE: FIRST WEEK

### 1. Discuss Service-Learning

Introduce the course syllabus and explain the rationale behind using service-learning in the course. Explain service at the sites, journal keeping, and class-related activities (reflection, critical analysis, etc.).

The most successful courses are those that weave service-learning into their fabric. Introducing service-learning as part of the regular syllabus emphasizes its integration into the course.

Nearly all faculty members who use service-learning have students keep some sort of journal. The journal serves as a basis for class-related activities and assignments that relate to the service experience. Two factors seem to be tied to the successful use of journals:

- Students should write their service-related journals as soon as possible after leaving the community sites. This assures that their memories and perceptions are the freshest and have the most detail.

- The format and purpose of journaling should be clearly explained to students in both the syllabus and orally in class.

### 2. Administer Community Service-Learning Pre-Evaluation

The Office of Community Service-Learning conducts ongoing research on student participation in the program. To assist in these efforts, the associate director requests that faculty members have students complete a service-learning survey prior to their first site visits. Copies of the survey are available in the Community Service-Learning Office, 225 Memorial Hall, or by calling 330-1775.

### 3. Hand Out and Discuss the "Guide to Service-Learning Sites and Student Responsibilities," the "Community Service-Learning Assignment Time Record," and the "Learning Contract" Forms

Students who have little work experience may not be aware of norms and expectations for workers, regardless of the fact that they are unpaid workers. The "Guide to Service-Learning Sites and Student Responsibilities" makes these expectations explicit.

Students must document their time at the community service site by turning in a Community Service Assignment Time Record. The completed record, including the site supervisor's signature for each site visit, should be turned in to the instructor at the end of the semester. After noting whether all students have completed their service assignment obligations, the instructor should give these records to the associate director.

### 4. Introduce Service-Learning Sites and Answer Questions

One of the responsibilities of the coordinator of the Community Service-Learning Program is to visit classes in order to describe community sites. She will describe sites that you have chosen for your class, tell about their histories and current status, and describe duties that students will perform. She will also answer questions that students have about the sites or about service-learning in general.

## DURING THE COURSE: SECOND WEEK

### 1. Students Choose Service-Learning Sites; Complete the Service-Learning Locator Form; Return the Form to the Associate Director

After the first week of class, but by the end of the second week, students should use the "Guidelines to Service-Learning Sites" handout to choose their top three service sites.

Students should be encouraged to limit their sites to those identified by the instructor and the associate director. These sites have worked to develop student activities that relate to course content. Students who choose sites because of their prior familiarity or convenience may have a less-than-satisfactory service experience.

Students should investigate the sites prior to choosing them. It is appropriate for students to call the site and discuss it and worker activities with the site supervisor prior to making a site choice.

Some sites may be more popular than others. It is important to assure each site of the number of workers that it expects. The use of a lottery can help assure a fair and equal distribution of students across sites.

On the day that students choose their sites, the instructor should have them fill out the Service-Learning Locator form which lists students by sites. A copy of this form should be returned to the associate director by the end of the second week of classes.

## 2. Assignment on Student Expectations

To get students thinking about the service sites prior to their first visit, it is useful to make an assignment about their expectations. This might be a written assignment that stands alone or serves as the basis for small group discussions.

**Course Name, Semester, Name**

Service Site _____

*About the site.*   What do you already know about the service site? What do you know about the community needs that the site serves?

(Provide space for written response.)

*About your work at the site.*   What do you expect to do at the site? What do you think will happen there? How do you think you will react? What are your hopes, expectations, and fears about going to the site?

(Provide space for written response.)

## DURING THE COURSE: THE FIRST MONTH

Despite their best intentions, students may not make their first service site visits in a timely fashion. This becomes a problem when service-related assignments are due in class and students have no service experiences upon which to base their work.

In order to assist students in making their first service visits, it is useful to provide a structure such as a deadline for having spoken in person to the site supervisor.

Students should be encouraged to schedule their first visit well in advance. Site supervisors are often very busy, have a number of students to supervise, and have numerous other duties in addition to working with students. Students should be proactive in contacting the site supervisor. It is not sufficient to call the service site and leave a message; the student needs to persist in directly contacting the supervisor.

## DURING THE SEMESTER

### 1. Reflection Activities, Critical Analysis Assignments, Other Assignments

Research on service-learning suggests that learning is facilitated by frequent structured opportunities to tie service activities to course concepts and theories. Reflection activities and critical analysis assignments should occur often and can be tied to other homework or assignments.

### 2. Mid-Semester Monitoring

Part of the mid-semester evaluation might be devoted to service activities and results used to make any necessary mid-course corrections.

## AT SEMESTER'S END

### 1. Final Projects Due

As with other service-related assignments, the more specific the project, the better. Final projects can take a variety of forms.

### 2. Administer the Community Service Experience Evaluation

This evaluation is part of the ongoing evaluation of the service-learning program conducted by the Office of Community Service-Learning. Multiple copies of the form are available from the associate director.

## AFTER THE COURSE

### 1. Thank You Letter to Site Supervisors

The faculty member should write a letter to the site supervisors; students should also be encouraged to express their thanks either orally or in writing.

### 2. Report Results to Sites

Students should send copies of their final projects or reports to the service sites. The site supervisors are very eager to obtain others' perspectives on their agencies; additionally, projects and reports provide supervisors with closure on the student workers' activities.

### 3. Debrief Sites with the Associate Director

After the end of the semester, arrange to meet with the associate director to discuss your impressions of the successes and challenges of each service site. Provide documentation when possible. The associate director provides ongoing feedback to the sites that allows them to improve their future interactions with student workers, so information from faculty perspectives is valuable.

# APPENDIX D

*President's Corner: Directions of Learning*

## Donald Harward, President
## Bates College

One of the bases of the curriculum at Bates is a thesis requirement, which includes an expectation that students take part in research. We believe that it is essential for undergraduates to experience this direction of learning—pointing inward to the individual learner as he or she defines an issue, discovers alternatives, and lays claim to what it is to know.

However, a second direction of learning is equally fundamental. Learning can point outward. It can point to the obligations that knowing brings to our encounters, how we must explore our connectedness to others and recognize that we are affected by them. In the broadest sense of what the ancients called the moral dimension of knowing, this outward direction of learning needs to be supported and encouraged by our pedagogy, our curriculum, and our educational rhetoric.

Undergraduate service should be understood as broader than what people of goodwill may be encouraged to do, or as extracurricular options for those motivated to participate. Undergraduate service is not a payment to those less fortunate, nor is it action motivated by *noblesse oblige.*

In our curricula and in the research we support, we need to think more creatively, more robustly, about the connections we establish to encourage the outward direction of learning, including civic education.

Undergraduate service is directly connected to the communal character of learning. Rather than being peripheral to an undergraduate's education, service reflects epistemological and pedagogical themes that are central to it.

In an essay entitled "Creating the New American College," Ernest Boyer wrote, "Higher education has more intellectual talent than any other institution in our culture. Today's colleges and universities surely must respond to the challenges that confront our children, our schools, and our cities." He wrote of a report that proposed a "new paradigm of scholarship, one that not only promotes the scholarship of discovering knowledge, but also celebrates the scholarship of integrating knowledge, of communicating knowledge, and of applying knowledge through professional service."

Boyer was suggesting what it could mean to take seriously the outward direction of learning. Attending to such consideration of what service could mean and how it could be connected to what we are about as liberal arts colleges, should result in the expression of two basic fundamental issues. One is epistemological: Service is connected to principles of learning. The other is democratic: Service is an essential link to principles of civic education. Both are communal.

Learning involves entering relationships—getting connected to what we know. We come to realize that knowing is not a means of controlling. What we learn forces us to examine the values, the categories of analysis, and the presuppositions we carry to the exchange. Encountering the other is to recognize the reciprocity of learning.

The democratic structure of community is one that is neither controlled nor objectified; it is cultivated. It does not happen naturally; it is substantiated through action. Service provides means of thoughtful and intentional action—conditions essential to both liberty and the public good.

We need to encourage the directions of learning that point both inward and outward. The perspectives of learning work both ways—there is no "other," no place, making its claim on us. As students and teachers, we shape and are shaped by the objects of our knowing. As citizens, we need to develop the habits of action that participate in the work of democratic community.

*(This speech originally appeared in the* Campus Compact Newsletter. *Reprinted with permission.)*

# APPENDIX E

## Selected Service-Learning Projects in Business
## Bentley College

**GR501 Management Systems in a Changing Environment (Graduate Level)**

*John Seeger, Professor of Management*

This course examines the theory and practice of managing organizations and their subunits in the context of a rapidly changing, global environment. The course focuses on the structure, design, and operation of organizations as interrelated systems and the integration of internal and external environments. Explores the changing relationship between business and its stakeholders, stressing political and legal, social and ethical, technological, and international environments. A centerpiece of the course is a semester-long team project analyzing a current management issue in an organization. Service-learning is a popular option, where teams conduct their analysis for a nonprofit organization. All analyses are written up in case form and are often submitted for publication.

**MG220 Comparative Management**

*Ed Wondoloski, Professor of Management*

The objective in this course is to strengthen students' knowledge and understanding of management as a process. The course explores the historical, current, and future perspectives of management regarding an organization's wellness, purpose, and its participation in and responsibility for sustaining a quality of civic life. The course affords students the opportunity to enhance their self-realization and direction through an integration of classroom study with an experience in nonprofit management. Topics include the traditional study of nonprofits, the need for management in voluntary organizations, and the role of the business community in civic life. A focus is on how management practices are similar and vary among the three sectors: nonprofit, business, and government. All students do 18–20 hours of community service, working on various projects with agencies or organizations that exist to serve the needs of the members of the community.

**OM280 Operations Management**

*Larry Dolinsky, Professor of Management*

This course presents an introduction to the operating component of a manufacturing or service organization where inputs such as raw material, labor, or other resources are transformed into finished goods and/or services. Addresses both strategic issues such as process selection, plant location, and capacity planning, as well as tactical issues that include inventory control, quality assurance, and operations scheduling. Identifies the various trade-off decisions that confront the operations manager and the resulting impact of these decisions on the marketing and financial components of the firm. Quantitative models and analytical tools are emphasized. Service-learning projects in this course consist of small group assessment of the current operations of an organization or a program within the organization. This assessment is done with a focus on a particular goal or issue, and a report is submitted which also provides recommendations to assist the organization in addressing this issue. A class presentation is also required.

### AC211/AC212    Intermediate Accounting I/Intermediate Accounting II
*Ralph McQuade, Associate Professor of Accountancy*

These are the first financial accounting courses at the professional level for the undergraduate accounting major. The first semester course intensively examines the generally accepted accounting standards related to the preparation of financial statements, with particular emphasis on balance sheet valuations and their relationship to income determination. The course studies in depth the valuation and disclosure problems associated with such topics as cash, receivables, inventories, plant assets, etc. The second course explores additional topics involving financial statement reporting and disclosure. Students may elect to participate in a service-learning project in either course. Students work 8–10 hours (depending on location of the site) at a nonprofit agency, assist in the completion of essential accounting work, and complete a four to five page report.

### AC340    Accounting Information Systems
*Jane Fedorowicz, Associate Professor of Accountancy*

This course examines the relationships and distinctions between accounting information systems (AIS) and the total management information system (MIS) environment, with major emphasis on computerized AIS. The course explores, in detail, several typical AIS application subsystems. All students work on team projects analyzing AIS systems in actual organizations, involving 1) systematic descriptions, 2) analysis of existing control measures, 3) recommendation of other appropriate controls, and 4) assessment of quality of actual AIS system. Each team produces an extensive written report and makes an oral presentation. Several teams elect service-learning projects involving community service/nonprofit organizations.

## AC351/AC361   Federal Taxation I/Federal Taxation II
*Mark Nixon, Assistant Professor of Accountancy*
*Ray Levesque, Senior Lecturer of Accountancy*

The first semester course gives a broad training in the federal income tax law and regulations of the treasury department. The course deals primarily with the basic philosophy of taxation, determination of taxable income, allowable deductions, and gains and losses on sales and exchange of property for the individual taxpayer. The second semester course examines federal income tax law and regulations applicable to partnerships, corporations, and fiduciaries. Basic tax research skills are developed. All students have a service-learning option to assist individuals in the Greater Boston area in the preparation of tax returns. Students are trained by CPAs who volunteer their time through the Community Tax Assistance Program (CTA).

## BC620   Managerial Communication (Graduate Level)
*Linda McJannet, Professor of English*

This course increases the student's effectiveness as a manager by providing opportunities to develop, practice, and reflect upon the process of communication with people inside and outside an organization. The course introduces aspects of rhetoric and communication theory relevant to managerial work, but the emphasis is on practice and reflection in both classroom and real-life settings. The centerpiece of the course is a field project, with most students electing a service-learning project. The project includes 1) a project proposal, 2) a letter to an outside party, 3) an interim presentation, 4) a written report, and 5) a reflective oral presentation.

## MK160   Marketing
*Debbie Easterling, Assistant Professor of Marketing*

This course explores the role of marketing both within the firm and within society. Examines concepts, functions, and institutions involved in the process of developing and distributing products and services to consumer, industrial, institutional, and international markets. Service-learning projects in this course consist of small group projects including analysis of current marketing strategies, a marketing plan, and production of marketing materials. A final report and class presentation are required.

## MK265   Marketing Research
*Andrew Aylesworth, Assistant Professor of Marketing*

This course introduces tools and techniques of marketing research as an aid to marketing decision-making. Covers definitions of research problems, research methodologies, design of research projects, analysis and interpretation of research results. Emphasizes practical aspects of conducting and evaluating marketing research studies. Service-learning projects consist of mainly whole-class projects which include designing, conducting, and analyzing research studies. Small group reports are generated along with recommendations for marketing strategies. Class presentations are required.

### BC620   Managerial Communications (Graduate Level)
*Terrance Skelton, Associate Professor of English*

This course approaches effective communication both as an essential professional skill and as an important function of management. Discusses the elements of communication (argumentation, structure, style, tone, and visual appeal) and presents techniques for increasing one's effectiveness in each area. Students read, discuss, and write about cases based on tasks that managers commonly face, such as explaining changes in policy; writing performance evaluations; analyzing survey results or other numerical data; and communicating with employees, shareholders, the press, and the public. Methods include group work, oral presentations, several writing assignments, and role playing. Drafting and revising and computerized word processing are stressed. Service-learning projects in this course consist of individual or group researched-based reports which address particular issues or tasks (as above) facing the organization's managerial staff.

# APPENDIX F

## Selected Administrative Forms
## Brevard Community College

### Appendix F-1
*Steps for Involvement: A Service Learner's Checklist*
**Brevard Community College**

❏ 1. Reflect on your educational and career objectives.

❏ 2. Find out from your instructor the evaluation criteria for service-learning credit option; i.e., reflective work, necessary amount of service hours, and class participation.

❏ 3. Contact a Center for Service-Learning (CSL) staff member in person or by telephone (632-1111): Cocoa Campus, Student Center 214, Ext. 62410; Melbourne Campus, Student Center 122, Ext. 33150; or Titusville Campus, Student Center 191, Ext. 42202; or Palm Bay Campus Room 1117G, Ext. 22020.

❏ 4. Peruse information about service opportunities.

❏ 5. Complete a short application form. CSL will supply you with a resource packet containing service-learning information, necessary forms, etc.

❏ 6. Talk with a CSL staff person to match your interests with community needs.

❏ 7. Arrange with a CSL representative dates and times of agency visitations.

❏ 8. Visit the agency or program of your choice.

❏ 9. Attend an orientation session (some sites have excellent training programs).

❏ 10. When you have accepted a service-learning position, complete the Placement Confirmation Notice with your agency supervisor and return it to the CSL office.

❏ 11. Devise your service-learning plan. CSL will provide you with resources for examples.

❏ 12. Choose your reflective methods (written and oral).

❏ 13. Give us feedback about your progress and concerns. This is as helpful to us as it is to you. Monitor and assess your service-learning progress.

❏ 14. Inform CSL if you wish to terminate or change positions. We will gladly help arrange a more suitable position for you.

❏ 15. You must, with the assistance of your agency supervisor, maintain hourly time sheets, turning them in to your instructor at the required times.

❏ 16. An evaluation of your contributions and performance during your service-learning experience will be compiled by the supervisor of your service site. You are to return these to your instructor at midterm and the end of each semester.

❏ 17. The completion of a questionnaire is required at the end of each semester in which you provide your services.

❏ 18. Integrate your experience with the rest of your life.

❏ 19. Enjoy your service-learning experience.

## Appendix F-2

### *Placement Confirmation Form* / Brevard Community College

Cocoa Campus, SC-214, 632-1111, X62410
Melborne Campus, CM-213, 632-1111, X33150
Palm Bay Campus, RM-134, 632-1111, X22219
Titusville Campus, SC-191, 632-1111, X42202

Student's Name: _____

Date: _____

Name of Organization: _____

Supervisor or Coordinator: _____

Is This Student Working as a
    Service-Learner in Your Organization? _____

Duties: _____

_____

_____

Days and Hours to Work: _____

Date Student Will Begin: _____

Termination Date: _____

Supervisor's Signature: _____

Dear Supervisor:

Those of us at the Center for Service-Learning, Brevard Community College, would like to thank you for taking the time to complete this form. If you have any questions, or if we can assist you in any way, please feel free to call us.

Thank you,

Service-Learning Faculty and
Center for Service-Learning Staff

## Appendix F-3
### *Service-Learning Contract, Fourth Credit Option*
### Brevard Community College

#### TO THE STUDENT:

Complete Section 1 of this form and ask your professor to complete Section 2 and the Center for Service-Learning staff to fill out Section 3. **When this form is filled out completely, give the white copy to your instructor, the yellow copy to the Service-Learning Center office, and keep the pink copy for yourself.**

**SECTION 1**
*(Please Print Clearly)*

Your Name_____ Phone _____

Address_____Best times to reach you _____

State your service and learning goals:

_____

_____

_____

Service:  What exactly do you expect to do? Briefly describe the nature of the volunteer service work you are choosing and why you have chosen it:

_____

_____

Learning:  What do you expect to learn from this experience? (e.g., information and understanding about the elderly, about teaching methods for 6th grade children, about environmental issues).

_____

_____

Skills:  What skills do you expect to develop and learn from this experience? (e.g., communication skills, writing, problem solving, teaching techniques, etc.)

_____

_____

I agree to devote at least 20 hours this semester between the dates of _____ and
_____at (community agency/volunteer project) _____.
I also agree to meet the academic or learning requirements that my professor has indicated in the next section in order to receive one hour of academic credit for this service-learning experience.

Signature:_____ Date: _____

• • • • • • • • • • • • • • • • • • • • • • • • • • • • • • • • • • • • • • • • • • • • • • • • • •

**SECTION 2**    *(To be completed by professor)*

The student named above has my permission to engage in this **4th credit option** service-learning experience to meet the requirements of Human Service-Experience. Please circle one: SOW 1051, SOW 1052, SOW 1053. In addition to the 20 minimum hours of service required, the student will complete the following service-learning related assignments or requirements for the course:

Journal _____     Oral Presentation _____

Final Essay _____    Other _____

**One midterm reflection seminar arranged by the Center for Service-Learning is required.**

**The Community Service-Learning Questionnaire must be completed at the end of the assignment.**

Elaboration of evidence or academic work needed:

Signature:_____    Date: _____

Instructor's Course _____

• • • • • • • • • • • • • • • • • • • • • • • • • • • • • • • • • • • • • • • • • • • • • • • • • • •

**SECTION 3**    *(To be completed by Center for Service-Learning staff person)*

Registration form completed _____    Fees Paid _____

SOW Course/Section _____

Service documentation forms given _____

Agency (organization confirmation) _____

Midterm seminar selection:  Campus _____

Date _____    Time_____    Room _____

The service-learning student has been given the necessary forms, has a completed confirmation form and registration form, and has chosen a reflection seminar to attend.

Signature:_____    Date: _____

• • • • • • • • • • • • • • • • • • • • • • • • • • • • • • • • • • • • • • • • • • • • • • • • • • •

## Appendix F-4
### *Service Hours on Academic Transcript (SHOAT) Guidelines*
### Brevard Community College

## PROCEDURES

1. **ENROLL:** Students must fill out a Center for Service-Learning Application. Stop by the center which is conveniently located on each campus or call 632-1111:
   Cocoa, Student Center 214, Extension 62410
   Titusville, Student Center 191, Extension 42273
   Melbourne, Student Center 213, Extension 33150
   Palm Bay, Room 134, Extension 22219

2. **VERIFY:** Pick up **SHOAT** Verification Card. At least 20 hours must be tracked each academic semester. Signature verification must be obtained from the agency supervisor or volunteer coordinator for each service activity.

3. **RETURN:** The **SHOAT** Verification Card must be returned to the center by the week before final examinations each academic semester.

### Service Activities to Be Considered for SHOAT

- Brevard Community College-sponsored service projects that meet a community need both for credit and noncredit (this includes service performed in service-learning courses and internships in nonprofit or state agencies, and service-learning clubs; i.e., Rotaract, PIC, AASU, etc., which meet a community need).

- Service sponsored by a community service agency including direct student involvement with local public service agencies.

- Church-sponsored service work where the goal is meeting secular needs (not proselytizing new members) including work ranging from assisting at a church soup kitchen or shelter for the homeless.

- Government-sponsored service work (federal, state, and local) including the AmeriCorps program at the federal level, conservation corps at the state level, and municipal programs such as serving in the school system.

- Independent service projects not sponsored by any agency in areas where legitimate human needs exist but no service agency exists or is equipped to meet those needs.

## Service Activities NOT to Be Considered for SHOAT

- Church-sponsored work where the goal is proselytizing new members.

- Work sponsored by a for-profit organization unless its mission involves meeting social needs of the community; e.g. nursing homes, and hospitals.

- Work in partisan political campaigns.

- Fundraising when there is not direct interaction with the organization. The hours of participation in car washes, dance marathons, and benefits are not counted. Organizing such events with direct interaction with a nonprofit agency will be allowed.

We do appreciate the diversity in philosophies of service across the campus. These guidelines serve only to define the boundaries of community service-learning for the SHOAT program. The definition originated with the Campus Compact, the coalition of over 550 colleges and universities established to create and enhance public service opportunities for students, and to develop an expectation of service as an integral part of student life and college experience.

## Appendix F-5
### *Student Volunteer Hour Report* / Brevard Community College

Please use this form to record the number of community service-learning hours per week. This report should be signed weekly by your agency supervisor.

STUDENT NAME _____

AGENCY SUPERVISOR _____

| DATE | M | T | W | R | F | S | S | TOTAL # HOURS | SERVICE PROVIDED | SUPERVISOR'S APPROVAL |
|---|---|---|---|---|---|---|---|---|---|---|
|  |  |  |  |  |  |  |  |  |  |  |
|  |  |  |  |  |  |  |  |  |  |  |
|  |  |  |  |  |  |  |  |  |  |  |
|  |  |  |  |  |  |  |  |  |  |  |
|  |  |  |  |  |  |  |  |  |  |  |
|  |  |  |  |  |  |  |  |  |  |  |
|  |  |  |  |  |  |  |  |  |  |  |
|  |  |  |  |  |  |  |  |  |  |  |
|  |  |  |  |  |  |  |  |  |  |  |
|  |  |  |  |  |  |  |  |  |  |  |
|  |  |  |  |  |  |  |  |  |  |  |
|  |  |  |  |  |  |  |  |  |  |  |
|  |  |  |  |  |  |  |  |  |  |  |
|  |  |  |  |  |  |  |  |  |  |  |

Ending Date:                    Total Hours Assignment:

Supervisor's Signature:

## Appendix F-6

### *Center for Service-Learning Volunteer Insurance Enrollment Record*
### **Brevard Community College**

I volunteer my service through the Center for Service-Learning and understand that I am not an employee of Brevard Community College.

_____          _____
            Date                          Signature of Volunteer

Person to notify in an emergency    _____

Relationship    _____    Place of work    _____

Phone    _____

If you will be driving to perform your volunteer work, please complete the following:

I, the Center for Service-Learning volunteer, understand that if I use my personal automobile in my volunteer service, I will arrange to keep in effect automobile insurance equal to the minimum limits required by our state.

Yes    _____    No    _____

Current Driver's License Number    _____

Issue Date    _____Expiration Date    _____

_____
                                          Signature of Volunteer

DESIGNATION OF BENEFICIARY
(for Accident Insurance)

Name(s)    _____    Relationship    _____

Address    _____

Place of employment    _____    Phone    _____

Enrollment forms should be signed and applications completed to enroll you as a prospective volunteer. Student volunteers do not receive benefits until their applications are completed and the enrollment forms signed.

---

## INSURANCE COVERAGE FOR
## CENTER FOR SERVICE-LEARNING VOLUNTEERS

The Center for Service-Learning Volunteer Program has secured accident and personal liability insurance coverage for our volunteers. Insurance coverage is provided to complement the insurance coverages already required of students of Brevard Community College and the state. This insurance is valid only while actually performing your volunteer duties. In no way is this insurance intended to replace your current insurance coverage.

If you need any more information or have any questions, please contact the Center for Service-Learning, 632-1111, ext. 62410; otherwise please complete this information sheet and return to the CSL office located on your campus, SC215B.

## Appendix F-7
### Student Volunteer Mid-Semester Progress Report
### Brevard Community College

STUDENT NAME:                               VOLUNTEER AGENCY/ORGANIZATION:

TODAY'S DATE:                           AGENCY/ORGANIZATION TELEPHONE:

SUPERVISOR'S NAME:                   SUPERVISOR'S SIGNATURE:

SERVICE HOURS TO DATE:              EVALUATION PERIOD (DATES):

| OVERALL PERFORMANCE | NEEDS HELP | AVERAGE | GOOD | EXCELLENT | CANNOT RATE | COMMENTS |
|---|---|---|---|---|---|---|
| **PUNCTUALITY:** gets to work on time Times Absent: Times Tardy: | | | | | | |
| **DEPENDABILITY:** prompt, trustworthy, follows directions, meets obligations | | | | | | |
| **ADAPTABILITY:** catches on fast, follows detailed instructions, can switch jobs | | | | | | |
| **ABILITY TO GET ALONG:** cooperative, well-mannered, socially and emotionally stable | | | | | | |
| **ATTITUDE:** enthusiastic, a good team worker, willing to cooperate, desires to improve | | | | | | |
| **INITIATIVE:** ability to work without supervision, self-motivating | | | | | | |
| **ACCEPTS SUGGESTIONS:** eager to improve, seeks assistance, follows through | | | | | | |

Do you think this individual is performing well at this stage of the program? YES _____    NO _____
Please explain:  (USE THE BACK OF PAPER IF NEEDED)
If there have been any problems, describe the circumstances and the outcome:
**THANK YOU FOR YOUR HELP!**

## Appendix F-8
### *Student Planning Guide* / Brevard Community College

I.  My volunteer service-learning choices:

AGENCY              PHONE NUMBER              CONTACT PERSON

_____

_____

_____


II.  Major learning objectives:

_____

_____

_____


III.  Important dates:  MONTH/DAY          TIME          PLACE

Volunteer Project:      start  _____

                        finish  _____

                        hours/weekly  _____

Orientation:  _____

Training:  _____

Placement Confirmation due:  _____

Mid-Term Performance Evaluation:  _____

Final Performance Evaluation:  _____

Hour Report Due:  _____

Seminars/Feedback Sessions:  _____

Written Reflective Work Turned In:  _____

Center's Questionnaire Completed:  _____


IV.  My service-learning reflective choices:

| <u>WRITTEN</u> | <u>NON WRITTEN</u> |
|---|---|
| _____ Service Learning Plan | _____ Instructor/Class Seminars |
| _____ Report Book | _____ Feedback from Agency Supervisor |
| _____ Journal | _____ Group Meeting(s) |
| _____ Essay | _____ Center/Service-Learning Sessions |
| _____ Critical Incidents | _____ Oral Presentation |
| _____ Other | |

# APPENDIX G
## Policies and Prodecures for the Evaluation of Faculty for Tenure, Promotion, and Merit Increases
### Portland State University

## INTRODUCTION

Policies and procedures for the evaluation of faculty are established to provide the means whereby the performance of individual faculty members and their contributions to collective university goals may be equitably assessed and documented. In the development of these policies and procedures, the university recognizes the uniqueness of individual faculty members, of the departments of which they are a part, and of their specific disciplines; and, because of that uniqueness, the main responsibility for implementation of formative and evaluative procedures has been placed in the departments.

Departmental guidelines should set forth processes and criteria for formative and evaluative activities which are consistent with the department's academic mission. For example, departmental guidelines might identify evaluative criteria which are appropriate to the discipline, or might delineate which activities will receive greater or lesser emphasis in promotion or tenure decisions. They should also include appropriate methods for evaluating the interdisciplinary scholarly activities of departmental faculty. The deans and the provost review departmental procedures in order to ensure that faculty are evaluated equitably throughout the university.

Evaluation instruments provide a means for gathering information that can provide a basis for evaluation, but these instruments do not constitute an evaluation in themselves. Evaluation is the process whereby the information acquired by appropriate instruments is analyzed to determine the quality of performance as measured against the criteria set by the department.

Policies and procedures shall be consistent with sections 580–21–100 through 135 of the Oregon Administrative Rules of the Oregon State System of Higher Education. Approval and implementation of these policies and procedures shall be consistent with the agreement between Portland State University (PSU) and the American Association of University Professors, Portland State Chapter, and with the internal governance procedures of the university. Each year the provost will establish a timeline to ensure that decision-makers at each level of review will have sufficient time to consider tenure and promotion recommendations responsibly.

## SCHOLARSHIP

### Overview of Faculty Responsibilities

The task of a university includes the promotion of learning and the discovery and extension of knowledge, enterprises which place responsibility upon faculty members with respect to their disciplines, their students, the university, and the community. The university seeks to foster the scholarly development of its faculty and to encourage the scholarly interaction of faculty with students and with regional, national, and international communities. Faculty have a responsibility to their disciplines, their students, the university, and the community to strive for superior intellectual, aesthetic, or creative achievement. Such achievement, as evidenced in scholarly accomplishments, is an indispensable qualification for appointment and promotion and tenure in the professorial ranks. Scholarly accomplishments, suggesting continuing growth and high potential, can be demonstrated through a variety of activities:

- Research, including creative activities

- Teaching, including delivery of instruction, mentoring, and curricular activities

- Community outreach

All faculty members should keep abreast of developments in their fields and remain professionally active throughout their careers.

At PSU, individual faculty are part of a larger mosaic of faculty talent. The richness of faculty talent should be celebrated, not restricted. Research, teaching, and community outreach are accomplished in an environment that draws on the combined intellectual vitality of the department and of the university. Department faculty may take on responsibilities of research, teaching, and community outreach in differing proportions and emphases. Irrespective of the emphasis assigned to differing activities, it is important that the quality of faculty contributions be rigorously evaluated and that the individual contributions of the faculty, when considered in aggregate, advance the goals of the department and of the university.

All faculty have a responsibility to conduct scholarly work in research, teaching, or community outreach in order to contribute to the body of knowledge in their field(s). Effectiveness in teaching, research, or community outreach must meet an acceptable standard when it is part of a faculty member's responsibilities. Finally, each faculty member is expected to contribute to the governance and professionally-related service activities of the university.

## Scholarly Agenda

*Individual faculty responsibility.*   The process of developing and articulating one's own scholarly agenda is an essential first step for newly-appointed faculty and is a continuing responsibility as faculty seek advancement. Each faculty member, regardless of rank, has the primary responsibility for planning his or her own career and for articulating his or her own evolving scholarly agenda.

The purpose of a scholarly agenda is not to limit a faculty member's freedom nor to constrain his or her scholarship, but, primarily, to provide a means for individuals to articulate their programs of scholarly effort. The scholarly agenda needs to be specific enough to provide a general outline of a faculty member's goals, priorities, and activities, but it is not a detailed recitation of tasks or a set of detailed, prescribed outcomes. A scholarly agenda accomplishes the following:

- Articulates the set of serious intellectual, aesthetic, or creative questions, issues, or problems which engage and enrich an individual scholar.

- Describes an individual's accomplished and proposed contributions to knowledge, providing an overview of scholarship, including long-term goals and purposes.

- Clarifies general responsibilities and emphases placed by the individual upon research, teaching, community outreach, or governance.

- Articulates the manner in which the scholar's activities relate to the departmental mission and programmatic goals.

As a faculty member grows and develops, his or her scholarly agenda may evolve over the years. New scholarly agendas may reflect changes in the set of questions, issues, or problems which engage the scholar, or in the individual's relative emphases on teaching, research, community outreach, and governance. The process of developing or redefining a scholarly agenda also encourages the individual scholar to interact with and draw upon the shared expertise of his or her departmental peers. This process promotes both individual and departmental development, and contributes to the intellectual, aesthetic, and creative climate of the department and of the university.

*Departmental, school, and college responsibilities.*   The development of a scholarly agenda supports a collective process of departmental planning and decision-making which determines the deployment of faculty talent in support of departmental and university missions. Departments, schools, and colleges have the primary responsibility for establishing their respective missions and programmatic goals within the context of the university's mission and disciplines as a whole. Recognizing that departments often accomplish such wide-ranging missions by encouraging faculty to take on diverse scholarly agendas, departments and individual faculty members are expected to engage in joint career development activities throughout each faculty member's career. Such activities must serve certain purposes:

- Recognize the individual's career development needs.

- Respect the diversity of individual faculty interests and talents.

- Advance the departmental mission and programmatic goals.

Departments shall develop processes for establishing, discussing, agreeing upon, and revising a scholarly agenda that are consistent with the focus upon individual career development and collective responsibilities and shall establish regular methods for resolving conflicts which may arise in the process of agreeing upon scholarly agendas. Finally, departmental processes shall include periodic occasions for collective discussion of the overall picture resulting from the combination of the scholarly agendas of individual faculty members.

*The uses of a scholarly agenda.*   The primary use of a scholarly agenda is developmental, not evaluative. An individual's contributions to knowledge should be evaluated in the context of the quality and significance of the scholarship displayed. An individual may include a previously agreed upon scholarly agenda in his or her promotion and tenure documentation, but it is not required. A scholarly agenda is separate from such essentially evaluation-driven practices as letters of offer, annual review of tenure-track faculty, and institutional career support-peer review of tenured faculty, and from the consideration of individuals for merit awards.

## Expressions of Scholarship

The term *scholar* implies superior intellectual, aesthetic, or creative attainment. A scholar engages at the highest levels of lifelong learning and inquiry. The character of a scholar is demonstrated by academic achievement and rigorous academic practice. Over time, an active learner usually moves fluidly among different expressions of scholarship. However, it also is quite common and appropriate for scholars to prefer one expression over another. The following four expressions of scholarship apply equally to research, teaching, and community outreach.

*Discovery.*   Discovery is the rigorous testing of researchable questions suggested by theory or models of how phenomena may operate. It is active experimentation, or exploration, with the primary goal of adding to the cumulative knowledge in a substantive way and of enhancing future prediction of the phenomena. Discovery also may involve original creation in writing, as well as creation, performance, or production in the performing arts, fine arts, architecture, graphic design, cinema, and broadcast media or related technologies.

*Integration.* Integration places isolated knowledge or observations in perspective. Integrating activities make connections across disciplines, theories, or models. Integration illuminates information, artistic creations in the literary and performing arts, or original work in a revealing way. It brings divergent knowledge together or creates and/or extends new theory.

*Interpretation.* Interpretation is the process of revealing, explaining, and making knowledge and creative processes clear to others or of interpreting the creative works of others. In essence, interpretation involves communicating knowledge and instilling skills and understanding that others may build upon and apply.

*Application.* Application involves asking how state-of-the-art knowledge can be responsibly applied to significant problems. Application primarily concerns assessing the efficacy of knowledge or creative activities within a particular context, refining its implications, assessing its generalizability, and using it to implement changes.

## Quality and Significance of Scholarship

Quality and significance of scholarship are the primary criteria for determining faculty promotion and tenure. Quality and significance of scholarship are overarching, integrative concepts that apply equally to the expressions of scholarship as they may appear in various disciplines and to faculty accomplishments resulting from research, teaching, and community outreach.

A consistently high quality of scholarship, and its promise for future exemplary scholarship, is more important than the quantity of the work done. The criteria for evaluating the quality and significance of scholarly accomplishments include the following.

*Clarity and relevance of goals.* A scholar should clearly define objectives of scholarly work and clearly state basic questions of inquiry. Clarity of purpose provides a critical context for evaluating scholarly work.

- Research or community outreach projects should address substantive intellectual, aesthetic, or creative problems or issues within one's chosen discipline or interdisciplinary field. Clear objectives are necessary for fair evaluation.

- Teaching activities are usually related to learning objectives that are appropriate within the context of curricular goals and the state of knowledge in the subject matter.

*Mastery of existing knowledge.* A scholar must be well-prepared and knowledgeable about developments in his or her field. The ability to educate others, conduct meaningful research, and provide high quality assistance through community outreach depends upon mastering existing knowledge.

- As researchers and problem solvers, scholars propose methodologies, measures, and interventions that reflect relevant theory, conceptualizations, and cumulative wisdom.

- As teachers, scholars demonstrate a command of resources and exhibit a depth, breadth, and understanding of subject matter allowing them to respond adequately to student learning needs and to evaluate teaching and curricular innovation.

*Appropriate use of methodology and resources.* A scholar should address goals with carefully constructed logic and methodology.

- Rigorous research and applied problem solving require well-constructed methodology that allows one to determine the efficacy of the tested hypotheses or chosen intervention.

- As teachers, scholars apply appropriate pedagogy and instructional techniques to maximize student learning and use appropriate methodology to evaluate the effectiveness of curricular activities.

*Effectiveness of communication.* Scholars should possess effective oral and written communication skills that enable them to convert knowledge into language that a public audience beyond the classroom, research laboratory, or field site can understand.

- As researchers and problem solvers, scholars make formal oral presentations and write effective manuscripts or reports or create original artistic works that meet the professional standards of the intended audience.

- As teachers, scholars communicate in ways that build positive student rapport and clarify new knowledge so as to facilitate learning. They also should be able to disseminate the results of their curricular innovations to their teaching peers.

Scholars should communicate with appropriate audiences and subject their ideas to critical inquiry and independent review. Usually the results of scholarship are communicated widely through publications (e.g., journal articles and books), performances, exhibits, and/or presentations at conferences and workshops.

*Significance of results.*   Scholars should evaluate whether or not they achieve their goals and whether or not this achievement had an important impact on and is used by others. Customarily, peers and other multiple and credible sources (e.g., students, community participants, and subject matter experts) evaluate the significance of results.

- As researchers, teachers, and problem solvers, scholars widely disseminate their work in order to invite scrutiny and to measure varying degrees of critical acclaim. They must consider more than direct user satisfaction when evaluating the quality and significance of an intellectual contribution.

- Faculty engaged in community outreach can make a difference in their communities and beyond by defining or resolving relevant social problems or issues, by facilitating organizational development, by improving existing practices or programs, and by enriching the cultural life of the community. Scholars should widely disseminate the knowledge gained in a community-based project in order to share its significance with those who do not benefit directly from the project.

- As teachers, scholars can make a difference in their students' lives by raising student motivation to learn, by developing students' lifelong learning skills, and by contributing to students' knowledge, skills, and abilities. Teaching scholars also can make a significant scholarly contribution by communicating pedagogical innovations and curricular developments to peers who adopt the approaches.

*Consistently ethical behavior.*   Scholars should conduct their work with honesty, integrity, and objectivity. They should foster a respectful relationship with students, community participants, peers, and others who participate in or benefit from their work. Faculty standards for academic integrity represent a code of ethical behavior. For example, ethical behavior includes following the human subject review process in conducting research projects and properly crediting sources of information in writing reports, articles, and books.

## Evaluation of Scholarship

Scholarly accomplishments in the areas of research, teaching, and community outreach all enter into the evaluation of faculty performance. Scholarly profiles will vary depending on individual faculty members' areas of emphasis. The weight to be given factors relevant to the determination of promotion, tenure, and merit necessarily varies with the individual faculty member's assigned role and from one academic field to another. However, one should recognize that research, teaching, and community outreach often overlap. For example, a service-learning project may reflect both teaching and community outreach. Some research projects may involve both research and community outreach. Pedagogical research may involve both research and teaching. When a faculty member evaluates his or her individual intellectual, aesthetic, or creative accomplishments, it is more important to focus on the general criteria of the quality and significance of the work than to categorize the work. Peers also should focus on the quality and significance of work rather than on categories of work when evaluating an individual's achievements.

The following discussion is intended to assist faculty in formative planning of a scholarly agenda and to provide examples of the characteristics to consider when evaluating scholarly accomplishments.

*Documentation.*   The accomplishments of a candidate for promotion or tenure must be documented in order to be evaluated. Documentation and evaluation of scholarship should focus on the quality and significance of scholarship rather than on a recitation of tasks and projects. Each department should judge the quality and significance of scholarly contributions to knowledge as well as the quantity.

In addition to contributions to knowledge, the effectiveness of teaching, research, or community outreach must meet an acceptable standard when it is part of a faculty member's responsibilities. Documentation should be sufficient to outline a faculty member's agreed-upon responsibilities and to support an evaluation of effectiveness.

Documentation for promotion and tenure normally includes several items:

- Self-appraisal of scholarly agenda and accomplishments including: 1) a discussion of the scholarly agenda that describes the long-term goals and purposes of a scholarly line of work, explains how the agenda fits into a larger endeavor and field of work, and demonstrates how scholarly accomplishments to date have advanced the agenda; 2) a description of how the agenda relates to the departmental academic mission, within the context of the university mission and the discipline as a whole; 3) an evaluation of the quality and significance of scholarly work; 4) an evaluation of the effectiveness of teaching, research, or community outreach when it is part of a faculty member's responsibilities.

- A curriculum vitae including a comprehensive list of significant accomplishments.

- A representative sample of an individual's most scholarly work rather than an exhaustive portfolio. However, a department may establish guidelines requiring review of all scholarly activities that are central to a faculty member's scholarly agenda over a recent period of time.

■ Evaluations of accomplishments by peers and other multiple and credible sources (e.g., students, community participants, and subject matter experts). Peers include authoritative representatives from the candidate's scholarly field(s).

*Research and other creative activities.* A significant factor in determining a faculty member's merit for promotion is the individual's accomplishments in research and published contributions to knowledge in the appropriate field(s) and other professional or creative activities that are consistent with the faculty member's responsibilities. Contributions to knowledge in the area of research and other creative activities should be evaluated using the criteria for quality and significance of scholarship. It is strongly recommended that the following items be considered in evaluating research and other creative activities:

■ Research may be evaluated on the quality and significance of publication of scholarly books, monographs, articles, presentations, and reviews in journals, and grant proposal submissions and awards. An evaluation should consider whether the individual's contributions reflect continuous engagement in research and whether these contributions demonstrate future promise. Additionally, the evaluation should consider whether publications are refereed (an important form of peer review) as an important factor. In some fields, evidence of citation or use of the faculty member's research or creative contributions by other scholars is appropriate.

■ The development and publication of software should be judged in the context of its involvement of state-of-the-art knowledge and its impact on peers and others.

■ In certain fields such as writing, literature, performing arts, fine arts, architecture, graphic design, cinema, and broadcast media or related fields, distinguished creation should receive consideration equivalent to that accorded to distinction attained in scientific and technical research. In evaluating artistic creativity, an attempt should be made to define the candidate's merit in the light of such criteria as originality, scope, richness, and depth of creative expression. It should be recognized that in music and drama, distinguished performance, including conducting and directing, is evidence of a candidate's creativity. Creative works often are evaluated by the quality and significance of publication, exhibiting, and/or performance of original works, or by the direction or performance of significant works. Instruments that include external peer review should be used or developed to evaluate artistic creation and performance. Including critical reviews, where available, can augment the departmental evaluations. The evaluation should include a chronological list of creative works, exhibitions, or performances.

- Contributions to the development of collaborative, interdisciplinary, or interinstitutional research programs are highly valued. Mechanisms for evaluating such contributions may be employed. Evaluating collaborative research might involve addressing both individual contributions (e.g., quality of work, completion of assigned responsibilities) and contributions to the successful participation of others (e.g., skills in teamwork, group problem solving).

- Honors and awards represent recognition of stature in the field when they recognize active engagement in research or creative activities at regional, national, or international levels.

- Effective participation in disciplinary or interdisciplinary organizations' activities should be evaluated in the context of their involvement of state-of-the-art knowledge and impact on peers and others. For example, this participation might include serving as editor of journals or other learned publications, serving on an editorial board, chairing a program committee for a regional, national, or international meeting, or providing scholarly leadership as an officer of a major professional organization.

*Teaching, mentoring, and curricular activities.* A significant factor in determining a faculty member's merit for promotion is the individual's accomplishments in teaching, mentoring, and curricular activities, consistent with the faculty member's responsibilities. Teaching activities are scholarly functions that directly serve learners within or outside the university. Scholars who teach must be intellectually engaged and must demonstrate mastery of the knowledge in their field(s). The ability to lecture and lead discussions, to create a variety of learning opportunities, to draw out students and arouse curiosity in beginners, to stimulate advanced students to engage in creative work, to organize logically, to evaluate critically the materials related to one's field of specialization, to assess student performance, and to excite students to extend learning beyond a particular course and understand its contribution to a body of knowledge are all recognized as essential to excellence in teaching.

Teaching scholars often study pedagogical methods that improve student learning. Evaluation of performance in this area thus should consider creative and effective use of innovative teaching methods, curricular innovations, and software development. Scholars who teach also should disseminate promising curricular innovations to appropriate audiences and subject their work to critical review. PSU encourages publishing in pedagogical journals or making educationally-focused presentations at disciplinary and interdisciplinary meetings that advance the scholarship of teaching and curricular innovations or practice.

Evaluation of teaching and curricular contributions should not be limited to classroom activities. It also should focus on a faculty member's contributions to larger curricular goals (for example, the role of a course in laying foundations for other courses and its contribution to majors, or contributions to broad aspects of general education or interdisciplinary components of the curriculum). In addition, PSU recognizes that student mentoring, academic advising, thesis advising, and dissertation advising are important departmental functions. Faculty may take on differential mentoring responsibilities as part of their personal scholarly agenda.

To ensure valid evaluations, departments should appoint a departmental committee to devise formal methods for evaluating teaching and curriculum-related performance. All members of the department should be involved in selecting these formal methods. The department chair has the responsibility for seeing that these methods for evaluation are implemented.

Contributions to knowledge in the area of teaching, mentoring, and curricular activities should be evaluated using the criteria for quality and significance of scholarship. It is strongly recommended that the following items be considered in the evaluation of teaching and curricular accomplishments:

- Contributions to courses or curriculum development

- Outlines, syllabi, and other materials developed for use in courses

- The results of creative approaches to teaching methods and techniques, including the development of software and other technologies that advance student learning

- The results of assessments of student learning

- Formal student evaluations

- Peer review of teaching, mentoring, and curricular activities

- Accessibility to students

- Ability to relate to a wide variety of students for purposes of advising

- Mentoring and guiding students toward the achievement of curricular goals

- The results of supervision of student research or other creative activities including theses and field advising

- The results of supervision of service-learning experiences in the community

- Contributions to, and participation in, the achievement of departmental goals, such as achieving reasonable retention of students

- Contributions to the development and delivery of collaborative, interdisciplinary, university studies, extended studies, and interinstitutional educational programs

- Teaching and mentoring students and others in how to obtain access to information resources so as to further student, faculty, and community research and learning

- Grant proposals and grants for the development of curriculum or teaching methods and techniques

- Professional development as related to instruction; e.g., attendance at professional meetings related to a faculty member's areas of instructional expertise

- Honors and awards for teaching

*Community outreach.*  A significant factor in determining a faculty member's advancement is the individual's accomplishments in community outreach when such activities are part of a faculty member's responsibilities. Scholars can draw on their professional expertise to engage in a wide array of community outreach. Such activities can include defining or resolving relevant local, national, or international problems or issues. Community outreach also includes planning literary or artistic festivals or celebrations. PSU highly values quality community outreach as part of faculty roles and responsibilities.

The setting of Portland State University affords faculty many opportunities to make their expertise useful to thecommunity outside the university. Community-based activities are those which are tied directly to one's special field of knowledge. Such activities may involve a cohesive series of activities contributing to the definition or resolution of problems or issues in society. These activities also include aesthetic and celebratory projects. Scholars who engage in community outreach also should disseminate promising innovations to appropriate audiences and subject their work to critical review.

Departments and individual faculty members can use the following guidelines when developing appropriate community outreach. Important community outreach can:

- Contribute to the definition or resolution of a relevant social problem or issue

- Use state-of-the-art knowledge to facilitate change in organizations or institutions

- Use disciplinary or interdisciplinary expertise to help groups conceptualize and solve problems

- Set up intervention programs to prevent, ameliorate, or remediate persistent negative outcomes for individuals or groups or to optimize positive outcomes

- Contribute to the evaluation of existing practices or programs

- Make substantive contributions to public policy

- Create schedules and choose or hire participants in community events such as festivals

- Offer professional services such as consulting (consistent with the policy on outside employment), serving as an expert witness, providing clinical services, and participating on boards and commissions outside the university

Faculty and departments should evaluate a faculty member's community outreach accomplishments creatively and thoughtfully. It is strongly recommended that the evaluation consider the following indicators of quality and significance:

- Publication in journals or presentations at disciplinary or interdisciplinary meetings that advance the scholarship of community outreach

- Honors, awards, and other forms of special recognition received for community outreach

- Adoption of the faculty member's models for problem resolution, intervention programs, instruments, or processes by others who seek solutions to similar problems

- Substantial contributions to public policy or influence upon professional practice

- Models that enrich the artistic and cultural life of the community

- Evaluative statements from clients and peers regarding the quality and significance of documents or performances produced by the faculty member

*Governance and other professionally related service.* In addition to contributions to knowledge as a result of scholarly activities, each faculty member is expected to contribute to the governance and professionally related service activities of the university. Governance and professionally related service create an environment that supports scholarly excellence and the achievement of the university mission. Governance and professionally related service actives include the following.

- Committee service. Service on university, school or college, and department or program committees is an important part of running the university. Department chairs may request a committee chair to evaluate the value a faculty member's contributions to that committee. Such service also may include involvement in peer review of scholarly accomplishments.

- University community. Faculty are expected to participate in activities devoted to enriching the artistic, cultural, and social life of the university, such as attending commencement or serving as adviser to student groups.

- Community or professional service. Faculty may engage in professionally related service to a discipline or interdisciplinary field, or to the external community, that does not engage an individual's scholarship. For example, a faculty member may serve the discipline by organizing facilities for a professional meeting or by serving as treasurer of an organization.

# APPENDIX H

## PSP 101 Syllabus
### Introduction to Service in Democratic Communities
### Providence College

Spring 1996-TR 11:30–12:45 (Series K)
Instructors:  Dr. Rick Battistoni
  Office: Feinstein Inst. for Pub. Service, FAC 402
  Phone: 865-2787 (direct line w/voicemail)
Dr. Kathleen Cornely
  Office: Sowa Hall 225
  Phone: 865-2866
Feinstein Institute Teaching Assistants: Liza Pappas, Lara Slachta

### Required Texts (available at PC Bookstore)

Barber, B. R., & Battistoni, R. M. (Eds.). (1993). *Education for democracy: citizenship, community, service*. Dubuque, IA: Kendall-Hunt. (B & B in course outline).

Kozol, J. (1995). *Amazing grace: The lives of children and the conscience of the nation*. (Kozol in course outline).

. . . and other readings to be provided in class

### Course Description and Requirements

This course serves two major purposes. First and foremost, it serves as the introductory survey or gateway course in a newly approved and unique interdisciplinary major and minor in public and community service studies. In addition, it serves as a lower level elective for students who are either determining whether or not they want to take other Feinstein Institute courses or eventually major or minor in public and community service studies, or who are intrigued by the notion of combining a community service experience with their academic study. Whatever your motivation, we are thrilled that you've chosen to join us at this, the beginning of an exciting exploration into a new academic area. However, please understand that while we have the experience of the past year's pilot courses to inform what we are doing this semester, we will still be experimenting with a variety of concepts, materials, assignments, and exercises.

As the introductory survey to a major and minor in public and community service studies, the course will focus on three concepts that are central to our studies: service, community, and democracy. Each concept or topic will be explored from three different perspectives (hence, the designation I, II, & III in the course outline) over the course of the semester: concrete and practical experiences (drawing on students' service and other experiences and observations); ideas, concepts, and theories (thoroughly discussed and critiqued in class and in written assignments); and challenges and commitments (the challenges posed for those interested in promoting service, community or democracy, and the individual and social commitments that must be made to produce quality service, meaningful community, or active democracy). Among the questions to be explored under each topic:

## Service

- Why do people serve? Why do I serve?
- Whom do we serve?
- What is service?
- What is good service? How is good service organized?
- Should I/we serve? or Can service be a bad thing?

## Community

- What is community?
- Who belongs and who doesn't? To what communities do I belong?
- What makes a community work—individuals, organizations, values, institutions?
- What helps and what hinders a community?
- Is community always a good thing?

## Democracy

- What is democracy?
- What makes communities and service democratic?
- What kinds of participation and responsibilities does democracy require?
- How and at what level can I participate?
- What does democracy require in terms of liberty, equality, and legitimate power?
- What promotes and what undermines democracy?
- Is democracy always a good thing (can the majority turn tyrannical)?

This course is about service, community, and democracy. Our class structure and pedagogy will therefore attempt to mirror these three concepts, in the following way.

## Service

In addition to the regular class meetings, you and other students in the class will participate in approximately 30 to 40 hours of community service over the course of the semester. Community service allows you the unique opportunity to apply theories and concepts discussed in class to your own practical experiences in serving others in the community. In this course, we intend to connect your service experience both to the other academic material discussed in class, and to weekly writing assignments. You will have a choice among several possible community service options and will be able to schedule your service around your other classes, work, or extracurricular activities. These options will be presented during the first week of class, and you should expect to begin your service in week two, continuing through the final week of classes.

Students working at a particular site will usually work with the assistance of one of the members of the Feinstein Institute Service Corps assigned to this course. Each teaching assistant will serve as a team leader for your service activity, acting as a liaison between your service site and this course, troubleshooting any problems that may occur, and leading a number of group activities and projects with the other students at your site.

## Community

Over the course of the semester, we hope that students and faculty will form a democratic community as we discuss and reflect upon the nature of democratic community. A democratic community depends much more on public reflection and action than on elections. To reinforce that, we have structured class experiences that will build community and public reflection. In addition to the service work, where you will be placed in teams, your service team will be asked to make group presentations or lead class sessions, and you will share your written reflections as a dialogue with the others from your service group.

*Group presentations.*   Over the course of the semester you will be responsible for contributing to and participating in several different group presentations to the rest of the class, or for leading class discussion on a particular day and topic. We will talk much more about each in class as they approach, but you will work with others placed at the same service site on some of these group projects.

*Structured writing assignments: Experiential journal.*   You will document your thoughts and experiences working in the community, reflecting critically on the assigned readings and class discussions, responding to specific questions presented for writing. You should aim for about five pages of freely written material per assignment; the writing will not be scrutinized for "quality" along typical academic lines—it can be loose, informal, associative, and in alternative forms to straight prose. Entries will be evaluated in light of the overall quantity of entries and the general quality of your intellectual explorations, responses to specific questions, and your integration of the readings and class discussions. We encourage you to conclude each entry with questions you would like to ask yourself, your fellow students, those you work with in the larger community, or us. These questions will be used to write the final exam. We'll respond to the written assignments along the way so that all will get feedback, and we will provide opportunities to share journals with other students, to enhance the seminar and community-building nature of the class.

## Democracy

Democracy is about participation, engagement, and responsibility. The following features of the course will contribute to your understanding of democracy.

*Seminar format.*　The class will be conducted as a seminar and will break into small groups often during the semester. Therefore, it is imperative that students come to class and come prepared to discuss class themes and reading assignments. The class will be an opportunity for us to reflect upon and analyze together critical questions about citizenship, democracy, and community. Students will be encouraged to bring into class discussions their community service experiences as they relate to topic themes. Class attendance and participation are crucial parts of your democratic responsibility to your fellow students: If you are not present and participating, not only are you losing out, but you are failing to contribute to other students' learning and understanding in the course. You have unique experiences and perspectives which we all want you to share.

*Reading assignments.*　We will be using an interdisciplinary anthology (Barber & Ballistoni) which spans a wide range of reading materials, from philosophy and theology to poetry and literature to politics and sociology. Readings from the anthology will be supplemented by Jonathan Kozol's *Amazing Grace* and other short pieces to be handed out in class. The readings are meant to serve as resources to you as you think about what it means to be a democratic citizen and a member of the communities in which you find yourself. You may not find all of the readings inspiring, and you may not agree with the perspective of some of the authors. But we hope they will provoke thought and discussion of the relevant matters of the course. We have chosen to focus on only a few readings for each topic to be discussed in class out of the 60-plus selections contained in the reader. That was our responsibility, given the other demands of this course. Your responsibility is to read each work by the time it is listed in the course outline, as well as to respond to journal questions about the reading in question. At the end of the semester, we will ask you to thoroughly evaluate the readings for the course, as part of our ongoing process of improving the course and the program.

## Evaluation

Your learning in this course will be somewhat different from a typical college course, and so the evaluation is also somewhat different. Since it is a service-learning course offered within the Feinstein Institute, a significant portion of our learning will come from structured individual and group reflection on our service experiences with community partners. We will also strive to create an energetic democratic learning community in the class. Accordingly, the evaluation in this course is designed to match the multiple and creative ways learning will take place. Your course grade will be determined as follows:

*Experiential journal.*   Worth 30% of the final grade.

*Final essay examination.*   30% of the final grade will be based on an essay final exam. We will discuss the format and the nature of the final later in the semester.

*Group presentations.*   20% of the final grade will be based on your contribution to group presentations and your group's leadership of class discussions as designated during the semester. More details on these to come . . .

*Community responsibility index.*   20% of your final grade will be based on your evaluation of your contribution to meeting the responsibilities of membership in this learning community. As in any community, members may gauge the extent to which they meet their own responsibilities in cooperating with other community members in meeting collective goals. We ask you to evaluate the extent to which you have met your responsibilities to our democratic learning community. To the extent that you live up to your agreed-upon commitments in the course, you will get full credit for this portion of your grade. To the extent that you, and we, feel that you have failed to meet the minimum level of commitment to your community responsibilities, you will get zero credit for this portion.

We want to emphasize your responsibilities to our academic community by making them part of your grade. The success of this class and our collective learning in it hinges on each of us taking shared ownership of the class. This means that each of us meet our responsibilities in the following areas:

- Living up to our commitments to our service placement

- Attending class attendance diligently and actively participating in our conversations

- Completing required reading by the date assigned

- Completing written assignments on time

- Deporting oneself as an equal member of a democratic community

Since you will be asked to take responsibility for your own learning, you will be the person best able to assess whether you have lived up to your responsibilities to this learning community. With responsibility for learning comes responsibility for evaluating that learning. Responsibility for learning is not given; it is taken. Only you can decide that you wish to be a full participant in the course and so, at the end of the course, you will be asked to do a self-evaluation of your contribution to this community. The Community Responsibility Index (CRI) is our vehicle for doing this.

Please feel free to raise concerns, questions, criticisms, and suggestions as we go along, either publicly or in private consultation with me. The course outline that follows is tentative and should be seen as a general guide, not a prison out of which none of us can escape.

## PSP 101
### Intro. to Service in Democratic Communities
### *Spring 1996*

### Course Outline

| Date | Topic under discussion | Reading assignment** |
|------|------------------------|----------------------|
| *Jan 18* | Orientation; Introduction to Class; Community Service Opportunities | |
| *Jan 23* | Service & Service-Learning: Expectations Service Placement Choices | |
| *Jan 25, 30* | Service I: What Is Service? | Mansfield. The Garden Party; King. Good Neighbor; Mother Teresa (all in B & B) |
| *Feb 1* | Why Do People Serve? Why Do I Serve? Whom Do We Serve? | Coles. *Method*; Fuller. *Theology of Enough*; article on Tzedakah |

| | | |
|---|---|---|
| *Feb 6* | Our Service Neighborhoods<br>Group Presentations | |
| *Feb 8, 13, 15* | Community I: What Is<br>Community? | Arendt. *The Public Realm*<br>Bellah. *Habits of the Heart* |
| | To What Community Do<br>I Belong? | Kemmis. Barn Raising ;<br>Kretzman & McKnight |
| | What Makes a Community<br>Work: A Field Exercise | Barber, Moffatt |
| *Feb 20, 22* | Democracy I: What Is<br>Democracy?<br>What Makes Communities<br>and Service Democratic?<br>What Kinds of<br>Participation and<br>Responsibilities Does<br>Democracy Require? | Barber & Boyte; U.S.<br>Constitution |
| *Feb 27, 29* | Service II: What Is Good<br>Service?<br>How Is Good Service<br>Organized?<br>How Is Service Organized<br>at Your Site? | Addams, *Hull House*;<br>Chi & Harkavy<br>Group Presentations |
| *Mar 5, 7* | Community II: Diversity<br>& Community | Lorde, Okin, Sacks,<br>Wilkinson, &<br>Jackson |
| *Mar 19,<br>21, 26* | Who Belongs and Who<br>Doesn't? | Kozol (read all by Mar 19) |
| *Mar 28* | How Is Community<br>Represented in the Media? | Group Presentations |
| *Apr 2* | Democracy II: Democracy<br>& Service | DeTocqueville. Putnam.<br>*Bowling Alone* |
| | National Service &<br>Democracy | Selected service essays.<br>Kennedy, Peace Corps<br>Announcement |
| *Apr 9* | Our Service and National<br>Service | Group Presentations |
| *Apr 11, 16* | Service III: Is Service a<br>Good Thing? | McKnight, Illich, Rand, &<br>Bloustein. |

| | | |
|---|---|---|
| *Apr 18,*<br>*23, 25* | Community/Democracy III<br>What Promotes/<br>Undermines Dem. Com?<br>How Much Liberty,<br>Equality Is Necessary?<br>Is Community, Democracy<br>Always Good? | Schaar; Boutros-Ghali; &<br>King. *Letter from*<br>*Birmingham Jail.*<br>Jackson. *The Lottery*<br>LeGuin. *The Ones Who*<br>*Walk Away* |
| *Apr 30,*<br>*May 2* | Final Service Site<br>Presentations | |
| *May 10* | Final Examination Date | |
| *Apr 30,*<br>*May 2* | Final Service | |

# APPENDIX I

*Educational Philosophy of the Eastside Project*
*Tony Sholander, S.J.*
Santa Clara University

There is a great deal of confusion about the Eastside Project, what it does, and how it does it. Most folks mistake us for a community service program, so agencies in the community call us for volunteers, and faculty from the university drop off old vacuums or clothes for distribution. But we are not a community service agency. We are an educational support program of the university, and we reside on the academic side of the university.

## MISSION

The mission of the Eastside Project is to create a lasting partnership between the university and the community that fosters continuing discussion between both parties so that the Eastside Project is directly responsive to and shaped by the community. We approach these goals and objectives in a variety of ways, one very potent form of which is experiential education. Experiential learning is a pedagogical tool available to instructors to further their classroom goals. In many respects, experiential education resembles community service. We do send students out into the community to work with agencies in the service of poor and often neglected people.

But we insist on a major distinction of purpose for our participants, a distinction that helps clarify some of the misunderstandings about the Eastside Project and demonstrates how this is an educational program. While we use experiential education to develop skills and abilities, we use service-learning first and foremost to foster a paradigm shift in the minds of the students, the result of which is significantly altered world views. Our purpose is to provide students with personal experiences of cultures other than their own so that their perceptions of the world will expand and become more accurate. To borrow a geographical metaphor, we are hoping to facilitate an intellectual earthquake, where cognitive and affective plates shift and realign to form a new conceptual terrain.

I-1

## ROLE OF THE PARTICIPANT

Our perception of the role of the Eastside Project participant might also help illustrate a difference in this program. The participants of the Eastside Project go into the community as students, not volunteers. They go out to listen and explore, question and wonder, observe, feel, and experience. That is why what they are doing is not adequately described as community service.

So they will have sufficient time for these activities, we place them in agencies that do not rely on them for survival, and we have them work in an unstructured capacity—because they are there primarily to learn.

All the wonders and riches and experiences of the larger community are hidden from the student until the student takes the chance and makes the effort to expose him or herself to what is really out there. From the perspective of the learner, great thinkers live agelessly, and experiences reside without cultural boundaries in the lives and memories of members of the community. Great treasures make themselves available to the willing student.

Further critical reactions center on the perceived nature of the relationship of the students to the community members. This is also a very important point of consideration. If Eastside Project participants enter into this relationship as volunteers, they go in from a position of prestige, status, and power over the community member. Wearing the volunteer's hat, the participant approaches the relationship with a sense of giving to others. In what sense does the volunteer encounter the community member as a person, as an equal, entering into a mutual partnership?

The reason we pursue this distinction is that the nature of the relationship of the participant to the community member is affected by the label or definition we apply. Eastside Project participants who enter these relationships as students, rather than volunteers, enter with the acknowledgment, at least at some level, that they are more vulnerable to what happens in the relationships than if they formed the relationships as volunteers.

There is one other reason for pursuing this distinction. Volunteers can walk away from their volunteer work with a sense of well-being and satisfaction. And rightly so. What they do is generous, needed, valuable, and good. But volunteerism and relief work address only the symptoms of social ills.

The student, on the other hand, must wrestle with questions that are not necessarily within the purview of the volunteer. Rigorous analysis and investigation into what causes and supports homelessness, bigotry, homophobia, sexism and racism, inequities in pay between men and women, and a whole host of other ills that affect our society, are the appropriate domain of the student. Students are being challenged to intellectually evaluate the structures of our society to see how well they respond to the needs of all humankind. That is why we send them into the community, that is what makes this an intellectual enterprise, and that is why we reside within the academic side of the university.

## EXPERIENTIAL EDUCATION AND LEARNING

Our application of the strategy of experiential education has two levels, the first of which resembles community service programs at other institutions which send people into the community. At the first level, our general plan of experiential education coordinates the learning objectives of classroom instructors with the service opportunities available within the community. At this level, students are provided with a first-hand experience of the theories, principles, data, models, and ideas that are presented in the classroom.

A deeper level of learning takes place in a less obvious manner but reflects some of the more significant aims of the project. This level of learning is reached partly as a result of the manner in which the service-learning is structured. We choose to have students come into contact with those persons in our society who are marginalized and powerless because these populations have been traditionally underserved. But more importantly, this preference reveals a core insight of the project: Those who are discarded, pushed aside, and discounted within our society are in a unique and privileged position to comment and reflect on the attitudes, values, and priorities of the dominant culture.

Every placement is designed in such a manner that each of the students develops a personal, one-to-one relationship with a person in one of our target populations. This personal interaction initiates a chain of events and experiences that challenges, sometimes dramatically, the ideas, attitudes, and backgrounds often cherished by the students. In the process, students will frequently perceive a role reversal, realizing that the person they have come to help has become their guide to a larger, more accurate and complex orientation to reality and has opened them up to the full range of human experience.

One helpful description of this learning process is a model developed by Albert Nolan as a result of his work among South Africa's disenfranchised Black Community. His model describes four stages of development:

### Compassion

The first stage is called compassion, because it occurs when students are moved by the struggles, issues, and concerns of the people they meet.

Often information, movies, etc., are sufficient to initiate this stage, but personal exposure is more powerful. The heightened anxiety at this level prompts a person to relief work and acts of charity. Here one is likely to answer "yes" to Cain's age-old question, "Am I my brother's keeper?"

The heightened effect is an important moment for the students. Sometimes students interpret the anxiety as guilt. Their lives are significantly more advantaged than these other people, and the guilt is often the motive for the charity response or change of lifestyle. Or the anxiety can be interpreted as proof that all the stereotypes the student brought into the relationship are true; that the community member is dangerous or lazy or bad. Neither lingering guilt nor negative attributions are desirable final outcomes of a learning process, and the students shift to the next stage when given an opportunity for self-expression through journals or discussion.

## Structural Change

The second stage of this process is called structural change, and it focuses on the causes and supports of poverty, homelessness, undocumented immigration, and other issues that affect our society. At this stage, students begin to see that these are all a result of choices we have consciously or unconsciously made in the way we structure and run our community, our nation, and our world. Since the focus is on structures, there is usually no blame or hatred, but instead, a desire to work for social change. Here, too, the answer to Cain would be, "Yes, you are your brother's keeper."

## Humility

The next level of development is called humility, and it takes some time to reach. Time is actually the central element that precipitates the shift. It is at this point that students begin to realize that if these issues are going to be resolved, the ones who are affected by them are the ones who will have to do the work. If we don't get in the way or actively interfere, the poor will save themselves, and they do not really need you or me.

The second aspect of this level is an awareness that I need to learn from poor people, from their experience, approach to life, and values. Students who participate in the Eastside Project initially expect that they will be helping others, but in the end they often discover that what they learned, what they received in the process, was a gift beyond price, unique and irreplaceable. At this stage, the response to Cain might be: "No, you are your brother's brother."

Romanticism is the hazard of the third stage. It takes some experience to recognize that even the poor have their share of liars, cheats, and thieves, just as they have their share of generous, honest, kind, and hardworking members.

## Solidarity

The final stage of Nolan's model is solidarity. It is facilitated by disillusionment and the insight that the lives of all human persons are inextricably bound together. At this stage, one would answer Cain thus: "No, you are your brother."

*(Adapted from Tony Sholander's article in* The Bridge, *Winter Quarter, 1994.)*

# Appendix J

## Educating the Good Citizen:
## Service-Learning in Higher Education
### University of Utah

This document, prepared in 1995 by the faculty advisory committee of the Lowell Bennion Center of the University of Utah, presents a proposal for enhancing the educational experience offered at the University of Utah by introducing service-learning into the curriculum on a broad scale. After reviewing the ways that higher education in America has changed over the last centuries, the document discusses the three types of knowledge that universities seek to instill: foundational knowledge, professional knowledge, and socially responsive knowledge. It focuses on how socially responsive knowledge has become extremely important in contemporary society, and how that form of knowledge can be instilled through service-learning. The document concludes by proposing a plan of action for developing the service-learning curriculum at the University of Utah and discusses the role of the Bennion Center in accomplishing this effort.

Higher education is at a crossroads. At few moments in our country's history have so many questioned the importance and relevance of higher education to contemporary society. Politicians and average citizens alike often share a view of the American university as a bastion for privileged intellectuals, not attending to social problems, teaching irrelevant (and irreverent) subjects, too little concerned with teaching and too much interested in research, and somehow not serving their local communities.

Though such an atmosphere might be viewed as threatening, in fact it offers a golden opportunity for the University of Utah to rethink the fundamental nature of the educational experience that it is offering to the next generation of our leaders. One important way for this university to continue making its vital contribution to our society is by developing and emphasizing the role of service-learning or socially responsive learning in the curriculum. By providing our students with an education that integrates classroom and laboratory experiences with opportunities to apply those experiences as concerned citizens in the community that surrounds us, the University of Utah can move to the forefront of American higher education. By developing educational programs that are intimately attuned to real world demands of our society, our institution will be more immune to assertions of irrelevance and obsolescence.

## THE HISTORICAL ROLE OF HIGHER EDUCATION IN AMERICAN LIFE

Throughout our country's history, higher education has aimed to accomplish two fundamental goals. First, universities have directed their educational mission to serving the social needs that were perceived to exist in the community during each period in our history. Second, universities have sought to develop their students into "good citizens," able to meet the public and private challenges of the society into which they would emerge.

Thus, in responding to the growth of technology in a previously agrarian society, the 19th century university perceived a need to provide a growing economy with the new professional citizen, by developing vocationally oriented programs in medicine, engineering, and agriculture. Following World War II, the demands of an increasingly complex society led our colleges and universities to perceive a need to expand their scope and extend their offerings to a greater number of young Americans. Accordingly, new forms of institutions developed—community colleges, four-year colleges, comprehensive universities, and research universities. These institutions embraced a new goal of educating the masses of the nation—the average citizen along with the future leader. In addition to meeting the ever-increasing social demand for scientists, engineers, pharmacists, nurses, physicians, teachers, and other well-trained professionals, American universities perceived a new social need that they educate broadly all who desired a college experience to be good citizens, able to make intelligent, socially responsible decisions. This expanded role was required by a burgeoning population needing access to housing, schools, and science-linked products and services, as well as by the increasing technological complexity of the world.

States and the federal government poured enormous resources into research programs, fellowships and stipends, loan programs, buildings, laboratories, and other forms of support to encourage higher education to contribute to the well-being of the nation and to the development of the student as a citizen able to meet the growing, complex challenges of our society. At the same time, issues of diversity and civil rights resulted in educational programs that expanded the curriculum to include ethnic studies, women's studies, and cross-cultural programs.

## TWO FUNDAMENTAL QUESTIONS OF HIGHER EDUCATION

Each era in American higher education has involved a continuing dialogue between universities and the communities in which they are situated. These exchanges occur at national, regional, and local levels and are aimed at addressing two questions:

- What are the current goals of higher education in light of the perceived social needs of the community?

- How can colleges and universities best teach and prepare students to become "good citizens" to serve their community?

In responding to these fundamental issues, institutions of higher education have, on occasion, been out of synch with changing social needs, as those needs are understood by the larger society. The process whereby a university comes to appreciate the needs of its surrounding society is a gradual one; such needs often become evident only after a period of time. Moreover, like other institutions, universities are prone to inertia and tend to change slowly. Thus, there is often a disjunction between what the members of a university community perceive as the goals of higher education and what persons in the larger society perceive those goals to be. In particular, this disjunction often relates to the attributes of the good citizen that institutions of higher education should be developing. Do we seek only liberally educated citizens, technically skilled citizens, or citizens with a sense of social responsibility, or some combination of these?

Given this tendency to be out of synch with the larger society, universities must maintain a strong commitment to an ongoing dialogue with the communities in which they are situated and must be willing to challenge regularly their current responses to the two fundamental questions of higher education.

## THE PRESENT STATE OF AFFAIRS

As illustrated by the number of books and articles calling for various reforms of colleges and universities, American higher education is in a state of uncertainty and disagreement about how to provide contemporary answers to the fundamental questions of higher education. Expressions of dissatisfaction are also emerging from legislatures and from the federal government, which tend to focus on budgets and teaching loads and voice vague concerns about the values being fostered by modern colleges and universities. But the disturbing message being sent is clear: Society is not getting its money's worth from its institutions of higher education. Faculties need to work harder, be more efficient, stop doing so much research, do more teaching, etc.

Rather than ignore these statements as mere cacophonous rantings, we in American higher education should view these disturbing statements as an invitation to reengage in an important dialogue over the two fundamental questions concerning higher education, and welcome this as an opportunity to articulate a vision for the role of the university in preparing the good citizen of today and the future.

## A Conceptual Model

There are three types of knowledge that may be appropriate in American society in the present and future: 1) Foundational Knowledge, 2) Professional Knowledge, 3) Socially Responsive Knowledge.

*Foundational knowledge* refers to knowledge of the basic concepts and substance of a traditional discipline. *Professional knowledge* refers to the substance and skills of what students learn in vocationally oriented fields, including medicine, business, engineering, architecture, and law. Professional knowledge aims at teaching the student to be a professional, with the practical ability to do certain tangible activities. To a great extent, American colleges and universities during the post-World War II era viewed their role in society as instilling foundational and professional knowledge in students.

The good citizen that institutions of higher education sought to turn out was broadly educated, steeped in foundational knowledge in one or more disciplines, and fit the image and identity of an educated person. Some members of the student population prepared to fulfill their roles as good citizens by being trained as professionals who could contribute immediately to societal needs in science, engineering, business, teaching, or other areas. Universities considered it important that these students be exposed not only to the professional knowledge necessary to enable them to pursue their careers, but also to foundational knowledge. By requiring professional students to take liberal education classes, universities have viewed their role as producing a well-rounded good citizen, one who is not merely a specialist in his or her professional sphere.

In imbuing professional knowledge, institutions of higher education historically have used classrooms, laboratories, and community settings (clerkships, practica, internships) to educate students. The goal has been to teach students to fulfill roles as good professional citizens. To a large extent, fundamental knowledge has been taught by universities and colleges in classrooms, laboratories, and on campus. Students emerge from these settings as educated citizens. In neither instance do these educational systems view service to the community as a central feature of the educational process.

A fundamental change, however, is occurring in higher education as we approach the 21st century. People are beginning to realize that a new kind of knowledge, *socially responsive knowledge*, is necessary if colleges and universities are going to be successful in preparing our students to assume the duties of good citizenship in the future. This newly evolving knowledge includes teaching students a sense of community; a sense of responsibility to others; sensitivity and aspirations to help resolve problems of society; a feeling of commitment and obligation to become involved in community affairs; and a general commitment that extends beyond oneself, one's family, friends, colleagues, and immediate reference groups to the broader concern for one's society. Although some features of this type of social knowledge have been implicit in certain aspects of higher education, historically universities have encouraged individuals to seek more self-focused foundational knowledge and professional skills.

Why does the task of educating our students to be good citizens now require that we pay more attention to socially responsive knowledge? To begin with, the needs that now challenge society are significantly different than those that have faced us in the past. Large-scale problems of the physical environment, health, homelessness, and underemployment have taken the forefront of our attention as never before. Moreover, changes in the demography of the nation and attendant issues of cultural, religious and ethnic diversity, changes in family structures and lifestyles, and the globalization of the economy and political systems force us as academicians to no longer assume that we can perform our teaching role without paying close attention to the impact of that role on the communities that surround us. And these questions simply cannot be addressed only by instilling traditional and professional knowledge in our students. New generations of students must be taught to accept social responsibility if they, as the "good citizens" of the future, are to make a meaningful contribution to the resolution of these newly emerging social problems.

Accordingly, colleges and universities must expand and enhance their curricula in order to offer new educational experiences for coming generations of students. Many students around the nation have already begun this process on their own through volunteer service activities. For example, the Lowell Bennion Community Service Center at the University of Utah currently sponsors more than 50 projects involving 5,000 students per year, who devote thousands of hours of service to community causes. Yet simply providing opportunities for volunteer service will not enable universities to meet the social demands of the coming decades. The transmittal of socially responsive knowledge needs to be integrated broadly into the entire educational enterprise. To take one example, the "good citizen" of the future needs to understand homelessness from a societal, cultural, family, and individual perspective. He or she needs knowledge of the root causes of homelessness, knowledge of potential social policy actions, and knowledge about possible legislation to address these issues. Equally important, students need to understand their roles in attacking the problem and how they are part of any solution. Such knowledge cannot be instilled in the classroom alone. It requires that the classroom experience be conjoined with the experience of providing frontline services to homeless people.

## SERVICE-LEARNING AS A WAY OF TEACHING SOCIALLY RESPONSIVE KNOWLEDGE

Joining of classroom experience with frontline community service experience is the foundational basis for the service-learning concept which has been introduced at the University of Utah by the Bennion Center. Service-Learning provides students with an interplay of acting, thinking, reading, and discussing the social issues of the era. Service-learning will provide students of the future with a blend of academic and action experiences necessary to develop an understanding of the issues facing our larger community, giving them the knowledge, skills, and tools necessary for dealing with emerging social issues. Service-learning does not supplant the teaching of foundational or professional knowledge. Rather, its goal is to enhance and capitalize on the teaching of that knowledge by coupling it with socially responsive knowledge.

Understanding community and societal issues and one's relationship to those issues requires active participation and involvement in community experiences. To gain socially responsive knowledge, a student needs an experience that enables her to sense that she is not merely a one-time observer on the periphery. By the time of graduation, the student needs the experience of having been in the midst of the community, assisting professionals, and consumers to act on and contribute to the resolution of societal problems. Service-learning seeks to make such contributions while at the same time developing a deeper understanding of those problems at a personal, professional, and conceptual level. It aims to develop a sense of responsibility, skills, and a substantive understanding of the specific societal problem being investigated and tackled. As a result, when students graduate from the university, they are far better oriented and more inclined to become citizens of the community with broad knowledge and leadership potential, in addition to serving as professional citizens and educated citizens.

Service-learning fosters the development of personal and interpersonal knowledge grounded in an interdisciplinary perspective that illuminates self-understanding and provides the basis for effective team work. Service-learning encourages students to be more self-reflective about who they are, what they value, and the reasons for their values. It promotes the development of interpersonal and communication skills related to effective and cooperative problem solving. This interdisciplinary approach to self-understanding and interpersonal understanding can 1) tap into and strengthen the interdisciplinary connections at the university (liberal education, ethnic studies, environmental studies, women's studies, etc.); 2) help the community to understand the value of the University of Utah and the relationship between the university's strong interdisciplinary-based curriculum and community problem solving; and 3) enable faculty to better understand the relevance of their own discipline to community problem solving, and to appreciate the interconnection between their own discipline and other disciplines in tackling community problems.

Adding service-learning to the university curriculum does not require homogenizing higher education. The way that service-learning is integrated into a student's academic program will vary greatly depending on the discipline in which the student is focusing. But regardless of major or discipline, we encourage the university to expand and enhance its educational mission to respond to society's emerging needs if we are to fulfill our role in educating the good citizen.

## KEY ELEMENTS OF SERVICE-LEARNING

### Service-Learning Involves Foundational and/or Professional Knowledge that Is Combined with "Experience In" and "Action On" Community Needs

In a service-learning experience, students learn about community problems firsthand, study foundational concepts and knowledge about the issue, develop professional skills, and participate in solving actual social problems and formulating social policy for the future. Students not only learn about social issues, study and discuss fundamental concepts in a discipline, and/or learn professional skills, but they combine these knowledge bases, apply them, and put them into action to address real problems in their own community.

### Service-Learning Combines Traditional Classroom and Laboratory Experiences with Significant Experiences in Field Placements Where Pertinent Social Issues Are Being Played Out

A part of the service-learning experience must occur in community sites such as shelters, hospitals, neighborhood social service agencies and social centers, and in homes. Absent such active participation at off-campus sites, students cannot hope to gain insight into and understanding of how the ways in which so many of our citizens are challenged by numerous difficulties in their daily lives. But it is also essential that service-learning involve some combination of university-based classroom, media, and/or laboratory settings in order for students to gain essential foundational and professional skills. An important aspect of learning in community settings is that students will necessarily interact with and work directly with professional service providers and consumers whose everyday lives are confronted by the difficult challenges posed by our complex society.

A fundamental aspect of service-learning is offering students an opportunity to step back and reflect on their firsthand experiences in various community settings, and to consider their role and responsibilities as a citizen of that broader community. Students need to develop the skills and insight necessary to identify community problems; they also need to develop the sensibility to ask how they can be a part of the solution to those problems.

### Service-Learning Requires a Special Tripartite Partnership Among Students, Faculty, and the Community

Faculty must be willing to develop partnerships with community groups, spend time in community settings, and work in an often unpredictable and shifting milieu—as the demands of a community issue change, as opportunities and barriers arise, and as circumstances shift. Service-learning is often fluid and dynamic, and requires a reflexive orientation to teaching and instruction.

In addition, faculty must conceive of themselves as team players in service-learning, and as co-teachers and co-students with students, community professionals, and community consumers. All parties are both knowledgeable and often uninformed about different aspects of a service-learning venture, and everyone must be capable of assuming varied roles at different times.

Students must also be willing to shift their often traditional role of passive learner to that of active participant, as they learn content and concepts, develop professional skills, and use their learning to understand and undertake problem solving actions on community issues. Thus, students must learn to relate to faculty as teachers, consultants, and co-students.

A student must come to consider community professionals and consumers as an equally important group of teachers in the service-learning educational process. Faculty must engage these community members in defining and refining course goals, in identifying potential experiences for students, in training and supervising students, and in evaluating student performance.

This tripartite partnership, an essential ingredient of service-learning, is challenging but essential, and is an opportunity to forge essential links between the university and the citizens it serves and educates.

## THE ROLE OF THE BENNION CENTER IN IMPLEMENTING SERVICE-LEARNING AT THE UNIVERSITY OF UTAH

Integrating service-learning into the curriculum at the University of Utah cannot be done casually or as a simple add-on to existing responsibilities of faculty and administrators. It will require a significant investment of planning time and finances to reshape and restructure existing and new courses and ultimately to test and revise these new forms of instruction. In order for an academic department to take seriously this new educational challenge, the investment of time to rethink an entire curriculum or even parts of a curriculum will be even greater, an endeavor that reasonably can be expected to extend over several years.

## The Bennion Center's Past Accomplishments in Service-Learning

The Bennion Center, its faculty advisory committee, and its faculty mentor have played a major role in developing service-learning at the University of Utah. Over the past five years the Bennion Center, with support from many sources, has been very active. Some of its activities include the following:

- Awarded 11 public service professorships which have enabled faculty members to develop simultaneously service-learning courses and projects that service the community.

- Worked with faculty to develop 45 service-learning courses in 23 different departments (these courses are identified for students in the class schedule with a "SL" notation).

- Created a Service-Learning Scholars program in which students must work with a faculty adviser to complete 15 credit hours of service-learning courses, 400 hours of community service, and a major capstone project that integrates the students' service and academic interests. Projects must meet a community need. Seven service-learning scholars graduated in 1994–95, and 60 are currently enrolled.

- Collected and analyzed data that document the learning outcomes of service-learning classes.

- Funded 23 Bennion Center teaching assistants trained in community service methodology to assist faculty teaching service-learning courses.

- Created a faculty mentor award which enables an experienced service-learning faculty member to help other faculty who desire to teach service-learning classes.

To date, these programs have engaged more than 1,800 students and more than 50 faculty members, all of whom have contributed more than 30,000 hours of service to our local community, while strengthening the undergraduate learning environment. The Bennion Center has raised more than $330,000 to create and support these service-learning programs since 1991.

## Student Perspectives on Service-Learning

In the minds of students who have taken service-learning classes at the University of Utah, the experience has been a significant academic and civic success. During the 1993–94 school year and the first two quarters of the 1994–95 school year, 503 student evaluations of service-learning were completed in 21 separate classes. The results show overwhelming support among students for more experiential, service-learning opportunities throughout the university. Also, results indicate that, in the perception of students, both academic and civic learning outcomes are greatly enhanced when service is joined with traditional class work.

Eighty-nine percent of students felt that the service they performed helped them to see the relevance of the course work to their everyday lives. A similarly high percentage (84%) felt that the service opportunities helped them to better understand class lectures and readings. Only 9% felt that they would have learned more if more time had been spent in the classroom. Ninety-two percent felt that they were able to experience real learning through the service-learning class because it had helped them to integrate the learning from the class into their own behavior.

The service-learning experience also bolstered students' sense of civic commitment. Over 80% reported that the class had made them more interested in performing community service than they were before. Only 26 students out of more than 500 (under 6%) reported that they would not be doing community service after the class was over.

It seems safe to say that from the perspective of students, service-learning is a tremendous success. The overwhelming majority of students find that service-learning courses provide a kind of learning experience that is not only exciting and provocative, but one which accomplishes more effectively the learning goals of individual courses. Students not only report increased learning, but improved retention from the practical real life experience. So great has been the effect of these courses that over 90% felt that more courses at the university should combine service and learning. Many, in fact, commented that service-learning courses should be available (even required) in all disciplines.

## The Bennion Center's Future Role in Service-Learning

The Bennion Center can continue to play a major role in assisting faculty and administrators in redesigning and creating new education offerings aimed at integrating service-learning into higher education. The center can make readily available the wealth of experience that it has developed in assisting individual faculty members to successfully integrate service-learning into their courses. The center can use its impressive network of community contacts to help departments identify appropriate community agencies and organizations, and to suggest ways that a service experience can be added as a rigorous component to an existing educational offering. In addition, the Bennion Center has the expertise to help academic units to identify potential federal, state, and foundation funding sources to aid in developing new classes.

In essence, the Bennion Center can serve as a resource for educational change at this university. The existing expertise and knowledge of Bennion Center staff, student leaders, faculty advisory committee (consisting of representatives from every college at the University of Utah), and community advisory board, coupled with this group's enthusiasm for service-learning, can provide an important talent pool in the university.

## A PROPOSED PLAN OF ACTION

Systematically incorporating service-learning into the university curriculum requires actions and initiatives at all levels—individual faculty, departments and colleges, other academic units; e.g., liberal education, honors and others, and the university central administration, notably the president and vice presidents.

### Individual Faculty

The Bennion Center has worked with individual faculty for several years, resulting in almost four dozen service-learning classes being offered during the 1994–95 academic year. In this bottom-up approach, the Bennion Center staff, with financial support from the university and outside sources, has assisted faculty in developing courses, providing TA assistance, and working with the instructor's department for release time and support.

We recommend that this grassroots, one-on-one approach be continued as one part of a multi-pronged effort to incorporate service-learning in the university curriculum. But this is not enough. Indeed, if this is all we do, the concept will wither, because service-learning ultimately requires a fundamental philosophical commitment of university departments, colleges, and the administration.

### Departments, Colleges, and Programs

Most instruction is organized around academic departments, colleges, and other academic programs. Any educational change must, therefore, eventually involve these units. If service-learning is to gain any significant role in the university, these units must be involved in an integrated and systematic way. The university administration needs to encourage, stimulate, and require these units to begin moving in this direction.

## University Leadership

The Bennion Center staff, faculty advisory committee, and students have been engaged in an ongoing discussion with individual faculty members about the role and development of service-learning at the University of Utah. In light of the powerful momentum that this discussion has engendered, this process of legitimation from the ground up will continue.

Now that a grassroots movement is in place, the faculty advisory committee of the Bennion Center believes that the next stage of momentum must come from the top—that is, from the president and appropriate vice presidents of the university. We believe that these leaders must now play an active role, announce their commitment to service-learning as an integral part of the university of the future, and openly commit resources to the development of such an initiative. With visionary leadership articulated at the highest levels of the university, and with their call for movement in this direction, coupled with some financial resources to do the planning, curriculum revision, evaluation, and fine tuning, we foresee dramatic progress in the enhancement of our educational activities.

To be specific, the faculty advisory committee of the Bennion Center recommends that the president and his cabinet, academic vice president, health sciences vice president, and vice president for student affairs publicly endorse the philosophy and plan outlined in this document (perhaps jointly with the faculty advisory committee if so desired); state a commitment to provide resources for pilot programs; and encourage deans, department chairs, program directors, and faculty to prepare initial proposals. As a next step, the faculty advisory committee anticipates meeting with the council of academic deans, the academic senate, and the associated students of the University of Utah in order to gain additional input and support for the expansion of service-learning at the University of Utah.

The Bennion Center Staff and faculty advisory committee are prepared to assist in whatever way is deemed appropriate. One possible model is for academic units to consult with Bennion Center staff and faculty advisory committee prior to preparing brief preliminary proposals. The Bennion Center staff and faculty advisory committee are also willing to advise the president and vice presidents regarding possible expanded proposals from some units and suggestions regarding financial needs for various proposals. In essence, one possible model involves the Bennion Center and its faculty advisory committee serving as an honest broker between academic units and the university administration, and assisting all parties in a reflexive process.

We ask for a good faith commitment by the administration to publicly support the introduction of service-learning in the university and to provide reasonable resources as faculty units commit to constructive evolution of their educational programs. At the same time, the Bennion

Center staff and faculty advisory committee are willing to act in good faith to stimulate curriculum change, and to work with the administration to achieve a process that is reasonable and realistic regarding resource requirements.

Given the exigencies of budgets and resource issues, the faculty advisory committee is willing to join the university administration as partners in communicating the general plan proposed here to the university community, including the gradual and iterative process to be followed in developing socially responsive learning opportunities.

It is not possible to be more specific at this time regarding the ideal scope of service-learning at the University of Utah, the rate at which the process will proceed, and the exact configuration of service-learning in the curriculum of various departments and academic units. Nor is it to be expected that the university administration and specific colleges and departments can specify exact resource requirements and exact resources available at this time. What we now need is a good faith commitment, and a step-by-step process that proceeds in an open and flexible fashion, with an opportunity for everyone to be partners in reshaping and enhancing education at the University of Utah in the present and future decades.

We welcome the opportunity to discuss these matters with you, are prepared to provide models of unit financial costs, and to invest our energies in launching a campus-wide initiative.

# INDEX